Aircraft
Dispatcher

ORAL
EXAM
GUIDE

Prepare for the FAA
oral and practical
exam to earn your
Aircraft Dispatcher
certificate

Dr. David C. Ison

Aviation Supplies & Academics, Inc.
Newcastle, Washington

Aircraft Dispatcher Oral Exam Guide
David C. Ison

Based on the *Oral Exam Guide Series* by Michael D. Hayes,
with excerpts from the *Airline Transport Pilot Oral Exam Guide*.

Aviation Supplies & Academics, Inc.
7005 132nd Place SE • Newcastle, Washington 98059-3153
asa@asa2fly.com • www.asa2fly.com

Visit the ASA website often to find updates posted due to FAA regulation revisions
that may affect this book.

Printed in the United States of America
2015   2014   9   8   7   6   5   4   3   2

ASA-OEG-ADX
ISBN 978-1-56027-900-6

Library of Congress Cataloging-in-Publication Data:

Ison, David C.
   Aircraft dispatcher oral exam guide : prepare for the FAA practical exam to earn your
aircraft dispatcher certificate / by David C. Ison.
      p. cm.
   Includes bibliographical references.
   ISBN 978-1-56027-900-6 (pbk.) — ISBN 1-56027-900-1 (pbk.)
   1. Air traffic control—Examinations—Study guides. 2. United States. Federal Aviation
Administration—Examinations—Study guides. 3. Air traffic controllers—
Certification—United States. I. Title.
   TL725.3.T7I86 2011   387.7'40426076—dc23
                                                    2011046476

03

Contents

6 Aircraft Systems, Performance, and Limitations

7 Navigation and Aircraft Navigation Systems

8 Practical Dispatch Applications

9 Manuals, Handbooks, and Other Written Materials

Introduction:
What to Expect for Your ADX Practical Test

The Aircraft Dispatcher Practical Test Process

As with any testing process, the more you know about it, the less stressful and overwhelming it is. The Aircraft Dispatcher (ADX) certification is not overly difficult to acquire. The information you must know prior to sitting for the ADX practical test is fairly straightforward; however, ADX certification does require knowledge in a wide range of subject areas which would necessitate a tremendous amount of study and preparation. Applicants who put in ample study time and take advantage of available preparation tools, such as this book, should be well prepared for the test.

While this book is an excellent means of preparing for the ADX practical test and is based upon actual questions used on ADX practical tests, it should not be the only source of study. Applicants should first participate in a ground school course specific to dispatchers and/or read the books listed under "References" (below), then conclude their study with a comprehensive review of this book.

Practical Test Standards (PTS)

The Federal Aviation Administration (FAA) publishes guides to the practical tests for each certification that they issue, known as the Practical Test Standards (PTS). The PTS guides tell applicants exactly what to expect, what subject areas or tasks will be covered, and what they need to bring with them on test day. The PTS for the ADX is designated FAA-S-8081-10 and can be found on the FAA website or in print, often combined with the PTS for Airline Transport Pilot (ATP).

The PTS are broken into several parts: areas of operation, tasks, and references. Areas of operation form an outline of what general subjects will be covered. Although they are presented in a logical sequence according to the FAA, examiners do not necessarily follow this order. Tasks are the actual knowledge areas or procedures that will be covered under each area of operation. References are provided for each area of operation and task in order to provide applicants the source documents examiners will defer to for the correct responses. Applicants should study these documents in preparation for the exam. The list below includes these PTS references, as well as additional resources helpful in preparing for your ADX exam.

Examiners are required to use the PTS. They are also technically required to cover all areas of operation and their associated tasks. Some omissions are permissible if, for example, a certain technology or piece of equipment is not available at the testing site. It is advisable, though, to be prepared for all areas of operation and tasks. It is also possible that the examiner will venture outside the confines of the PTS to probe the applicant in subjective areas such as judgment, decision making, and ethics.

References

The following is a list of ADX references to source books, documents, handbooks, etc., that are useful in preparing for certification:

14 CFR Part 1 Definitions and Abbreviations

14 CFR Part 65 Certification: Airmen Other than Flight Crewmembers

14 CFR Part 91 General Operating and Flight Rules

14 CFR Part 119 Certification: Air Carriers and Commercial Operators

14 CFR Part 121 Operating Requirements: Domestic, Flag, and Supplemental Operations

14 CFR Part 135 Commuter & On Demand Operations

14 CFR Part 139 Airport Certification

49 CFR Part 175 Carriage by Aircraft

49 CFR Part 830 Notification and Reporting of Aircraft Accidents or Incidents and Overdue Aircraft, and Preservation of Aircraft Wreckage, Mail, Cargo, and Records

49 CFR Part 1544 Aircraft Operator Security: Air Carriers and Commercial Operators

AC 00-6 *Aviation Weather*

AC 00-45 *Aviation Weather Services*

AC 60-22 *Aeronautical Decision Making*

AC 120-42 *Extended Operations (ETOPS and Polar Operations)*

AC 121-32 *Dispatch Resource Management Training*

Aeronautical Chart User's Guide

AIM *Aeronautical Information Manual*

Air Traffic Control Command Center (ATCCC) website (www.fly.faa.gov)

ARINC website (Aeronautical Radio, Inc.) (www.arinc.com/products/voice_data_comm/)

Airport/Facility Directory legend (aeronav.faa.gov)

Aviation Weather Center (aviationweather.gov)

Boeing (www.boeing.com)

Boeing 737 Flight Manual

Defense Internet NOTAM Service (https://www.notams.faa.gov)

Eurocontrol (www.ecacnav.com/content.asp?CatID=24)

European Space Agency (ESA) (www.esa.int/esaNA/egnos.html)

FAA (www.faa.gov)

FAA-H-8083-2 *Risk Management Handbook*

FAA-H-8261-1 *Instrument Procedures Handbook*

FAA-H-8083-25 *Pilot's Handbook of Aeronautical Knowledge*

FAA-S-8081-10 *Aircraft Dispatcher Practical Test Standards*

Flight Standards Information Management System website (fsims.faa.gov)

ICAO website (www.icao.int)

Jeppesen navigational charts, introductory section

National Weather Service (NWS) website (www.nws.noaa.gov)

North Atlantic MNPSA Operations Manual, 8th edition

Turbulence: A New Perspective for Pilots, by Peter F. Lester

FAA Examiners

Each FAA practical test examiner is a unique individual. Some are laid back and amicable, while others are more formal and serious. Try to find out as much information as you can about your examiner prior to the practical experience. But do not let your guard down even if the rumor is that a particular examiner is "easy." The ADX practical test will still be an arduous process, no matter who your examiner is on test day. Get a feel for the personality of the examiner when you first meet, then try to mirror their general demeanor.

Here are few tips concerning examiners:

- Never argue with an examiner.
- Never be belligerent with an examiner.
- Most examiners will want to teach you something at some point during the testing process—let them do so.
- Answer questions thoroughly, but avoid saying too much. Let the examiner ask for more if they want more. Do not dig yourself into a hole.
- Be polite and courteous.
- Ask about how they got into dispatch, their experiences, and their career.
- Do not be afraid of saying "I don't know." An examiner will prefer that you say this rather than try to bluff your way out of a question. It is okay to not know *everything*; however, of course, if you say "I don't know" too much, you might fail the test.

Prerequisites for the ADX Practical Test

The most certain way to fail the ADX practical test is to not fulfill the required prerequisites. According to the PTS, in order to sit for the ADX practical test you must:

1. Be at least 23 years of age;
2. Have passed the required aircraft dispatcher knowledge test within the preceding 24 calendar months prior to completion of the practical test; and
3. Have obtained the applicable experience prescribed for the Aircraft Dispatcher Certificate under 14 CFR §65.57 and provide documentary evidence of such experience, or
4. Have successfully completed an FAA-approved aircraft dispatcher-training course within the past 90 days, or received revalidation in accordance with 14 CFR §65.70 (b).

To be eligible to take the Aircraft Dispatcher Knowledge Test, an applicant is required by 14 CFR Part 65 to be at least 21 years of age. If there are questions concerning English language requirements, refer to AC 60-28; English Language Skill Standards Required by 14 CFR Parts 61, 63, and 65; or your local FSDO. Determination that English language requirements have been met should be accomplished prior to beginning the practical test.

If you are at least 21 years old, but less than 23 years old, you can still sit for the ADX practical test, but you will not receive a certificate if you pass. Instead, you will get a letter that you can trade in for a certificate following your twenty-third birthday.

Although the examiner will decide the circumstances upon which you will plan a flight, it is up to the applicant to bring all necessary forms, charts, and other documents to the test. These include, but are not limited to, the following:

1. Aircraft Flight Manual
2. General Operating Manual and Operations Specifications
3. Enroute low/high altitude charts

4. Standard instrument departures
5. Standard terminal arrival routes
6. Standard instrument approach procedure charts
7. ATC flight plan form
8. Navigation log/flight log
9. Load manifest form
10. Weight and balance form
11. Dispatch release form
12. *Aeronautical Information Manual*
13. Computer and plotter
14. Notices to Airman (NOTAM) information
15. 14 CFR Parts 1, 25, 61, 65 Subpart C, 71, 91, 121, and 139
16. 49 CFR Parts 175, 830, and 1544
17. Completed FAA Form 8400-3, Application for an Airman Certificate and/or Rating*
18. Airman Knowledge Test Report
19. Pilot certificate (if applicable)
20. Statement of graduation certificate (if applicable)
21. Identification—photo/signature ID
22. Notice of Disapproval/Letter of Discontinuance (if applicable)
23. Examiner's fee (if applicable)

*(This can be downloaded from the Internet; check with the examiner to see if they would prefer the applicant use the Integrate Airman Certification and/or Rating Application [IACRA] system.)

A basic rule is that applicants should bring everything they would need to dispatch a flight in the real world. It is paramount that these items be in the possession of the applicant, particularly if they are not readily available at the facility where the test takes place. Not having the required forms, documents, charts, etc., could result in failing the practical test.

Test Day

On test day, the applicant should arrive early; *never* be late for an FAA practical test. He or she should be well dressed, which means a coat and tie for men and business attire for women. If the examiner wants to relax things a little, he or she will say, "you can take off your tie," or something of the sort. Applicants should also be well rested and have recently eaten a meal or snack to ensure they have ample energy to work through the test.

ADX practical tests typically last from four to eight hours. Usually, stronger applicants have shorter tests; on the other hand, some examiners push strong applicants further. Normally, the test begins with a review of the prerequisites, application, and other documents. Then the examiner will typically begin the oral portion of the test, which will cover all applicable subject areas listed in the PTS.

Upon successful completion of the oral portion, the examiner will assign a route for which the applicant must plan a flight. Examiners often assign a route that will be near the performance limits of the aircraft (in terms of fuel). Also, they generally will select a route with poor weather at the departure airport, en route, at the destination airport, or any combination thereof. It is not uncommon for examiners to include an inoperative item on the aircraft to be used for the flight that may affect the dispatchability of the flight.

For the flight planning portion of the test, it is best if the applicant has a set plan or checklist to follow to ensure that the process proceeds in a logical, organized manner and covers all of the required items. Many an applicant has failed the test due to poor organization or time management. While there normally is no set time limit to the flight planning portion of the test, examiners can get a feel for the applicant's flight planning fluency by how long the process takes. However, applicants should not rush through it as it is obvious that a concise, organized flight planning methodology can help you to efficiently complete the flight planning task in a reasonable period of time.

The end product of the flight planning exercise will be a route of flight, a cruise altitude, a fuel burn, weight and balance data, performance data, a dispatch release, a flight plan, and other applicable documents, forms, and items. Applicants should present the flight to the examiner as though they were briefing the pilots that would be operating the flight. This should begin with an overview of the weather and any applicable NOTAMs, and how each relates to the planned route. The examiner should be informed as to how each decision was made—such as how the weight and balance data affected the selection of the departure runway, why a particular departure procedure was selected, why the cruise altitude is the best choice, why the route was planned around adverse weather, and so on. The fewer questions the examiner has, the better.

As the applicant goes through their briefing, the examiner will probably ask several "what if" questions. For example, "What if the aircraft had an engine failure over XYZ VOR, what would you do?" Or perhaps, "What if the weather at the destination airport suddenly goes below the forecasted conditions?" The examiner will be looking more for good judgment, sound decision making, and adherence to regulations/policies rather than some particular "right answer." Upon completing the flight briefing, the examiner will probably ask some more hypothetical or situational questions. Following this line of questioning, the applicant will be informed of the decision about whether or not they passed.

Pass or Fail

If an applicant makes it through the flight briefing, it is likely that they have passed. Upon successfully passing the test, the examiner will issue either a letter (for individuals not yet 23 years old) or a temporary ADX certificate. If the applicant is unsuccessful, they will instead receive a letter of discontinuance. Normally, if things are not going well, the examiner will stop the test and inform the applicant that they will not pass but they can elect to continue the test. This allows the examiner to cover more areas of operation and tasks so that when the applicant returns to retake the test, the examiner can elect to only cover the items that they found to be deficient.

Summary

The ADX practical test is a strenuous and demanding event that will consume much of an applicant's day. However, it is not some insurmountable task at which only a few succeed. With the proper preparation, perseverance, and positive attitude, applicants will be successful at passing the test. Aircraft dispatching can be a very interesting and rewarding career, therefore the pursuit of the ADX certificate is certainly worth every minute of preparation and study. Good luck!

Note: Many of the definitions noted in this book are verbatim from the regulations. Quotation marks were omitted for simplicity of presentation.

Acknowledgments

The author wishes to express thanks to Dan Hargrove, Director of Aviation, Rocky Mountain College, and to Scott Wilson, Professor of Aviation, for their contributions in reviewing and commenting on the *Aircraft Dispatcher Oral Exam Guide*.

About the Author

Industry expert David C. Ison has been involved in aviation for over 25 years, during which he has flown as a flight instructor and as an ATP for both regional and major airlines flying domestic and international routes. He holds ATP multi-engine land, commercial single-engine land and sea, Gold Seal Certified Flight Instructor, instrument flight instructor, multi-engine flight instructor, ground instructor—instrument and advanced, and aircraft dispatcher certifications.

Dr. Ison has been in aviation higher education for over 8 years and is currently the Program Chair of the Master's of Aeronautical Science and an Assistant Professor of Aeronautics at Embry-Riddle Aeronautical University–Worldwide. He holds a Master's degree in Aeronautical Science—Operations Specialization from Embry-Riddle Aeronautical University and a Ph.D. in Educational Studies/Higher Education Leadership with a Specialization in Aviation Education.

1

Dispatch Resource Management

1. What is "dispatch resource management" (DRM)? (AC 121-32)

Successful DRM is defined by the Federal Aviation Administration (FAA) as a "dispatcher who coordinates a wide array of resources for the flight crew. DRM addresses the challenge of optimizing the person/machine interface and related interpersonal issues. These issues include effective teambuilding and maintenance, information transfer, problem solving, decision making, maintaining situational awareness, and dealing with automated systems."

2. What are the various interactions with the operational environment that dispatchers must make? (AC 121-32)

To successfully maximize the positive effects of DRM, dispatchers should effectively and openly interact with the following:

- Pilots
- Other dispatchers
- Maintenance personnel
- Load planners
- Crew schedulers
- Aircraft routers
- Air traffic controllers
- Managers
- Station personnel
- Communications systems and personnel
- Flight planning systems and personnel
- Meteorological systems, sources, and personnel
- Written documents such as operations specifications, operations manuals, regulations, company procedures, etc.
- Any other sources that may be helpful to the safe and efficient conduct of flights

3. How does the FAA define "dispatcher situational awareness"? (AC 121-32)

The FAA defines this as "the ability to absorb information in a dynamic environment, to evaluate and refine that information, to anticipate contingencies, and to initiate appropriate actions as necessary."

4. When dispatchers communicate with the various available resources, special emphasis should be made in what three areas? (AC 121-32)

- Inquiry—don't be afraid to ask questions.
- Advocacy—try to work together in a positive manner.
- Assertion—do not be afraid to bring up concerns or to be proactive.

5. Why is conflict resolution so important for dispatchers? (AC 121-32)

There will come a time when dispatchers encounter conflict when communicating with available resources. For example, pilots might want to carry more fuel, or maintenance personnel might want a flight dispatched even in light of an aircraft with an inoperative component that could negatively affect operations. Dispatchers often have to serve as negotiators and diplomats. While there is something to be said for being as tactful and non-abrasive as possible, this doesn't mean dispatchers have to be pushovers. Remember that as a dispatcher, you are legally responsible for safety of flight—it's your neck on the line. No matter how much a pilot wants to do something or how much a maintenance manager tries to convince you how things should be done, you must decide that it is safe and agree to "sign your name" to the result.

6. What types of briefings are dispatchers required to conduct? (AC 121-32)

Dispatchers are responsible for briefing flight crews on the applicable items associated with a flight, such as weather, route, and operational considerations. Dispatchers must also brief the other dispatchers replacing them concerning the flights for which they will be responsible. All normal and abnormal circumstances should be conveyed, including weather conditions, aircraft status, and air traffic control system status.

7. What should dispatchers consider regarding interpersonal relationships when dealing with available human resources? (AC 121-32)

Dispatchers should consider the following:
- Diversity among personality styles
- Diversity among operating styles
- Sensitivity to coworker personalities and styles
- Maintaining a relaxed, friendly, yet task-oriented workplace environment

8. How can dispatchers best prioritize tasks when workload is high? (AC 121-32)

Generally, safety oriented tasks should be first and foremost, followed by (in order of priority) regulatory tasks, operational tasks, and convenience. For example, assume a flight needs to be diverted because of an emergency. The safest course of action might be to land at the nearest airport, timewise; however, if the weather is extremely poor at this airport, it might be wise to go to a different airport. If a diversion is due to a non-emergency issue, it might be helpful to choose an airport that is a company station to ensure proper and inexpensive aircraft and passenger handling. Lastly, if the passengers will need to be disembarked, it would be convenient to land at an airport with services available to handle them.

9. Use the list of typical resources available to the dispatcher to work through the following example maximizing DRM: An aircraft you are responsible for dispatching must divert to an alternate airport following the inability to conduct an approach to the destination airport.

- *Pilots*
  The dispatcher will need to coordinate with the pilots to determine the current fuel status of the aircraft. Once this is verified, the best alternative destination should be determined and discussed. The closest suitable airports should be considered, not just the alternate listed on the flight plan. This will require the dispatcher to check the weather conditions at the alternate as well as enroute weather. This information should be passed on to the flight crew. Once a new destination is agreed upon, the release will need to

be amended. Flight crews should request the new destination and then convey the new route and estimated time of arrival to the dispatcher. The dispatcher should also provide the pilot with any other pertinent information such as Notices to Airmen (NOTAMs), where they can expect to park, station servicing/handling capabilities, and how to secure maintenance services (if applicable).

- *Other dispatchers*
  In a high workload situation such as a diversion, it is helpful to have the assistance of other dispatchers. These individuals can help collect resources needed to make the diversion possible, make phone calls, coordinate services, or help handle other flights for which you are responsible.

- *Maintenance personnel*
  If a maintenance issue exists, maintenance should be notified so they can coordinate with personnel at the new destination to handle the problem.

- *Load planners*
  Load planners can be notified to begin new calculations for the departure of the flight from the alternate airport.

- *Crew schedulers*
  Crew schedulers should be notified so that they can coordinate the schedules of the crews affected by the diversion. Depending upon the duty and flight time experienced by the crew up to this point, a diversion may entail sending the flight crew to rest, which will cause a major delay or possible cancellation of the flight. Schedulers could work on securing a replacement crew, rescheduling crews expected to use the delayed aircraft, or simply reworking the schedule of the affected crewmembers.

- *Aircraft routers*
  If an aircraft does not arrive where it is supposed to, this obviously disrupts the air carrier's schedule. These individuals should be notified of the diversion and the expected delay so that they can begin to shuffle aircraft as necessary to cover any gaps in the day's schedule.

- *Air traffic controllers*
  The pilots should handle the communications with air traffic control, although some consultation on routing or delays could be requested from air traffic control or related resources.

- *Managers*
  Your manager should be notified of the diversion as soon as practical. They may even help in the alternate decision process and/or with relieving some of your workload.

- *Station personnel*
  Station personnel at the new destination should be contacted immediately following the decision to use the station. This is particularly important if your airline does not normally serve the airport, as it will require the use of the employees and gate of another air carrier. The availability of both may play a part in the alternate decision-making process. Most air carriers will service their own aircraft first, which might cause delays for your aircraft. Ideally, the aircraft can be diverted to a mainline airport. Lastly, any required services (such as fuel) should be coordinated to prepare for the arrival of the diverted aircraft.

- *Communications systems/personnel*
  Various communications systems may be used, including Aircraft Communications Addressing and Reporting System (ACARS), selective calling (SELCAL), radio, and phone.

- *Flight planning systems and personnel*
  Flight planning systems can be referenced to assist in routing and fuel planning to the diversionary airport. You will need to work on the flight planning for the aircraft's departure from the alternate airport. This should be done following completion of all the tasks required to get the aircraft to the alternate and handled once on the ground.

- *Meteorological systems, sources, and personnel*
  Obviously, you will need to reference various weather reports, forecasts, and images to select the diversionary airport and to re-dispatch the aircraft to its final destination later.

- *Written documents such as operations specifications, operations manuals, regulations, company procedures, etc.*
  The selection of an alternate will require you to reference Ops Specs for the airports authorized for use as alternates. Other manuals may have established procedures for dealing with this type of situation. Station manuals may be helpful in providing information about available services, radio frequencies, phone numbers, etc.

- *Any other sources that may be helpful to the safe and efficient conduct of flights*
  Any other available persons or references should be utilized to prioritize tasks, maintain situational awareness, and maintain a manageable workload.

10. **Use the list of typical resources available to the dispatcher to work through the following example maximizing DRM: An aircraft you are responsible for dispatching just had an engine failure while enroute. The engine is shutdown and secured and the aircraft appears to have no other damage or associated problems.**

- *Pilots*
  The pilots in this case will be very busy. They will need your help to line up everything that's necessary to get the aircraft on the ground. You should immediately assist them in selecting a suitable alternate that is as close as possible, timewise. You should also communicate to them the current weather conditions, NOTAMs, and other pertinent information. Try not to task the pilots with superfluous requests, but be sure to inquire about the fuel status. You might also need to assist them in calculating fuel dumping requirements (if applicable) to get to a diversionary airport.

- *Other dispatchers*
  You should enlist the help of other dispatchers to coordinate everything needed to handle the emergency (e.g., contacting the arrival station, making calls to emergency response to back up calls from air traffic control, etc.). These individuals should take the remaining aircraft for which you are responsible so that you can concentrate on dealing with the emergency.

- *Maintenance personnel*
  You should notify maintenance personnel about the situation. They may be patched to the pilots to assist in troubleshooting any issues and discussing potential solutions. Maintenance will need to begin coordinating the repair or replacement process for the engine once the aircraft is on the ground. This will likely require the transport of maintenance personnel and equipment to the diversionary airport if it is not a maintenance station of your air carrier.

- *Load planners*
  Load planners should be notified as needed, although in this case, they probably will not be tasked with dealing with a departure from the diversionary airport anytime soon.

- *Crew schedulers*
Schedulers should be contacted so they can mitigate the effects on the system of a crew that will probably be unavailable for duty in the near future. They can begin to reschedule crews to cover gaps in the schedule.

- *Aircraft routers*
Aircraft routers should be contacted so that they can mitigate the effects on the system of an aircraft that will likely be unavailable for duty in the near future. They can begin to reschedule aircraft to cover gaps in the schedule.

- *Air traffic controllers*
The pilots will handle the communications with air traffic control, although it might be necessary to help coordinate with controllers at the airport of arrival. If time permits, calls can help ensure emergency services have been properly notified.

- *Managers*
Dispatch management should be notified immediately upon receipt of a notice of an aircraft in an emergency. These individuals will assist in the overall coordination process and oversee the entire abnormal operational process. They will be the one(s) responsible for filing a report with their supervisor/boss and will coordinate the filing of report(s) with the FAA and/or NTSB. Ensure that you keep all documents associated with the flight for use in the report-filing process. Further, try to make notes of the chronology of events throughout the emergency for later use.

- *Station personnel*
Arrival station personnel should be notified to coordinate services and handling of the arriving aircraft and its passengers.

- *Communications systems and personnel*
All applicable personnel should be notified so as to communicate the delay of the flight. Communication systems that will be used include phone, radio, ACARS, and SELCAL.

- *Flight planning systems and personnel*
Flight planning systems can be referenced to assist in routing and fuel planning to the diversionary airport. No further flight planning will probably be required.

- *Meteorological systems, sources, and personnel*
Weather reports, forecasts, and images should be referenced to assist crews in safely arriving at the diversionary airport.

- *Written documents such as operations specifications, operations manuals, regulations, company procedures, etc.*
The corporate emergency manual should be referenced throughout this process. It will likely have a checklist showing who to contact, what to do first, and guidance on where to send the aircraft.

- *Any other sources that may be helpful to the safe and efficient conduct of flights*
Any other available persons or references should be utilized to prioritize tasks, maintain situational awareness, and maintain a manageable workload.

2

Aeronautical Decision Making

A. Hazard and Risk Management

1. What is the definition of a hazard? (FAA-H-8083-2)

According to the FAA, "a hazard is a present condition, event, object, or circumstance that could lead to or contribute to an unplanned or undesired event such as an accident. It is a source of danger."

2. What is the first step in the risk management process? (FAA-H-8083-2)

Hazard identification is the first step. This means realizing that a hazard exists. For example, a maintenance issue that could affect the safety of flight is a potential hazard. Another example of risk is severe weather along the route of flight.

3. What four things affect a person's ability to recognize a hazard? (FAA-H-8083-2)

- Personality
- Education
- Regulations
- Experience

4. How might a person's personality affect the ability to recognize a hazard? (FAA-H-8083-2)

Research has shown that one of the primary characteristics exhibited by accident-prone pilots is their disdain toward rules. People who seek thrills may push beyond normal procedures or regulations in order to fulfill their desire for emotional rushes. Further, individuals who have problems evaluating risk and hazards in one part of their lives, (e.g., driving) tend to bring this with them into other areas. Dispatchers should be aware of potential negative influences of their personality and the personalities of their coworkers and take action to mitigate the effects on the safety of flights.

5. How might education affect the ability to recognize a hazard? (FAA-H-8083-2)

Hazards to the safety of flight can be more easily recognized when you have learned well the reasons behind why a certain situation or circumstance of flight may be dangerous. For example, a clear understanding about the interaction of the jet stream with other meteorological conditions could lead a dispatcher to identify the risk of severe turbulence and take this into account during the flight-planning process. In contrast, a lack of education could prevent a dispatcher from identifying a potential risk to the safety of flight. Whenever something is questionable, a dispatcher should check the reference materials or query more experienced dispatchers for assistance.

6. How might regulations affect the ability to recognize a hazard? (FAA-H-8083-2)

Regulations set a threshold or marker for individuals to recognize when an operation is outside of what is considered acceptable or safe. For example, air carrier aircraft are not allowed to initiate an instrument approach if the visibility is below landing minimums. This sets a barrier against the flight crew taking the risk of attempting an approach into poor conditions that is not likely to end successfully.

7. How might experience affect the ability to recognize a hazard? (FAA-H-8083-2)

Seeing something that is dangerous firsthand can make a lasting impression. It is much less likely that a dispatcher will release an aircraft with minimum fuel when there are widespread thunderstorms if previously doing so with another aircraft resulted in a low-fuel emergency. Dispatchers should recognize circumstances in which they have minimal experience and seek assistance in the form of reference materials and more experienced dispatchers.

8. What is the definition of risk? (FAA-H-8083-2)

If a hazard is not addressed, risk exists. In short, risk is the potential future consequence of neglecting a hazard. Risk can also be described as uncertainty.

9. What are the six types of risk? Define each. (FAA-H-8083-2)

- *Total risk*—all identified and unidentified risks.
- *Identified risk*—those areas of uncertainty/risk that can be readily identified (e.g., thunderstorms or a maintenance issue).
- *Unidentified risk*—those areas of uncertainty/risk that are not known or readily identifiable (e.g., a hidden defect in an engine part or unforecast freezing rain)
- *Acceptable risk*—those risks that are tolerable under normal operations and conditions. There is always a certain level of risk in aviation, just as in driving or playing a sport. Some risk is tolerated, though every effort is made to mitigate any risks associated with the activity.
- *Unacceptable risk*—those risks that are not practical to accept. For example, dispatching a flight with an engine leaking a substantial amount of oil is simply not acceptable as it will likely end in failure of the engine, potentially cascading into much worse.
- *Residual risk*—this is the risk that remains following all the actions taken to mitigate risk. Residual risk is equal to the sum of acceptable risk and unidentified risk.

10. What four items should a dispatcher evaluate prior to releasing a flight in order to assess the potential for risk? (FAA-H-8083-2)

For pilots, the acronym "PAVE" is used to assess risk with an organized process:

  P Pilot
  A Aircraft
  V enVironment
  E External pressures

Dispatchers can also use this model, substituting the "P" with a "D" for dispatcher, and using the acronym "DAVE" to help remember this process.

11. Using the DAVE risk assessment process, what should dispatchers evaluate about themselves in terms of potential for risk? (FAA-H-8083-2)

Dispatchers should review the following:

- Experience
- Currency
- Physical health
- Emotional health

12. What is the "I'M SAFE" checklist? How can this assist dispatchers in evaluating their ability to safely conduct themselves in the workplace?

The I'M SAFE checklist is designed for pilots, but is applicable to everyone in a safety sensitive aviation job function, including dispatchers. The I'M SAFE checklist is a mnemonic to recall what issues dispatchers should consider in their self-evaluation before allowing themselves to go to work. I'M SAFE stands for:

I   Illness

M   Medication

S   Stress

A   Alcohol

F   Fatigue

E   Emotion and/or Eating

Dispatchers should use this checklist to appraise their overall fitness to work. A dispatcher who is very sick or on a sedative medication may not function to the best of his/her ability, raising the risk for the overall operation. Stress, fatigue, and emotional issues can distract dispatchers from conducting flight safely. Alcohol, of course, has no place in a dispatch center. Moreover, a dispatcher with a hangover is not able to function as safely as if he or she were feeling well. Lastly, dispatchers should remember to keep well fed and hydrated so their brains function at the highest possible level. Only after checking all of these factors and feeling confident that none could potentially negatively affect performance should a dispatcher agree to work releasing and controlling flights.

13. Using the DAVE risk assessment process, what should dispatchers evaluate about the aircraft in terms of potential for risk? (FAA-H-8083-2)

There are many aircraft-related issues to consider when assessing risk. What is the maintenance status of the flight? What if the cross-feed valve is inoperative—how might this raise the risk of operation? Is this risk tolerable? Is the fuel load correct, legal, and safe? Can the aircraft take off and land safely under the current conditions, including weather, field conditions, and aircraft loading? Each potential risk should be identified and assessed. Unacceptable risk should lead to the cancellation of the flight, adjustment of loading, selection of an alternate aircraft, or other risk-mitigating decision.

14. Using the DAVE risk assessment process, what should dispatchers evaluate about the environment in terms of potential for risk? (FAA-H-8083-2)

For dispatchers, weather is one of the most important considerations when planning a flight. Are the weather conditions good enough for the flight to be legally and safely completed? Are there any ways that the dispatcher can take advantage of the weather to augment fuel efficiency? Are there any areas of dangerous weather that should be avoided? How might the snowfall and high winds at the destination potentially affect the safety and dispatchability of the flight? The environment also includes other critical factors such as terrain around the airports of operation and en route; airports (runways, lighting, etc.); airspace; flight over remote or inhospitable areas; and even time of day.

15. Using the DAVE risk assessment process, what should dispatchers evaluate about external pressures in terms of potential for risk? (FAA-H-8083-2)

External pressures might tempt dispatchers to conduct flights with elevated levels of risk or to hurry the flight-planning process. Such conditions must be identified so that the associated risks can be properly handled. Examples of external pressures are company mandates to dispatch aircraft with minimum fuel for cost savings, delayed flights prompting pressure to hurry to get the flights out, approaching or deteriorating weather, and personal pressures such as the desire to get off of work.

B. Aeronautical Decision Making (ADM)

1. What is "aeronautical decision making" (ADM)? (FAA-H-8083-2)

ADM is a methodical process that is used to produce a positive (safe) outcome in response to encountered risks.

2. What is the "DECIDE" model? (FAA-H-8083-2)

The DECIDE model is an analytical decision-making process used to deal with hazards. DECIDE stands for:

D Detect
E Estimate
C Choose
I Identify
D Do
E Evaluate

3. Describe the "detect" step of the DECIDE model. (FAA-H-8083-2)

Of course, the detection of a hazard or change is necessary in order to identify the need to take any action. An example would be the failure of an engine anti-ice protection system while an airplane is enroute. What does this mean to the pilots and to the dispatcher? How might this affect safety? How might this affect operations?

4. Describe the "estimate" step of the DECIDE model. (FAA-H-8083-2)

Upon detecting a hazard, the need for a reaction to this hazard must be estimated. Using the example of the engine anti-ice system failure, if the weather was clear all the way to the destination, there would be little need to do anything other than have the problem addressed by maintenance on the ground. However, if the weather at the destination was cloudy and near freezing, it would be unwise to allow the flight to continue to that point, thus prompting a need for a reaction to the hazard.

5. Describe the "choose" step of the DECIDE model. (FAA-H-8083-2)

In this step, dispatchers choose an action (or choose inaction, as appropriate). In the case of the engine anti-ice system failure, the dispatcher and flight crew must come to an agreement on the choice of action. Of course, the best choice is that which is legal, practical, and safe.

6. Describe the "identify" step of the DECIDE model. (FAA-H-8083-2)

Dispatchers should identify the action that could best control the change/hazard. Of course, the best choice is that which is legal, practical, and safe.

7. Describe the "do" step of the DECIDE model. (FAA-H-8083-2)

Once a decision is made about the best alternative, the dispatcher should do whatever was decided upon to handle the hazard. In the case of the aircraft with an inoperative engine anti-ice system, the dispatcher could plan for the flight to divert to an alternate.

8. Describe the "evaluate" step of the DECIDE model. (FAA-H-8083-2)

After the decision is made and the action(s) taken, dispatchers should evaluate their decisions. How is the weather at the alternate and original destination? If the weather improves at the destination, perhaps a change in plans is in order. Or if the weather deteriorates at the alternate, further action and hazard management will be necessary.

9. What is "situational awareness"? (FAA-H-8083-2)

Situational awareness is a person's overall awareness of all aspects of their current circumstances. Dispatchers would be considered to have good situational awareness if they knew the status of all of the aircraft for which they were responsible, including the aircrafts' positions, fuel status, maintenance conditions, and limitations, while also maintaining awareness of enroute and destination weather conditions, the impact of Air Traffic Control delays, and other operational factors. Put simply, good situational awareness is the ability of a dispatcher to be aware of what has happened, what is happening, and what may happen in the near future.

10. What is the "3P model"? (FAA-H-8083-2)

The 3P model is a means to assess risk. The 3P's are:
- Perceive
- Process
- Perform

11. Define each of the components of the 3P model. (FAA-H-8083-2)

- *Perceive*—this step is where dispatchers identify the existence of a risk.
- *Process*—in this step, dispatchers evaluate the impact of the risk on the safety of the operation.
- *Perform*—this step is when a dispatcher takes action (or instead takes no action) in response to the identified risk.

3

Regulatory Requirements

A. 14 CFR Part 1

1. What is the definition of an "air carrier"? (14 CFR §1.1)

An air carrier is a person (or entity) who directly undertakes to engage in air transportation by lease or other arrangement.

2. What is the definition of "air commerce"? (14 CFR §1.1)

Interstate, overseas, or foreign air commerce or the transportation of mail by aircraft or any operation or navigation of aircraft within the limits of any Federal airway or any operation or navigation of aircraft which directly affects, or which may endanger safety in, interstate, overseas, or foreign air commerce.

3. What is an "air traffic control clearance"? (14 CFR §1.1)

An air traffic control clearance is an authorization by air traffic control, for the purpose of preventing collision between known aircraft, for an aircraft to proceed under specified traffic conditions within controlled airspace.

4. What is an "air traffic service (ATS) route"? (14 CFR §1.1)

A specified route designated for channeling the flow of traffic as necessary for the provision of air traffic services. The term "ATS route" refers to a variety of airways, including jet routes, area navigation (RNAV) routes, and arrival and departure routes. An ATS route is defined by route specifications.

5. What is the definition of "air transportation"? (14 CFR §1.1)

Air transportation is defined as interstate, overseas, or foreign air transportation or the transportation of mail by aircraft.

6. What is the definition of an "alternate airport"? (14 CFR §1.1)

An airport at which an aircraft may land if landing at the intended airport becomes inadvisable.

7. What is "area navigation" (RNAV)? (14 CFR §1.1)

Area navigation is a means of navigation that allows for direct and random routes. This type of navigation allows for the selection of essentially any routing permitted by Air Traffic Control.

8. What are some examples of RNAV capable avionics?

Global positioning system (GPS), flight management system (FMS), distance measuring equipment (DME)/DME navigation, and VOR/DME RNAV.

9. What is a Category II ILS? (14 CFR §1.1)

This type of instrument landing system (ILS) allows for lower minimums than Category I, but not less than a 100-foot decision height (DH) and normally not less than 1,200 runway visual range (RVR).

10. What are the different types of Category III ILS approaches and what minimums are associated with each type? (14 CFR §1.1)

Category III approaches allow for approach minimums lower than Category II ILS procedures. Category IIIa approaches allow operations down to a DH as low as 100 feet and to an RVR as low as 700 feet. Category IIIb approaches allow operations down to a DH as low as 50 feet and to an RVR between 700 feet and 150 feet. Category IIIc operations are permitted without a DH or visibility requirement.

11. What is the definition of a "ceiling" in terms of weather reporting? (14 CFR §1.1)

A ceiling is the lowest reported cloud layer that is broken, overcast, or obscured. Clouds that are reported as thin or obscurations that are reported as partial are not considered a ceiling.

12. What is a "clearway"? (14 CFR §1.1)

For turbine aircraft built after August 29, 1959, the clearway is an area beyond the runway that is clear of obstacles (in an upward slope of 1.25 degrees) and under control of the airport. It is a minimum of 500 feet wide and centered on the runway centerline. Threshold lights no higher than 26 inches can protrude into the clearway. For aircraft built before the aforementioned date, the clearway must be 300 feet wide and have no obstacles (there is no allowance for a slope or threshold lights).

13. What is the definition of "controlled airspace"? (14 CFR §1.1)

Controlled airspace is airspace in which IFR traffic is subject to Air Traffic Control. In the United States, controlled airspace is designated Class A, B, C, D, or E.

14. What are some examples of crewmembers? (14 CFR §1.1)

Crewmembers are individuals who are assigned a duty during flight. A flight attendant is considered a crewmember. Pilots are also considered crewmembers, though they are typically differentiated by the term "flight crew." A dispatcher riding in the jump seat is normally not considered a crewmember unless participating in required dispatcher training.

15. What is the difference between a decision altitude (DA) and a decision height (DH)? (14 CFR §1.1)

A DA is the altitude above mean sea level (MSL) that pilots fly to on a precision approach. The DH is the height above the touchdown zone of the runway at which the aircraft will be located when the altimeter indicates arrival at the DA. The DA/DH is the point on a precision approach at which a pilot must decide to land or execute a missed approach.

16. How is the critical engine determined in an aircraft? (14 CFR §1.1)

The engine, if it were to fail, that would most adversely affect the controllability and/or performance of the aircraft is termed the critical engine. Most twin-engine jet aircraft have no critical engine as the failure of either engine has identical effects. In four-engine jet aircraft, the outboard engines are considered critical because the failure of one will cause a larger yaw moment than the failure of an inboard engine. Also, wind and aircraft system failures that accompany an engine failure are sometimes take into consideration when determining the critical engine.

17. What is ETOPS? (14 CFR §1.1; AC 120-42)

Extended Operations (ETOPS) refers to flights that have a portion of their route beyond one-hour flying time, with one inoperative engine, from the nearest suitable airport for emergency landing. Up until 1985, twin-engine aircraft could not be more than 60 minutes from a suitable alternate. This precluded their use on long-haul oceanic routes. Specific aircraft and engine combinations can now be certified to allow for the operation of flights up to 240 minutes from a suitable alternate. (Certification testing is currently underway to allow for 330-minute ETOPS.)

18. What is considered an extended overwater operation? (14 CFR §1.1)

For fixed-wing aircraft, an extended overwater operation is when an aircraft flies beyond 50 NM from the nearest shoreline. This type of operation requires the installation of special equipment. If an aircraft is not properly equipped, it must remain within 50 NM of a shoreline. For example, air carriers that fly to the Caribbean will often plan routes that remain close to or overhead island chains so that they can utilize aircraft in their fleet that do not have the necessary overwater equipment.

19. What is a "flight level"? When is this term used? (14 CFR §1.1)

Cruise altitudes of aircraft are referred to flight levels (FL) above 17,999 feet in the United States. Flight levels are indicated by three numbers. For example, FL240 is a cruise altitude of 24,000 feet. FLs are determined when the altimeter is set to 29.92". Other countries have different, usually lower, thresholds to begin using FLs.

20. What is a "flight plan"? (14 CFR §1.1)

A flight plan is a standard form that conveys critical flight data to Air Traffic Control. Flight plans include information such as the departure airport, destination airport, route of flight, estimated time of departure, estimated time enroute, flight rule type (IFR/VFR), and fuel onboard. The FAA now requires flights using random and/or RNAV routes to use the ICAO flight plan form (FAA form 7233-4), which differs from the typical FAA form 7233-1.

21. When is the operation of aircraft considered to be flight time? (14 CFR §1.1)

Flight time is counted from when an aircraft is first moved under its own power for the purpose of flight until it comes to rest after landing.

22. What does it mean if an airport or an aircraft is said to be experiencing IFR conditions? (14 CFR §1.1)

This would mean that conditions are lower than those authorized to conduct VFR flight. In general, an airport is considered to be IFR when the weather is reported to be less than 3 SM visibility and the ceiling is less than 1,000 feet.

23. What is an "instrument approach procedure" (IAP)? (14 CFR §1.1)

An instrument approach procedure is a set of maneuvers that safely guide an aircraft to an airport. IAPs can be used anytime, but are intended to assist in landing during poor weather conditions.

24. What is a "long-range communication system" (LRCS)? What are two examples of this type of system? (14 CFR §1.1)

A LRCS provides aircraft with the capability to communicate in remote areas beyond the line of site of typical very high frequency (VHF) radio stations. Examples include satellite and high frequency (HF) communications systems. The latter bounces radio waves off of the atmosphere to ensure constant communication over long distances.

25. What is a "long-range navigation system" (LRNS)? What are some examples of this type of system? (14 CFR §1.1)

A LRNS is a navigation device that is suitable as the sole means of navigation over long distances that are out of range of typical ground-based navigation sources. These systems have at least one, but often more than one, input from GPS, inertial navigation, or LORAN (which, however, is currently deactivated).

26. High altitude flight planning airspeeds are given as Mach numbers. How is Mach number defined? (14 CFR §1.1)

Mach number is the ratio of the true airspeed of an aircraft to the ambient speed of sound. The true airspeed (TAS) of an aircraft increases as altitude increases. The speed of sound decreases as temperature decreases (which occurs with increases in altitude). Thus, TAS and Mach converge as an aircraft climbs. If a constant indicated airspeed (IAS) is held as an aircraft climbs, Mach number will gradually increase.

27. Define V_{EF}. (14 CFR §1.2)

V_{EF} is the speed at which an engine is assumed to fail during takeoff (for certification and performance purposes).

28. Define V_{MO} and M_{MO}. (14 CFR §1.2)

These are maximum operating speeds. V_{MO} is expressed in knots and M_{MO} is expressed in Mach number.

29. Define V_1. (14 CFR §1.2)

V_1 is often referred to as takeoff decision speed. This is the speed at which first action must be taken to abort a takeoff following an engine failure in order to successfully stop an aircraft within the calculated accelerate-stop distance. Pilots must continue a takeoff if they have not initiated an abort at or below V_1.

30. Define V_R. (14 CFR §1.2)

V_R is the rotation speed during takeoff.

31. Define V_2. (14 CFR §1.2)

V_2 is takeoff safety speed. This is an airspeed that will allow an aircraft to continue a takeoff with a positive slope (i.e., be able to climb). This speed must be achieved by an altitude of 35 feet no later than reaching the departure end of the runway.

32. What is an "MDA"? (14 CFR §1.1)

The minimum descent altitude (MDA) is the lowest altitude to which an aircraft is authorized to descend during a non-precision or circling IAP. Pilots can descend from MDA if they have the runway environment in sight, have the required visibility to land, and can make a normal descent to the runway.

33. What is a "non-precision approach"? Name some examples of this type of procedure. (14 CFR §1.1)

Any approach procedure without vertical guidance, typically in the form of an electronic glide slope, is considered non-precision. Examples include VOR, NDB, SDF, and Localizer approaches. LNAV, LP GPS approaches, and Airport Surveillance Radar (ASR) approaches are also considered non-precision.

34. What is "operational control"? (14 CFR §1.1)

Operational control is the authority to initiate, conduct, and terminate a flight. Dispatchers must be able to exercise operational control over a flight over its entire route at all times.

35. Why is operational control important?

Operational control ensures that aircraft are operated under safe conditions and are monitored throughout a flight. The FAA also requires that flights always remain under control of the company operating them. Flights must always be able to be communicated with by dispatch in order to guarantee these aforementioned provisions.

36. What is the definition of the term "pilot-in-command"? (14 CFR §1.1)

The pilot-in-command (PIC) is the person responsible for the operation and safety of flight. While this part of the regulation states that the PIC is the final authority to these ends, the PIC shares the responsibility of safe conduct of the flight with the aircraft dispatcher.

37. What is a "precision approach"? Name some examples of this type of procedure. (14 CFR §1.1)

Precision approaches are IAPs that have glide slope guidance. Examples include ILS, precision approach radar (PAR), LNAV/VNAV, LPV, and some LDA approaches.

38. What is a "stopway"? (14 CFR §1.1)

A stopway is an area beyond the end of a runway that must be at least as wide as the runway. The surface must be able to support an aircraft without resulting in structural damage. Stopways are designed to be used during aborted takeoffs. The stopway can be counted as usable surface for the calculation of accelerate-stop distances.

39. What is TCAS II? (14 CFR §1.1)

Traffic Alert and Collision Avoidance System (TCAS) II is an electronic device that notifies pilots of proximate aircraft and can issue vertical escape instructions if an aircraft is deemed to be a collision hazard. TCAS cannot detect aircraft without transponders.

40. What is "true airspeed" (TAS)? (14 CFR §1.1)

True airspeed is the speed at which an aircraft is moving through the air. A simpler explanation is that in a no-wind condition, TAS will equal ground speed.

41. What is an "AFM"? (14 CFR §1.2, 121.141)

An airplane flight manual (AFM) is basically an instruction manual for how to operate a particular aircraft.

42. Define AGL. (14 CFR §1.2)

AGL stands for above ground level, or the height of an aircraft above the ground. This is also referred to as absolute altitude.

43. Define ALS. (14 CFR §1.2)

An approach light system (ALS) is used to guide aircraft from an area off the end of the runway to the threshold and is typically used in poor weather or at night.

44. What is an "APU"? (14 CFR §1.2)

An auxiliary power unit (APU) is a miniature jet engine, usually in the tail of a transport aircraft, that is used for electric and/or bleed (pneumatic) air on the ground and in the air (typically in emergency or abnormal situations).

45. What is DME? (14 CFR §1.2)

Distance measuring equipment (DME) is used to determine how far an aircraft is flying from a particular NAVAID. GPS can be used as a substitute for DME under certain circumstances. DME is a requirement for flights above FL240 in the U.S.

46. What is a GS? (14 CFR §1.2)

A glide slope (GS) is an electronically produced vertical guidance system used by aircraft during landing. GS can also be used to represent aircraft ground speed.

47. What is HIRL? (14 CFR §1.2)

High intensity runway light (HIRL) systems are very bright lights that line the edge of the runway.

48. What is the ICAO? (14 CFR §1.2; ICAO Website)

The International Civil Aviation Organization (ICAO) is an international entity that aims to help standardize aviation operations in a global environment. Its objectives are to augment safety, security, environmental protection, efficiency, continuity, and rule of law.

49. What is IFR? (14 CFR §1.2)

Instrument flight rules (IFR) govern aircraft operations when weather is less than required to conduct a flight under visual flight rules (VFR) and/or anytime an aircraft is operated on an IFR flight plan. Most air carrier operations are conducted under IFR.

50. What is an "ILS"? (14 CFR §1.2)

An instrument landing system (ILS) approach is a precision approach that provides lateral guidance to the runway in the form of a localizer and also provides vertical guidance to runway in the form of a glide slope.

51. What is an "MAA"? (14 CFR §1.2; FAA-H-8261-1)

A maximum authorized altitude (MAA) is the maximum altitude an aircraft can fly over a certain segment of an airway while en route. These are published, as necessary, on IFR enroute charts.

52. What is an "MCA"? (14 CFR §1.2; FAA-H-8261-1)

A minimum crossing altitude (MCA) is the minimum altitude at which an aircraft must cross a point (waypoint/intersection) along an airway.

53. What is an "MEA"? (14 CFR §1.2, 91.177; FAA-H-8261-1)

A minimum enroute altitude (MEA) is the minimum altitude an aircraft must typically fly along a published route such as an airway. Flight at or above the MEA provides 1,000 feet of obstacle protection in non-mountainous areas and 2,000 feet in mountainous areas. Except where there is an MEA Gap, flight at or above the MEA also assures navigation signal coverage. Flight at the MEA does not ensure radio communication or radar coverage.

54. What is a "MOCA"? (14 CFR §1.2, 91.177; FAA-H-8261-1)

A minimum obstruction clearance altitude (MOCA) is another minimum altitude used along published routes such as an airway. The MOCA provides 1,000 feet of obstacle protection in non-mountainous areas and 2,000 feet of obstacle protection in mountainous areas, much like the MEA. However, the MOCA only assures ground-based navigation (e.g., a VOR) coverage within 22 NM of the NAVAID. Therefore, an aircraft using VOR navigation cannot descend to the MOCA unless within 22 NM of the station. Regulations now include a provision that allows an aircraft with RNAV (e.g., GPS) to descend to the MOCA regardless of the distance from the defining NAVAID.

55. What is an "MRA"? (14 CFR §1.2; FAA-H-8261-1)

A minimum reception altitude (MRA) is the minimum altitude an aircraft must maintain in order to identify a specific intersection/waypoint if relying upon certain types of ground-based navigation. For example, if the only way an aircraft could identify an intersection along an airway was to tune a distant VOR to use a particular radial, and the aircraft could only receive that VOR at 8,000 feet, an MRA of 8,000 feet would be published. However, an aircraft that could identify that intersection through other means, such as GPS, would not need to comply with the MRA.

56. What is a "NM"? (14 CFR §1.2)

A nautical mile (NM) is the typical measure used for aeronautical flight planning, distances and speed measurement. A NM is 6,080 feet as compared to a statute mile (SM), which is 5,280 feet. SM is usually used for weather reports and for approach minimums.

57. What is "NAT MNPSA"? (*North Atlantic MNPSA Operations Manual*)

The North Atlantic Minimum Navigation Performance Specifications Airspace (NAT MNPSA) is a region that most aircraft transiting to and from Europe and the U.S. traverse. Special rules apply as to how aircraft operate in NAT airspace, the equipment requirements, and the training required to operate flights in such airspace. NAT MNPSA is located over the North Atlantic from FL285 to FL420. Air traffic services in this airspace are provided by Reykjavik, New York, Gander, Shanwick, or Santa Maria depending upon where the aircraft is located within the NAT MNPSA.

58. What is a "NAT track"? (*North Atlantic MNPSA Operations Manual*)

A NAT (North Atlantic) track is a route for aircraft flying between Europe and the United States. These change on a daily basis to take advantage of winds and to avoid turbulence and other adverse weather conditions. NAT tracks are defined by entry points that are named fixes (waypoints). Over the Atlantic, fixes are defined by latitude and longitude (for example 50N/30W).

59. What is "NOPAC"? (14 CFR §1.2; AC 90-70)

NOPAC is the Northern Pacific area of operation. It is a set of organized routes between the Alaska/Canada region and Asia.

60. What are "Ops Specs"? (14 CFR §1.2, 119.49)

Operations specifications (Ops Specs) are a series of publications that an air carrier produces to indicate to the FAA how it will comply with regulations and how it will conduct its operations.

61. What is "PACOTS"? (14 CFR §1.2; Defense Internet NOTAM Service)

PACOTS is the Pacific Organized Track System. These are set routes between Japan and the Western U.S. and between Japan and Hawaii. These are much like NAT tracks in that they are changed regularly to take advantage of ambient weather conditions.

62. What is an "RCLS"? (14 CFR §1.2)

A runway centerline light system is a series of lights embedded in the pavement of runways to mark the centerline at night and in poor visibility.

63. What is "RVR"? (14 CFR §1.2)

Runway visual range (RVR) is a visibility measurement for a specific runway given in feet (in the U.S.; some other countries report this in meters). RVR can be specified as the minimum visibility necessary to land on an IAP.

64. What is "SATCOM"? (14 CFR §1.2)

Satellite communication (SATCOM) is a means of communication via satellites. It is not limited by line-of-sight restrictions, as are VHF radios.

65. What is "TACAN"? (14 CFR §1.2)

Ultra-high frequency tactical air navigational (TACAN) aid is a type of navigation avionics used by military aircraft. Civilian aircraft can also use TACAN to provide DME when properly equipped.

66. What are "TDZL"? (14 CFR §1.2)

Touchdown zone lights (TDZL) are a series of lights on each side of the runway centerline spanning the first 3,000 feet of the runway to assist pilots landing in poor visibility and at night. TDZL, coupled with runway centerline lights, can reduce the required visibility to land from certain types of IAPs. For example, typical ILS approaches require ½ SM or 2,400 RVR to land. With RCLS and TDZL, this requirement could possibly be reduced to 1,800 RVR. (1,800 RVR must be published as the approach minimums to use this value.)

67. What is a "VOR"? (14 CFR §1.2)

A very high frequency omni-directional range (VOR) station is a common NAVAID and is commonly used to define airway routes.

68. What is a "VORTAC"? (14 CFR §1.2)

This is a VOR co-located with a TACAN station. For civilian pilots, this means the VOR can be used to provide DME if the aircraft is properly equipped.

B. 14 CFR Part 65

1. Aircraft dispatcher certification requirements are covered under what part of the 14 CFR? (14 CFR §65.1)

The requirements associated with becoming and serving as an aircraft dispatcher (ADX) are found in 14 CFR Part 65.

2. If your ADX certificate is suspended, can you apply for any additional certifications or ratings? (14 CFR §65.11)

No, you must wait until the suspension period has ended.

3. If your ADX certificate is revoked, can you reapply for the certification? (14 CFR §65.11)

Yes, you may reapply after a one-year period following the date of revocation.

4. If you are convicted of any federal or state statute concerning alcohol or drugs, what can you expect as a penalty? (14 CFR §65.12)

You can expect prohibition of applying for certification or ratings for a year following the date of the final conviction. Certifications and ratings that you currently hold may also be suspended or revoked.

5. How long is your temporary ADX certificate effective? (14 CFR §65.13)

The temporary certificate is good for 120 days following its issuance.

6. What is a security disqualification for an ADX certification? (14 CFR §65.14)

If the Transportation Security Administration (TSA) deems you to be a security threat, the FAA can revoke or suspend your certification or rating. You will also be ineligible to apply for certifications or ratings.

7. How long is your ADX certificate valid? (14 CFR §65.15)

ADX certificates are valid until they are surrendered, suspended, or revoked.

8. You are about to go to work to dispatch flights for your air carrier employer and realize you have lost your ADX certificate. What should you do? (14 CFR §65.16)

You can request a temporary replacement certificate from the FAA. This will be sent via telegram and will be valid for 60 days.

9. What is the minimum passing score for the ADX written exam? (14 CFR §65.17)

70 percent.

10. You do not need an endorsement for taking the ADX written exam. What do you need to do if you fail the exam? (14 CFR §65.19)

You can wait 30 days and retake the exam without special endorsement. If you wish to retake the exam earlier than 30 days following failure, you must receive an endorsement stating you have received instruction in the areas deemed deficient.

11. How long do you have to notify the FAA of a change of address? (14 CFR §65.21)

Thirty (30) days. Note this is for a change in your permanent address, which may be different than your mailing address.

12. When are you required to have your ADX certificate in your personal possession? (14 CFR §65.51)

Your ADX certificate must be in your personal possession whenever you are acting as an aircraft dispatcher and exercising authority in coordination with the pilot in command for a flight operating under air commerce.

13. How old must you be to take the ADX written exam? (14 CFR §65.53)

You must be 21 years old.

14. How old must you be to take the ADX practical exam? (14 CFR §65.53)

You must be 21 years old.

15. How old must you be to act as an aircraft dispatcher?
(14 CFR §65.53; FAA Document 8900.1 Vol. 5 Chap. 5)

23 years old. If you take the practical exam at an age less than 23 (but a minimum of 21) you will receive a letter that you can exchange for a certificate at a local Flight Standards District Office when you turn 23.

16. What are the eligibility requirements to earn the Aircraft Dispatcher certificate?
(14 CFR §65.53, 65.55)

You must have passed the ADX knowledge exam within the past 24 calendar months, be 23 years old (or 21 years or older and aware that you will not receive a certificate until age 23), be able to read, speak and understand English, meet the experience requirements as outlined in §65.57, and take and pass the practical exam outlined in §65.59.

17. What are the aeronautical experience prerequisites for taking the ADX practical test? (14 CFR §65.57)

A minimum of two years out of the previous three years acting in:
• Military operations as a pilot, flight navigator, or meteorologist, or
• Part 121 aircraft operations as a pilot, flight engineer, or meteorologist, or
• In aircraft operations as an air traffic controller or flight service specialist, or
• In aircraft operations serving in a capacity deemed equivalent by the administrator.

The other option, in lieu of the above, is graduation from an approved aircraft dispatcher course.

18. **The ADX practical test must include the assessment of skill in dispatching what type of aircraft?** (14 CFR §65.59)

At least one type of large aircraft used in air carrier operations.

19. **How many hours of instruction are required in an approved aircraft dispatcher course?** (14 CFR §65.61)

A minimum of 200 hours of instruction must be given.

20. **Upon graduation from an approved aircraft dispatcher course, how long is the letter of graduation valid (in other words, how long does an individual have to take the practical)?** (14 CFR §65.70)

90 days. However, revalidation can take place if the course provider determines the individual is still competent to take the test.

C. 14 CFR Part 91

1. **What is the maximum speed allowed within Class B airspace?** (14 CFR §91.117)

250 knots.

2. **What is the maximum speed allowed within Class C airspace?** (14 CFR §91.117)

250 knots, except when within 4 NM and 2,500 feet of the primary airport, in which case the limit is 200 knots.

3. **What is the maximum speed allowed within Class D airspace?** (14 CFR §91.117)

200 knots.

4. **When flying a U.S.-registered large transport aircraft outside the U.S., which rules apply—those of the U.S. or those of the host country?** (14 CFR §91.703)

Pilots and dispatchers should abide by the rules of the host country, ICAO convention, or appropriate applicable U.S. FARs (as long as they are not inconsistent with the regulations of the host country).

5. **What is required of an operator to conduct flights in Minimum Navigation Performance Specifications (MNPS) airspace?** (14 CFR §91.705)

The aircraft must be equipped with the appropriate navigation system(s) necessary to comply with MNPS standards and authorized by the administrator to conduct flights in MNPS airspace.

6. **What is required of an operator to conduct flights in reduced vertical separation minimums (RVSM) airspace?** (14 CFR §91.706)

The aircraft must be equipped with the appropriate navigation system(s) necessary to comply with RVSM standards and authorized by the administrator to conduct flights in RVSM airspace. Pilots and dispatchers also must be properly trained to operate in or release flights into RVSM airspace.

D. 14 CFR Parts 110 and 119

1. What is the definition of a "domestic operation"? (14 CFR §110.2)

A domestic operation is any operation fitting the following constraints:

- Type of aircraft: turbojet aircraft; or an aircraft with more than 9 passenger seats (excluding crewmember seats); and/or an airplane with a payload capacity of more than 7,500 pounds.

- Operating in the following area(s): between any point within the 48 contiguous U.S. (or in the District of Columbia); operations solely within the 48 contiguous U.S. (or the District of Columbia); operations within any state, territory, or possession of the U.S.; or any flight route designated by the Administrator as domestic.

2. What is the definition of a "flag operation"? (14 CFR §110.2)

A flag operation is any operation fitting the following constraints:

- Type of aircraft: turbojet aircraft; or an aircraft with more than 9 passenger seats (excluding crewmember seats); and/or an airplane with a payload capacity of more than 7,500 pounds.

- Operating in the following area(s): between any point(s) in the State of Alaska or Hawaii to any point outside these states; between any point in a U.S. territory or possession to any point outside these areas; between any point in the 48 contiguous U.S. (or the District of Columbia) and any point outside the 48 contiguous U.S. (or the District of Columbia); or any point outside the U.S. to another point outside the U.S.

3. Is a turbojet flight from Anchorage, AK, to Seattle, WA, a domestic or a flag flight? (14 CFR §110.2)

This would be considered a flag flight because it is from the state of Alaska to a point outside the state.

4. Is a turbojet flight from Honolulu, HI, to Maui, HI, considered a domestic or a flag flight? (14 CFR §110.2)

This would be considered a domestic flight because it operates entirely within the state of Hawaii.

5. What is a "provisional airport"? (14 CFR §110.2)

A provisional airport is an airport to which service can be provided when the regular airport of use is not available.

6. What is a regular airport? (14 CFR §110.2)

A regular airport is an airport used by a scheduled operator and listed in the operations specifications.

7. What is the definition of a "supplemental operation"? (14 CFR §110.2)

Any operation fitting the following constraints:

- Type of aircraft: turbojet aircraft; or an aircraft with more than 30 passenger seats (excluding crewmember seats); and/or an airplane with a payload capacity of more than 7,500 pounds; a propeller aircraft with 9 to less than 31 seats (excluding crewmember seats) designated for supplemental use in operations specifications; a turbojet aircraft with 9 to less than 31 seats (excluding crewmember seats) designated for supplemental use in operations specifications.

- Operated in the following manner: in a scenario when the departure time, departure location, and arrival location are negotiated with the customer (or their representative); an all-cargo flight; or a public charter.

8. Operations specifications (Ops Specs) must contain what minimum items? (14 CFR §119.7)

Ops Specs must contain the authorizations, limitations, and procedures for each type of operation conducted, and operational procedures for each class and size of aircraft utilized.

E. 14 CFR Part 121

1. A U.S.-registered aircraft governed by 14 CFR Part 121 is operated outside the U.S. What regulations apply to such an operation? (14 CFR §121.11)

The most restrictive of FARs or the regulations of the host country apply.

2. Can an aircraft dispatched under 14 CFR Part 121 ever be outside direct two-way (or suitable) communication with the operator? (14 CFR §121.99)

No. Under normal conditions, reliable and rapid communication capabilities must exist between the aircraft and the company.

3. What additional communication requirement is necessary for ETOPS? (14 CFR §121.99)

Voice communication capability is a requirement for ETOPS, except when voice communication is not possible or is of such poor quality that it is not deemed reliable, in which case a substitute communication system can be used. For example, datalink communication may be used as a substitute. For ETOPS beyond 180 minutes, satellite-phone (or equivalent) voice capability is required for communication between aircraft and both the company and air traffic services. If it is determined that satellite-phone (or equivalent) voice communication is not possible or is of such poor quality that it is not deemed reliable, a substitute communication system can be used.

4. Can a dispatcher use any weather source when conducting domestic or flag operations, such as a commercial weather website? (14 CFR §121.101)

Weather reports used to control flights must be provided by the U.S. National Weather Service or be prepared by a source approved by the FAA Administrator. Also, operators must have a means of being informed of adverse weather conditions (such as turbulence and thunderstorms) for each route and airport used. Such weather information sources must be secure so that they cannot be tampered with by outside parties.

5. What is the minimum level of navigation aid coverage required to dispatch a flight on domestic or flag routes? (14 CFR §121.103)

A suitable number and type of NAVAIDS needed to fly a route per the expectations of accuracy demanded by ATC. NAVAIDS are not required for certain VFR operations, if authorized in Ops Specs.

6. Do ETOPS alternate airports have specific rescue and fire-fighting service (RFFS) requirements? (14 CFR §121.106)

Yes. All ETOPS alternates must have RFFS. For ETOPS flights of up to 180 minutes, an ICAO Category 4 or better RFFS rating is required. For flights beyond 180 minutes, each alternate must have at least a Category 4 rating, but aircraft must remain within the authorized maximum flight time from a Category 7 RFFS airport. In cases in which such requirements cannot be met by services immediately available at the airport, local RFFS can be counted towards meeting those requirements, as long as a 30-minute or better response time is possible and local RFFS can be notified of inbound emergency aircraft.

7. Can an aircraft be dispatched on a route outside of controlled airspace? (14 CFR §121.113)

Yes, as long as it is deemed safe and approved by the Administrator. Of course, this authorization would be in Ops Specs.

8. Can single-engine airplanes be operated under CFR 14 Part 121? (14 CFR §121.159)

No.

9. For the purposes of takeoff, a turbine aircraft cannot takeoff at a weight that exceeds what values? (14 CFR §121.189, 121.191, 121.195)

- Aircraft structural limits.
  - The maximum takeoff weight listed in the Airplane Flight Manual.
- Runway limits (based on runway lengths and ambient conditions).
  - A weight that will cause the aircraft to exceed the accelerate-stop distance plus any stopway.
  - A weight that will prevent the aircraft from having a takeoff distance that is greater than the length of the runway plus a clearway (which cannot be longer than one-half the length of the runway).
  - A weight which will cause the aircraft to have a ground roll in excess of the length of the runway.
- Aircraft climb limit(s).
  - A weight which will prevent the aircraft from having a net takeoff path that clears all obstacles by 35 feet vertically and 200 feet horizontally within the airport boundaries (300 feet horizontally outside airport boundaries).
- Enroute driftdown maximum allowable weight(s). (*See* 121.191)
- Landing runway limits. (*See* 121.195)
- Landing climb (go-around) limits. (*See* 121.195)

10. Can a wet runway ever be considered to be dry? (14 CFR §121.189)

Yes, if the runway is grooved or has a porous friction course (PFC) surface and is acceptable to the Administrator. This exemption would be listed in the carrier's Ops Specs.

11. What is "driftdown"? (14 CFR §121.191)

Driftdown is the concept that if an aircraft loses an engine en route, it will slowly drift from its original cruising altitude down to a lower service ceiling. Because this often is gradual and takes many miles to occur, aircraft can be dispatched over routes where their service ceiling with an engine inoperative is less than the highest minimum safe altitude along the route, but the aircraft is expected to reach an area after completing a driftdown where the minimum safe altitude is lower, or is able to avoid the area of concern altogether before completing the driftdown.

12. What are the two ways that dispatchers can ensure that an aircraft can comply with the driftdown requirements of CFR 14 Part 121? (14 CFR §121.191)

Dispatchers must use the method approved in the carrier's Ops Specs, which will utilize one of the two driftdown methods:

* Aircraft will not exceed a weight (for ambient conditions) that will prohibit it from maintaining a positive slope (it can climb) and clear all obstacles within five statute miles either side of the aircraft route by 1,000 feet. The aircraft must also have a positive slope upon arrival at 1,500 feet above the airport to which it diverts following the engine failure (if certificated after 8/29/1959).

* Aircraft will not exceed a weight that would prohibit a net flight path that clears all obstacles within five statute miles either side of the aircraft flight path by 2,000 feet. The aircraft must also have a positive slope upon arrival at 1,500 feet above the airport to which it diverts following the engine failure (if certificated after 9/30/1958).

The easiest way to distinguish between these two methods is to think of the first as if the aircraft falls immediately from its cruise altitude to its new service ceiling. The second method assumes that the aircraft slowly drifts down following a curved path to its new service ceiling. In the first case, an aircraft must be able to maintain altitude (and even climb slightly) if it lost an engine. The altitude that it falls to must exceed 1,000 feet above all obstacles within five SM either side of the route. The second method is much more complicated to calculate. As the aircraft descends it will burn fuel and become lighter and descend at a slower rate. Its new service ceiling also changes as it loses weight. Further, the aircraft is moving along its route, and obstacles that might be issues at some point along the route could end up not being issues depending upon the weight of the aircraft as it drifts by those points.

Thus for simplicity, method one is easiest to calculate and use. Unfortunately, in some parts of the world, this simpler method might prohibit certain routes, so the more complex method might have to be utilized to take advantage of the more gradual driftdown that aircraft actually make in such an emergency.

13. If using the net flight path method for driftdown, what assumptions must be made to determine if the aircraft is capable of complying with this method? (14 CFR §121.191)

* The engine fails at the most critical point on the route.
* The aircraft will pass the critical obstacle and will be the same distance or closer to a nearby NAVAID than this obstacle.
* Most adverse winds are used.
* Fuel dumping will occur (if applicable).
* A legal enroute alternate airport is specified.
* Fuel (and oil) consumption can be considered when determining the net flight path (i.e., you get credit for the aircraft losing weight as it descends).

14. What are the driftdown requirements for a turbine aircraft with two inoperative engines en route (certificated after 8/29/1959)? (14 CFR §121.193)

The aircraft will never be more than 90 minutes from an airport that complies with 121.197. Also, the aircraft will not exceed a weight that will prevent it from maintaining a net flight path that will clear the highest obstacle 5 SM either side of the intended route by at least 2,000 feet. It is also assumed that this aircraft will lose both engines at the most critical point in flight, will have a positive slope at 1,500 feet above the alternate airport, and have enough fuel to fly at this altitude/location for 15 minutes or more, and that fuel dumping will occur (if applicable and the consumption of fuel/oil can be considered).

15. A turbine aircraft is not permitted to exceed a weight that prevents it from landing within ____ percent of the effective length of a runway (from a point 50 feet above the intersection of the obstruction clearance plane and the runway). (14 CFR §121.195)

60 percent.

16. Which runway(s) can/should be considered when calculating maximum weights for landing? (14 CFR §121.195)

- Most favorable runway (still air).

- Most suitable runway in consideration of ambient conditions, the aircraft, available approaches/facilities, and terrain.

17. A turbopropeller aircraft is not permitted to exceed a weight that prevents it from landing within ____ percent of the effective length of a runway (from a point 50 feet above the intersection of the obstruction clearance plane and the runway). (14 CFR §121.195)

70 percent.

18. If a runway is considered to be wet or slippery, what additional consideration must be made in terms of the length of runway that must exist? (14 CFR §121.195)

In the case of a wet or slippery runway, aircraft must be able to stop within 115 percent of the length required by the regulation applicable to the type of aircraft (i.e., within 60 percent of the available runway for turbojets; 70 percent for turboprops).

19. At its current weight, the data you have on the turbojet aircraft you are dispatching indicates that it can land within 5,000 feet. How long must the runway be in order to dispatch the flight? (14 CFR §121.195)

According to regulations, a turbojet must be able to land within no more than 60 percent of the available runway. You must consider how long a runway must be so that 60 percent of this value is 5,000 (the actual aircraft capability). So the unknown runway length multiplied by 60 percent would yield 5,000. Simply divide 5,000 by .6 to get the required runway length of 8,333 feet.

20. **At its current weight, the data you have on the turbojet aircraft you are dispatching indicates that it can land within 5,000 feet. It has been raining all day and the runway is reported as wet. How long must the runway be in order to dispatch the flight?** (14 CFR §121.195)

According to regulations, a turbojet must be able to land within no more than 60 percent of the available runway. For wet runways, this value must be 115 percent of this aforementioned requirement. As noted in question 19, the dry runway requirement would be 8,333 feet. Multiply this by 1.15 to get the requirement for wet conditions. The runway must therefore be at least 9,582 feet to dispatch the aircraft under these conditions.

21. **You are planning to dispatch a flight to an airport with runway 9/27 (8,000 feet long) and runway 18/36 (9,200 feet long). Winds are 360 at 30 knots. The maximum demonstrated crosswind for your aircraft is 25 knots. Your Ops Specs state that no operations can be conducted in excess of demonstrated limits or when tailwinds exceed 10 knots. The weather is poor and the only instrument approach is to runway 18. Landing data indicates your aircraft could land in 5,500 feet in dry conditions. Can you legally dispatch your flight?** (14 CFR §121.195)

Yes. You need 9,166 feet to comply with regulations. Don't forget that you have to consider landing on the most suitable runway per ambient conditions. However, 121.195(e) allows you to neglect this requirement if you list an alternate airport. If authorized by your Ops Specs, you and your flight crew could consider the option to do the approach to runway 18 and circle to runway 36.

22. **At its current weight, the data you have on the turbojet aircraft you are dispatching indicates that it can land within 5,000 feet. How long must the runway be in order to dispatch the flight to an alternate airport?** (14 CFR §121.197)

To use an alternate airport with a turbojet, the aircraft cannot weigh more than a value that will allow it stop within 60 percent of the effective length of a runway at the time of arrival (from a point 50 feet above the intersection of the obstruction clearance plane and the runway). The runway must therefore be 8,333 feet long to allow this airport to be used legally.

23. **At its current weight, the data you have on the turboprop aircraft you are dispatching indicates that it can land within 5,000 feet. How long must the runway be in order to dispatch the flight to an alternate airport?** (14 CFR §121.197)

To use an alternate airport with a turbojet, the aircraft cannot weigh more than a value that will allow it stop within 70 percent of the effective length of a runway at the time of arrival (from a point 50 feet above the intersection of the obstruction clearance plane and the runway). Therefore, the runway must be 7,142 feet long to allow this airport to be used legally.

24. **How much oxygen must be aboard for crewmembers on a turbine, pressurized aircraft?** (14 CFR §121.333)

When flying above 10,000 feet, a two-hour supply of oxygen must be available for each flight crewmember (jump seat riders are typically considered "on duty").

25. How much portable oxygen must be available for use by flight attendants when operating above FL250? (14 CFR §121.333)

At least a 15-minute supply must be available, unless it is determined that there are enough portable oxygen and spare masks throughout the cabin to allow flight attendants to have access to oxygen regardless of their position in the cabin.

26. What equipment is required in order for an aircraft to be considered "overwater equipped"? (14 CFR §121.339)

- Life preservers for each occupant (with locator lights).
- An adequate number of life rafts to fit everyone onboard plus one additional raft (at a minimum) in case one does not work or is lost.
- A survival-type emergency locator transmitter.
- All items must be clearly marked in terms of their location and use.
- A survival kit appropriate for the route (i.e., polar, overwater, jungle, etc.).

27. Can cargo be carried in the passenger compartment? (14 CFR §121.285)

Yes, if approved in the Ops Specs, and if the following provisions are met:
- Cargo bin must be able to withstand appropriate load factors.
- Maximum cargo weight is clearly marked and not exceeded.
- Bin does not cause undue stress on aircraft structure.
- Bin must be secured to floor so that it can withstand appropriate loads.
- Bin must be closed and flame resistant.
- Provisions must be made to prevent shifting of cargo.
- Bin cannot block passenger view of necessary signage, including marked exits.
- If cargo is carried aft of the passenger compartment, it cannot in any way cause injury to occupants.

28. Can a transport-category airplane be dispatched on a flight with an inoperative airborne weather radar? (14 CFR §121.357)

For IFR flights (or night VFR flights) when thunderstorms are reasonably expected, an aircraft cannot be dispatched with an inoperative airborne weather radar. Exemptions are available for operations in Hawaii and Alaska.

29. How many flight attendants are required to be onboard an aircraft with 75 seats and only 50 people onboard? (14 CFR §121.391)

Two flight attendants are required. The number required is based on the number of seats, not the number of people aboard. For aircraft up to 51 seats, one flight attendant is needed; from 51 to 100 seats, two are required; and for every additional unit (or part thereof) of 50, one more flight attendant is required.

30. You are responsible for an aircraft that required five flight attendants. The flight you are planning has an intermediate stop. How many flight attendants are required to stay on the aircraft during such a stop? (14 CFR §121.393)

In this case, two. The regulation states that the number of flight attendants required for the flight, divided by two and rounded down (if necessary), is the number that must stay on the aircraft during a stop. The engines must be shut down and a floor-level exit must remain open. A qualified individual (such as a flight crewmember) may be substituted for one of the flight attendants.

31. You are responsible for an aircraft that required one flight attendant. The flight you are planning has an intermediate stop. How many flight attendants are required to stay on the aircraft during such a stop? (14 CFR §121.393)

In this case, one. The regulation states that the number of flight attendants required for the flight, divided by two and rounded down (if necessary)—but never less than one—must stay on the aircraft during a stop. The engines must be shut down and a floor-level exit must remain open. A qualified individual (such as a flight crewmember) may be substituted for the flight attendant.

32. How many dispatchers are required for each domestic or flag operation flight? (14 CFR §121.395)

There is no set number. The regulation just states that there must be enough to maintain operational control.

33. What is the minimum training program course content for dispatchers? (14 CFR §121.415)

The training curriculum must cover the duties and responsibilities of dispatchers, applicable Federal Aviation Regulations, and the operator's certificate authorizations and Ops Specs, as well as the certificate holder's operating manual.

34. When would a dispatcher need to go through differences training? (14 CFR §121.418)

Whenever a variant of an existing aircraft is brought into operation, dispatchers must be given training on the ways that particular aircraft is different from existing type(s). For example, if your carrier was operating Boeing 757-200 aircraft and purchased 757-300 aircraft, instruction would be required on the nuances of the new aircraft.

35. What subjects must be covered during initial and transition dispatch training? (14 CFR §121.422)

- Communication systems
- Meteorology/aviation weather
- Notices to Airmen (NOTAMs)
- Navigation aids and publications
- Dispatcher-pilot responsibilities
- How to determine "appropriate airports"
- Weather phenomenon and weather sources
- ATC
- Instrument approach procedures
- Dispatch resource management (DRM)

36. What additional training is required for each aircraft that the dispatcher may be required to dispatch? (14 CFR §121.422)

- General information and operational aspects
- Flight operation procedures
- Weight and balance
- Dispatch performance issues
- Flight planning (speed and fuel consumption)
- Emergency procedures

37. How does initial and transition training typically culminate? (14 CFR §121.422)

Dispatchers must pass a competency check to demonstrate required knowledge.

38. What is a Group I airplane? (14 CFR §121.422)

A Group I airplane is a propeller (reciprocating or turboprop) airplane.

39. What is a Group II airplane? (14 CFR §121.422)

A Group II airplane is a turbine (other than turboprop) airplane.

40. How many hours of instruction are typically required for initial dispatcher training for Group I airplanes? For Group II airplanes? (14 CFR §121.422)

- Group I: reciprocating propeller, 30 hours; turbopropeller, 40 hours.
- Group II: (jets) 40 hours.

41. What are the requirements to complete dispatcher recurrent training? (14 CFR §121.427)

The requirements are a quiz or review, instruction on the subjects found in initial training, and a competency check.

42. What is the minimum number of hours of instruction required for dispatcher recurrent training? (14 CFR §121.427)

- Group I: reciprocating propeller, 8 hours; turbopropeller, 10 hours.
- Group II: 20 hours.

43. You are planning to dispatch a flight to Aspen Colorado Airport. This airport is considered a "special airport" per 14 CFR §121.445. What is required of your pilot in command (PIC) to fly this flight? (14 CFR §121.445; FSIMS website)

Within the last 12 calendar months the PIC must have flown into Aspen, or familiarized himself with the airport using pictorial means (e.g., Jeppesen publishes picture approach plates that visually describe an airport). The exception to this rule (if allowed by Ops Specs) is if the weather at the airport is 3 miles visibility and a ceiling at least a 1,000 feet above the lowest MEA or MOCA, initial approach altitude.

44. Your airline has Saab 340 turboprops and Boeing 737 and 757 turbojets. As a dispatcher, you must have completed operating familiarization on which of these aircraft? (14 CFR §121.463)

You only need operating familiarization in one aircraft in each group. The Saab is a Group I airplane and the Boeing aircraft are Group II airplanes. Therefore, you must make familiarization flights on the Saab and one of the Boeing types.

45. What amount of operating familiarization flight time is required for dispatchers? (14 CFR §121.463)

Five hours must take place each year unless within the first 90 days of the initial introduction of the airplane into the carrier's operations.

46. Can the amount of required operating familiarization be reduced? (14 CFR §121.463)

The five-hour requirement can be reduced to a minimum of 2½ hours by substituting one additional takeoff and landing for an hour of flight.

47. Where must the dispatcher sit during operating familiarization flights?
(14 CFR §121.463)

Dispatchers must sit in the flight deck jump seat. If one is not available, they may sit in a forward passenger seat with a headset or speaker to hear operational communications.

48. How often must dispatchers complete operating familiarization flights?
(14 CFR §121.463)

Operating familiarization flights are required every 12 calendar months.

49. Can operating familiarization requirements be met in a simulator in lieu of riding in an airplane? (14 CFR §121.463)

Yes.

50. You are looking to complete your operating familiarization requirements, but have the opportunity to do so in a simulator. Can you reduce your hour requirements under these circumstances? (14 CFR §121.463)

No. When you use a simulator to fulfill operating familiarization requirements, no reduction is allowed.

51. Can you dispatch a flight on a route (and with operating procedures) with which you are not familiar? (14 CFR §121.463)

No, unless you coordinate with dispatchers who are familiar/qualified for such routes/ operations.

52. As a dispatcher, what is the maximum number of consecutive hours that you can be on duty? (14 CFR §121.465)

Unless there are circumstances beyond the control of the carrier or there is an emergency, dispatchers cannot be on duty for more than 10 consecutive hours.

53. Can a dispatcher be scheduled for more than 10 hours of duty in a 24-hour period?
(14 CFR §121.465)

Yes, as long as they have a rest period of at least eight hours at or before the end of 10 hours of duty.

54. You are scheduled to report to dispatch duty at 1:00 a.m. and scheduled to go home at 11:00 a.m. You employer wants you to come back to work at 6:00 p.m. Is this legal? (14 CFR §121.465)

No. You require eight hours of rest, meaning you could return no earlier than 7:00 p.m. But you can work more than 10 hours within a 24-hour period.

55. Your employer has you scheduled to work seven days in a week. On Tuesday night, you are scheduled to duty out at 10:00 p.m. You are scheduled to return to duty at 10:00 p.m. on Wednesday. Is this a legal schedule? (14 CFR §121.465)

Yes. You are not required to have a calendar day off. Instead, you only need 24 consecutive hours off during every seven calendar days (or their equivalent).

56. You are working for an air carrier that operates flag flights and has a dispatch center in Puerto Rico. Yesterday you worked until 10:00 p.m. Today you are assigned to report to work at 8:00 a.m. and are scheduled to work until 11:00 p.m. Is this a legal schedule? (14 CFR §121.465)

Yes. As a dispatcher employed outside the contiguous U.S. and D.C. and working under the aforementioned conditions, you may work for more than 10 consecutive hours as long as you have eight hours of rest within a 24-hour period. You were off for eight hours prior to coming to work, so you have the minimum eight hours within the 24-hour period you are working today.

57. What must an aircraft dispatcher do in terms of responsibility for operational control of domestic operations? (14 CFR §121.533)

- Monitor the progress of each flight.
- Deliver safety related information to the flight.
- Cancel or re-dispatch the flight if it cannot continue safely.

58. Can a dispatcher declare an emergency? (14 CFR §121.557)

Yes. The dispatcher should notify the PIC as soon as possible. If the dispatcher cannot communicate with the PIC, they must do whatever is necessary to deal with the emergency.

59. What reporting requirements exist when a dispatcher uses emergency authority? (14 CFR §121.557)

A report must be sent to the operations manager (usually via the dispatcher's supervisor) who will then pass the report on to the FAA. This report must be sent within 10 days following the emergency.

60. A twin-engine jet flight that you are responsible for dispatching notifies you that it has lost an engine. Where must the PIC land, according to regulation? (14 CFR §121.565)

The PIC must land at the nearest suitable airport, timewise, where it can land safely. For example, if the closest airport has a grass runway, it is not considered a suitable airport for the airplane to safely use.

61. What is the difference between landing at the "nearest airport" versus at the "nearest suitable airport, in point of time"? (14 CFR §121.565)

If a twin-engine aircraft loses an engine while en route, it is required to land at the nearest suitable airport, timewise. This implies that the airport is usable by the airplane (i.e., the runway is long enough, the weather is good enough, etc., to make it "suitable"). However, the closest airport in terms of distance may not necessarily be reachable in the shortest period of time. If the engine failure occurs at high-altitude cruise directly over a suitable airport, one might assume that airport is the natural choice for diversion. Yet it might take a long time to circle down and maneuver for the approach to that airport. On the other hand, if the aircraft were to continue straight ahead in a high-speed descent, it might be able to reach another suitable airport in a shorter period of time, even though it is physically located further away. Moreover, if one airport has better weather than another, a flight may be able to land in a shorter period of time if it does not have to conduct an instrument approach. Aircraft with more than two engines can continue to an airport other than the closest ("in point of time" or, with regard to time), as long as proceeding to this other airport is as safe as landing at the nearest suitable airport, timewise.

62. How can a dispatcher know if their flights are authorized to use RNAV GPS approaches? (14 CFR §121.567)

The carrier's Ops Specs specifically lists all of the approaches that are authorized for use.

63. For a domestic flight with an intermediate stop, how long is a dispatch release valid? (14 CFR §121.593)

One hour. As always, no flight may start unless authorized by the dispatcher.

64. For a flag flight with an intermediate stop, how long is the dispatch release valid? (14 CFR §121.595)

Six hours. Following this, the flight must be re-dispatched. As always, no flight may start unless authorized by the dispatcher.

65. You arrived to work late and have a domestic (or flag) flight to dispatch and you have not looked at the reported and forecast weather for this flight. Another dispatcher who is on duty states that the weather is favorable for the flight. Can you dispatch the flight under these circumstances? (14 CFR §121.599)

No. The dispatcher must be thoroughly familiar with all weather associated with the flight.

66. Prior to each flight, what information must a dispatcher provide each PIC? (14 CFR §121.601)

The dispatcher must provide current reports or information about airport conditions, weather reports and forecasts, and any issues with navigation facilities to be used. Anything that might affect safety must be explicitly conveyed. Examples include thunderstorms, turbulence, and wind shear.

67. During a flight, what information must a dispatcher relay to each PIC? (14 CFR §121.601)

The dispatcher is responsible for relaying any supplementary weather information, particularly any adverse conditions, as well as any abnormal issues that may affect the safety of flight.

68. Can a flight be dispatched if it will be out of communication range for a period of time while enroute? (14 CFR §121.607)

No.

69. Can you dispatch a flight to operate under visual flight rules (VFR)? (14 CFR §121.611)

Yes, if authorized in Ops Specs and the weather reports/forecasts show that the flight will be able to maintain VFR throughout the flight.

70. While collecting weather information for an upcoming flight, you notice that the forecast is calling for a 200-foot ceiling and ½ SM visibility. The lowest approach minimums available at the destination airport are an MDA of 500 HAT and 1 SM visibility. Can you dispatch this flight? (14 CFR §121.613)

No. In order to release the flight, weather reports or forecasts must indicate that the weather meets or exceeds the minimums for an approach at the estimated time of arrival.

71. **While collecting weather information for an upcoming flight, you notice that the forecast is calling for a 200-foot ceiling and 2 SM visibility. The lowest approach minimums available at the destination airport are an MDA of 500 HAT and 1 SM visibility. Can you dispatch this flight?** (14 CFR §121.613)

Yes. In order to release the flight, weather reports or forecasts must indicate that the weather meets or exceeds the minimums for an approach at the estimated time of arrival. The visibility, not the ceiling, is the approach minimum determinant.

72. **When is a takeoff alternate required to be included on a release?** (14 CFR §121.617)

Whenever the airport of departure is reporting weather below landing minimums for that airport.

73. **You are planning a flight out of an airport that is reporting a 100-foot ceiling and 1 SM visibility. The lowest approach minimums for that airport are a 200-foot DH and ½ SM visibility. Do you need a takeoff alternate?** (14 CFR §121.617)

No. The weather exceeds approach minimums (visibility).

74. **What is the maximum distance a takeoff alternate can be from the departure airport when flying a Boeing 757?** (14 CFR §121.617)

For two-engine aircraft, the maximum is the distance equivalent to one hour cruise with one engine inoperative assuming there is no wind. A specific distance is usually mentioned in Ops Specs to simplify flight planning.

75. **What is the maximum distance a takeoff alternate can be from the departure airport when flying a Boeing 747?** (14 CFR §121.617)

For aircraft with three or more engines, the maximum is the distance equivalent to two hours cruise with one engine inoperative assuming there is no wind. A specific distance is usually mentioned in Ops Specs to simplify flight planning.

76. **When is an alternate destination airport required for a domestic flight?** (14 CFR §121.619)

An alternate airport is always required, except if within one hour of the estimated time of arrival, weather reports and/or forecasts show that the ceiling will be equal to or exceed 2,000 feet above the airport and the visibility is equal to or better than three SM.

77. **When must a dispatcher include two (an additional) alternates on the release?** (14 CFR §121.619)

Whenever weather at the destination and first alternate is marginal. The definition of marginal is typically noted in Ops Specs.

78. The following TAF (terminal forecast) exists for your destination. Do you need an alternate if your ETA is 1700 Zulu? (14 CFR §121.619)

KBGM 091131Z 0912/1012 14004KT P6SM OVC150

    TEMPO 0912/0915 -RA BKN060 OVC100

    FM091500 16008KT 2SM -SHRA OVC040

    FM091700 16010KT 5SM -RA BR OVC020

    FM100300 16012KT 3SM -DZ BR OVC006

Yes. The forecast from 1700 Zulu (on the 9th of the month) to 0259 Zulu (on the 10th) indicates that you do not need an alternate. However, you must also look an hour prior to 1700 Zulu, which would include the part of the forecast from 1500 Zulu indicating that the weather will be less than 3 SM. Therefore, an alternate is required.

79. The following TAF (terminal forecast) exists for your destination. Do you need an alternate if your ETA is 0000 Zulu? (14 CFR §121.619)

KCLT 091129Z 0912/1012 VRB04KT P6SM SCT060 BKN250

    FM091400 20010KT P6SM FEW050 BKN250

    FM092000 22010G16KT P6SM VCSH BKN040

    FM100000 23004KT 2SM RA BKN030

Yes. The weather at the ETA is forecast to be less than a 2,000-foot ceiling and 3 SM visibility.

80. When is an alternate airport required for flag operations? (14 CFR §121.621)

Always, except if the flight is six hours or less and the weather reports/forecasts indicate:
- Ceiling
  - 1,500 feet above the lowest circling minimums; or
  - 1,500 feet above the lowest instrument approach minimums or 2,000 feet above the airport elevation, whichever is greater.
- Visibility
  - 3 SM; or
  - 2 SM above the lowest approach minimums, whichever is greater.

81. You are planning to dispatch a flag flight to an airport with a circling approach with an MDA of 800 feet and required visibility of 2 SM, and a straight-in approach with an MDA of 300 feet and a required visibility of ¾ SM. What weather must exist for you to be legally able to omit an alternate from the release? (14 CFR §121.621)

You are not required to assume that a circling approach will be used even though one exists for the destination. Therefore you would want to consider the lowest available minimums for determining if an alternate is required. Add 1,500 to the 300 MDA, which equals 1,800. This is less than the minimum value of 2,000 feet spelled out in the regulation; the required ceiling would be 2,000 feet. Add ¾ SM to the 2 SM noted in the regulation for a total of 2¾ SM. This is less than the mandated 3 SM; use 3 SM. In summary, the weather would have to be 2,000-foot ceiling and 3 SM or better to omit an alternate on the release.

82. What are the requirements for alternate airports for an ETOPS flight?
(14 CFR §121.624)

Alternates must be listed for ETOPS flights that meet the weather requirements specified in Ops Specs and must allow for a safe landing. These alternates must be within the maximum diversion time limit specified for the operation. Once airborne, the weather must remain above the specified minimums.

83. What is the minimum weather required to list an airport as an alternate?
(14 CFR §121.625)

The weather at the alternate airport must meet the minimum values listed in Ops Specs. This will typically involve the ability to derive alternate minimums, which allow for weather lower than the usual 800-foot ceiling/2 SM visibility for airports with non-precision approaches, and 600-foot ceiling/2 SM visibility for airports with precision approaches.

84. How does a dispatcher know if an inoperative instrument or equipment will affect the dispatch of a flight? (14 CFR §121.628)

A minimum equipment list (MEL) must be consulted. This publication lists items that can be inoperative and specifies what special restrictions or procedures must be used in such cases. Dispatchers typically use an alternative publication, termed the Dispatch Deviation Guide (DDG), that mimics the MEL.

85. How might snow at the departure airport affect the dispatch of a flight?
(14 CFR §121.629)

No frost, snow, or ice is allowed to adhere to the wings, control surfaces, engine inlets, or similar safety sensitive aircraft components. Therefore, the aircraft will likely need to be deiced, resulting in longer-than-usual ground/taxi times.

86. What action should be taken if the weather at the listed alternate airport goes below required minimums while a flight is en route? (14 CFR §121.631)

The release must be amended to reflect a new alternate that is within fuel range of the aircraft.

87. When selecting an ETOPS alternate, what restriction(s) exist when considering time-limited systems? (14 CFR §121.633)

For ETOPS flights, time-limited systems—namely fire suppression systems—must be considered in terms of the maximum distance from an alternate airport. The airplane must remain within a flying time from an alternate equal to the maximum time limit for such a system minus 15 minutes.

88. How much fuel is required for a domestic IFR flight? (14 CFR §121.639)

A domestic IFR flight is required to carry enough fuel to fly to the destination, then on to the most distant alternate (if required), and then another 45 minutes at cruise fuel consumption rates.

89. How much fuel is required for a turbine jet flag IFR flight operated in the contiguous 48 United States? (14 CFR §121.645)

When flown within the contiguous 48 states, domestic fuel requirements can be used. Therefore, this flight would require enough fuel to fly to the destination, then on to the most distant alternate (if required), and then another 45 minutes at cruise fuel consumption rates.

90. How much fuel is required for a turbine jet flag IFR flight (outside the contiguous 48 United States)? (14 CFR §121.645)

Enough fuel to fly to and land at the destination, to fly for a period of 10 percent of the total time required to fly to the destination, and after that, to fly to and land at the most distant alternate airport specified in the flight release, if an alternate is required; and after that, to fly for 30 minutes at holding speed at 1,500 feet above the alternate airport (or the destination airport if no alternate is required) under standard temperature conditions.

91. How much fuel is required for a turbine jet flag IFR flight if no alternate is required? (14 CFR §121.645)

Enough fuel to fly to the destination and then an additional two hours at normal cruise.

92. What enroute fuel supply considerations must be made for an airplane with more than two engines flying on a flag flight? (14 CFR §121.646)

That airplane should have enough fuel required for the flag flight per 121.646 and also has enough to reach an enroute diversionary airport. When calculating the fuel to reach this diversionary airport, the dispatcher must consider wind and weather, a rapid depressurization at the most critical point, and a descent to an altitude that allows for compliance with supplemental oxygen requirements. Further, the aircraft must be able to hold at the diversionary airport for 15 minutes at 1,500 feet.

93. When computing fuel requirements for a flight, what additional considerations must be made by a dispatcher other than simply how much fuel is necessary to reach the destination (and alternate, if required) plus reserve? (14 CFR §121.647)

Forecasted winds and weather, air traffic delays, the conduct of one instrument approach and one missed approach, and any other delaying factors.

94. Can a flight operating under 14 CFR Part 121 begin an instrument approach if the reported weather is less than the minimums required to land? (14 CFR §121.651)

No, this is prohibited. However, if the weather drops below minimums after the aircraft has begun the approach (after the final approach fix), the aircraft can continue.

95. What is the minimum weather for takeoff for a flight operating under 14 CFR Part 121? (14 CFR §121.651)

Whatever is permitted in Ops Specs. Usually this is a minimum of ¼ SM visibility or adequate visual reference, though some operations with much lower visibility requirements may be permitted.

96. You are dispatching a flight for which the PIC has less than 100 hours in the type of aircraft being flown. Are there any special considerations for the dispatcher? (14 CFR §121.652)

The weather requirements for such a PIC are augmented by 100 feet and ½ SM visibility. For example, if flying to an airport with an ILS with minimums of 200 feet and ½ SM, a "high minimums" captain would require 300 feet and 1 SM to fly to this airport.

97. You are viewing a METAR to determine the viability of conducting operations into an airport. The body of the report indicates that the visibility is ½ SM but the RVR for the runway in use indicates visibility is 1,600 feet. Can you expect your flight to legally be able to conduct an approach into this airport? (14 CFR §121.655)

No. RVR, if reported, is controlling.

98. What minimum altitude is required for all IFR flights operated under 14 CFR Part 121? (14 CFR §121.657)

Airplanes operated under IFR must fly 1,000 feet above all obstacles within five miles in non-mountainous areas and 2,000 feet above all obstacles within five miles in mountainous areas.

99. What minimum altitude is required for all IFR flights operated outside the U.S.? (14 CFR §121.657)

Section 121.657 rules apply unless the host country has higher requirements.

100. Can a dispatcher delegate the authority to sign the dispatch release? (14 CFR §121.663)

Yes. However, they cannot delegate their authority to actually dispatch the flight.

101. What elements need to be included in every dispatch release for flag and domestic operations? (14 CFR §121.687)

- Weather reports and forecasts.
- Aircraft identification number.
- Trip number.
- Airports of operation (departure, destination, alternates, intermediate stops).
- Type of operation (VFR or IFR).
- Minimum fuel.
- For ETOPS flights, the diversion time for ETOPS.

102. What elements need to be included on the load manifest? (14 CFR §121.693)

- Weight of aircraft (including fuel, oil, cargo, baggage, passengers, and crew)
- Maximum allowable weight (which cannot exceed known limits).
- Total weight.
- Evidence aircraft is within the center of gravity envelope.
- Names of passengers (unless maintained by carrier, which most large companies do through their reservation/ticketing system).

103. What documents must the PIC have in the airplane until reaching the destination? (14 CFR §121.695)

- Load manifest
- Dispatch release
- Flight plan

104. How long must copies of all flight documents be kept by the operator?

A minimum of three months.

105. How long are operators required to keep records of all radio communications between operations and flights?

30 days.

F. 14 CFR Part 135

1. What types of weather providers are authorized for use by 14 CFR Part 135 operators? (14 CFR §135.213)

U.S. National Weather Service or a source approved by this agency, or some other provider that is approved by the Administrator.

2. When is a takeoff alternate required under this part? (14 CFR §135.217)

A takeoff alternate is required whenever the weather meets or exceeds takeoff minimums but is less than landing minimums.

3. How far away can a takeoff alternate be from the departure airport? (14 CFR §135.217)

One hour at normal cruise with no wind. This applies to all airplane sizes/types.

4. Can you dispatch a flight to a destination where the weather forecast indicates the weather will be below landing minimums at the ETA? (14 CFR §135.219)

No.

5. When is an alternate required when operating under this part? (14 CFR §135.223)

An alternate is always required, except if there is an instrument approach at the destination airport and the weather forecast indicates that within one hour of the ETA, the ceiling is expected to be at least 1,500 feet above the lowest circling MDA or 1,500 feet above the lowest straight-in approach minimums (or 2,000 feet above airport elevation, whichever is higher), and the visibility is at least three miles (or two miles above the lowest approach minimums).

6. Can an airplane operated under this part begin an approach if the weather at the airport is below landing minimums? (14 CFR §135.225)

No, but if the aircraft has already begun the approach (within the final approach fix), it can continue.

7. The calculated accelerate-stop distance can never exceed the length of _____. (14 CFR §135.379)

The length of the runway plus the stopway (if available).

8. The calculated takeoff distance must not exceed _____. (14 CFR §135.379)

The length of the runway plus the clearway (if available). The clearway credit cannot be more than one-half the length of the runway.

9. The takeoff run cannot exceed _____. (14 CFR §135.379)

The length of the runway.

G. Miscellaneous

1. What are the dimensions of Class A airspace? (AIM)

Class A airspace extends from 18,000 feet to 60,000 feet.

2. What are the dimensions of Class B airspace? (AIM)

The dimensions of Class B airspace can vary, but usually extend up to 10,000 feet and laterally up to 30 NM. The base of the airspace rises the further one gets from the primary airport.

3. What are the dimensions of Class C airspace? (AIM)

The dimensions of Class C airspace can vary, but usually extend up to 4,000 feet above the primary airport and laterally to 10 NM. The base of the airspace typically rises from the surface to 1,200 feet at 5 NM from the primary airport.

4. What are the dimensions of an airway? (AIM)

A low altitude airway is 8 NM wide and normally extends from 1,200 feet AGL to 17,999 feet. A high-altitude airway (jet airway) extends from 18,000 to 60,000 feet and is also 8 NM wide. Beyond 51 NM from a defining NAVAID, airways widen due to the angular nature of radials and are thus wider than 8 NM beyond such a point.

5. When must an airport be certified under 14 CFR Part 139? (14 CFR Part 139)

The following airports must be 14 CFR Part 139 certified:

- Airports served by scheduled and unscheduled air carrier aircraft with more than 30 seats;
- Airports served by scheduled air carrier operations in aircraft with more than 9 seats but less than 31 seats.

Note: Airports designated for use solely as alternates are not required to comply with these requirements.

6. What special equipment and services does an airport certified under 14 CFR Part 139 have compared to a non-certified airport? (14 CFR Part 139)

Essentially, the FAA is concerned about rescue and fire-fighting capabilities of airports that receive air service. Thus, Part 139 airports will have a minimum amount of such services.

7. Is it possible to conduct air carrier operations into an airport not certified under 14 CFR Part 139? (14 CFR Part 139)

Yes, if such service is infrequent or "small," but the FAA must evaluate this on a case-by-case basis.

4

Weather Theory and Hazards

A. The Atmosphere

1. What is the gas composition of the atmosphere? (AC 00-6)

- 78% nitrogen
- 21% oxygen
- 1% other gases, including water vapor

2. Where is the troposphere the thickest—at the poles or the equator? (AC 00-6)

It is thickest at the equator, where it stretches to 55,000 to 65,000 feet. At the poles it only extends up to 25,000 to 30,000 feet. In mid-latitudes, it is around 35,000 to 40,000 feet.

3. What is the standard atmosphere? (AC 00-6)

This is a standard construct model of the Earth's atmosphere in terms of temperature and pressure. Simply, it is an average of atmospheric conditions.

4. What is "hypoxia"? (AC 00-6)

Hypoxia is a deficiency of oxygen in the tissues of the body.

5. At what altitude is hypoxia typically considered to be a factor? (AC 00-6)

Although effects of hypoxia may occur at a lower altitude, 10,000 feet is considered the "magic number," with many regulations and recommendations revolving around this height.

B. Temperature

1. What is standard temperature at sea level? (AC 00-6)

15°C or 59°F.

2. What is standard temperature in Denver (elevation 5,280 feet)? (AC 00-6)

The standard atmosphere lapse rate (rate of change of temperature for change in altitude) is 2°C per 1,000 feet. Since standard temperature at sea level is 15°C, and Denver is at approximately 5,000 feet, the standard temperature there is 5°C (5,000 × 2°C = 10°C; 15°C at sea level minus 10°C lapse rate = 5°C).

3. The temperature at an airport is reported to be 75°F. What is this temperature in Celsius? (AC 00-6)

The formula for conversion is $C = 5/9 (F - 32)$. Therefore the temperature is 24°C. The formula for conversion from Celsius to Fahrenheit is $F = 9/5 (C + 32)$.

4. What is primary cause of all weather? (AC 00-6)

Uneven heating of the Earth's surface.

5. What is "diurnal variation"? (AC 00-6)

Diurnal variation is the differences in temperature caused by daytime heating versus nighttime cooling.

6. **What are some examples of the causes of temperature variations across the planet?** (AC 00-6)

   - Diurnal variation
   - Seasonal variation
   - Latitude (angle of sun exposure)
   - Topographical issues
   - Altitude effects

7. **What is the standard lapse rate?** (AC 00-6)

   This is the rate at which temperature changes with changes in altitude per the standard atmosphere. The standard lapse rate is 2°C per 1,000 feet.

8. **Which type of topographical surface will heat up faster—a ploughed field or a swamp?** (AC 00-6)

   Typically, dry objects will heat up faster, thus the field will heat up more quickly than the swamp. Water tends to be an insulator and is not affected by exposure to heat as fast as solid, dry objects.

9. **What is an "inversion"?** (AC 00-6)

   Generally, the temperature of the air in the troposphere decreases as altitude is increased. However, if the temperature increases with altitude, the lapse rate is said to be inverted. This is referred to as an "inversion," or alternatively as a "temperature inversion."

10. **What effect does temperature have on aircraft performance?** (AC 00-6)

    As temperatures increase, aircraft performance is reduced due to a decrease in air density.

11. **What is "density altitude"?** (AC 00-6)

    Density altitude is the altitude at which the aircraft "thinks" it is flying. Simply, the aircraft will perform as though it is at the current density altitude regardless of the actual altitude at which it is flying. Density altitude changes with temperature, pressure, and humidity. As temperature increases, density altitude increases. As pressure decreases, density altitude increases. As humidity increases, so does density altitude.

12. **Standard temperature at the airport of departure is 10°C. The ambient temperature is 15°C. What is true about density altitude and aircraft performance on this day?** (AC 00-6)

    Density altitude will be higher than field elevation (disregarding other factors) and aircraft performance will be reduced.

13. **What potential issues might arise when an inversion exists at an airport?** (AC 00-6)

    Inversions often are associated with reduced visibility and possible wind shear as an aircraft passes through the inversion layer.

C. Pressure and Altitude

1. What are the common units used to measure or present atmospheric pressure? (AC 00-6)

- Inches of mercury (Hg)
- Millibars (mb)
- Hectopascals (hPa)
  - hPa are equivalent to mb.

2. How does pressure vary with altitude? (AC 00-6)

Pressure decreases as altitude increases. In the standard atmosphere the rate of decrease is 1 inch Hg per 1,000 feet.

3. The altimeter setting in Denver is reported at 30.00" Hg. What is the actual atmospheric pressure at the station? (AC 00-6)

Altimeter settings are reduced to sea level. Therefore, the actual atmospheric pressure in Denver is 5" less (since Denver is about 5,000 feet above sea level and pressure decreases at about 1" per 1,000 feet). Therefore actual barometric pressure is around 25.00" Hg.

4. At which airport would an aircraft have the best performance: Key West at sea level, 15°C, and an altimeter setting of 29.92" Hg, or Atlanta at 1,000 feet, 15°C, and an altimeter setting of 29.92"? (AC 00-6)

The density altitude (disregarding other factors) at Atlanta would be higher as the airport is 1,000 feet higher than Key West. The true barometric pressure at Key West is 29.92, but in Atlanta it is 28.92. Thus the aircraft in Key West would have better performance.

5. What is an "isobar"? (AC 00-6)

An isobar is a line of equal pressure used to display pressure systems and distributions on weather maps.

6. Describe a low-pressure system. (AC 00-6)

Lows are areas of reduced pressure and have counterclockwise wind that flows inwards and upwards in the northern hemisphere (opposite in the southern hemisphere). These are commonly associated with poor weather.

7. Describe a high-pressure system. (AC 00-6)

Highs are areas of increased pressure and have clockwise wind that flows outward and downward in the northern hemisphere (opposite in the southern hemisphere). These tend to be associated with good weather.

8. What is a "trough"? (AC 00-6)

A trough is an elongated area of low pressure. Weather systems often develop in association with troughs.

9. What is a "ridge"? (AC 00-6)

A ridge is an elongated area of high pressure.

10. What is a "col"? (AC 00-6)

A col is a neutral area between high- and low-pressure systems, or it is where a ridge and a trough meet.

11. Weather maps often refer to height contours. What does this describe? (AC 00-6)

Weather maps use isobars or lines that connect areas of equal pressure height (contours) to indicate pressure systems. These are much like topographical maps, showing high points and low points in the atmosphere. If a map for the 10,000-foot level (about 3,000 meters) indicates an area where the ambient pressure height equivalent to 10,000 feet is actually at a lower altitude, this is indicative of a low-pressure system.

12. What is "true altitude"? (AC 00-6)

True altitude is an aircraft's height above sea level. It is also known as mean sea level (MSL).

13. What is "indicated altitude"? (AC 00-6)

Indicated altitude is an aircraft's height based on the altimeter reading in the cockpit.

14. What is "pressure altitude"? (AC 00-6)

This is altitude in reference to the standard datum plane of 29.92" Hg. When the aircraft altimeter is set to 29.92" Hg, it reads pressure altitude. Aircraft fly at pressure altitude at and above 18,000 feet in the U.S.

15. Why does a high density altitude reduce aircraft performance? (AC 00-6)

Due to the reduction in the number of air molecules in a given volume of air (reduced density), such conditions:
- Reduce engine thrust/power.
- Reduce the amount of lift that is produced by the wing.

D. Wind

1. What causes wind? (AC 00-6)

Uneven heating of the Earth's surface causes changes in density, which results in pressure gradients. These differences in pressure try to equalize through the flow of air molecules. This movement, of course, is what is known as wind.

2. What determines the speed of wind? (AC 00-6)

Pressure gradient force, or how much pressure changes over a given distance. The larger the pressure difference, particularly if occurring over a limited space, the stronger the wind. An easy way to see this is by looking on a weather map. Areas with closely spaced isobars have a strong pressure gradient (change over distance) and will therefore have stronger winds.

3. What is "Coriolis force"? (AC 00-6)

The Coriolis force is a phenomenon that occurs due to the rotation of the Earth that causes wind in the Northern Hemisphere to be deflected to the right.

4. Why is wind speed usually slower near the surface as compared to aloft? (AC 00-6)

This occurs due to friction between the terrain at the surface and the wind. Winds aloft move relatively unrestricted.

5. How does wind flow in relation to isobars near the surface? Why? (AC 00-6)

At the surface, winds tend to flow perpendicular to isobars as a result of frictional forces and negligible Coriolis effect.

6. How does wind flow in relation to isobars aloft? (AC 00-6)

Winds aloft tend to flow parallel to isobars due to Coriolis force turning the wind to the right (in the Northern Hemisphere).

7. How does wind flow locally in mountain/valley regions during the day? At night? (AC 00-6)

During the day, the air along the mountain slopes warms, forcing winds to flow up from the valley. This is known as valley wind. At night, the air aloft cools and then sinks, moving from the mountains into the valley. This is known as mountain wind.

8. What is "katabatic wind"?

Katabatic wind is wind flowing along an inclined surface. This is common in mountainous areas and is caused by cold, dense air aloft rapidly sinking downwards along the sloping terrain.

9. How does wind flow locally in coastal areas during the day? At night? (AC 00-6)

During the day, the land surface heats up quickly and air over the land become less dense. Air flows from the sea in towards the land. This is referred to as a sea breeze. At night, the water remains warmer than the land because water resists temperature change more so than land, therefore the wind flows from the land out to the sea. This is called a land breeze.

10. What is "wind shear"? (AC 00-6)

Wind shear occurs anytime there is a rapid shift in wind speed or direction. The presence of wind shear is unfavorable for aircraft operations.

E. Clouds and Precipitation

1. What happens to the ability of air to hold moisture as its temperature decreases? (AC 00-6)

As temperature decreases, the air cannot hold as much water vapor. The relative humidity of this parcel of air will increase.

2. What is the dew point? (AC 00-6)

The dew point is the temperature at which air reaches water vapor saturation.

3. How can water vapor get into the air? (AC 00-6)

- Evaporation (liquid to gas)
- Sublimation (solid to gas)

4. How can water vapor be removed from the air? (AC 00-6)

- Condensation (gas to liquid)
- Sublimation or deposition (gas to solid)

5. What is "latent heat"? (AC 00-6)

Latent heat is the extra amount of energy that must be added (or removed) from water to force it to change state. For example, once the temperature of water is reduced to freezing, the water does not immediately freeze. A small amount of additional energy must be removed for the water to solidify. This is called the latent heat of fusion. When water evaporates from a surface, it requires additional energy to do so, called the latent heat of vaporization. The energy that is removed results in a cooling of the surface from which evaporation took place.

6. When does frost form? (AC 00-6)

Frost will form whenever the collection surface and dew point are below freezing and the humidity is high.

7. What danger does frost impose on aircraft? (AC 00-6)

Frost can disrupt airflow and prevent an aircraft from becoming airborne.

8. How do clouds and fog form? (AC 00-6)

When the air reaches its saturation point, water vapor condenses on small particles called condensation nuclei. This moisture becomes visible in the form of clouds or fog.

9. How thick must a cloud normally be to produce precipitation? (AC 00-6)

4,000 feet

10. A flight is about to depart enroute to Cleveland Hopkins International just inshore from Lake Erie. It is October and a cold front just moved through, leaving a strong, cold wind from the northwest. How might this potentially affect dispatch of the flight? (AC 00-6)

There is a possibility that lake effect precipitation may occur. In the fall, the lake is still warm, but cold air invades from Canada. As this occurs, the cold air picks up moisture and it quickly condenses into clouds. As this moisture continues to be fed into the local atmosphere, precipitation develops in the form of rain or snow. The same phenomenon can cause fog to form downwind from a cold lake when warm air is blown over its surface.

11. What is the weather east of a mountain range typically like (compared to the area to the west) in North America? (AC 00-6)

Areas to the east of mountain ranges tend to be drier and often warmer than areas to the west. This is not only because the mountains "block" the moisture but also due to the katabatic winds that often form and flow down the eastern slopes.

12. What do the following cloud descriptors mean: cirrus, alto, and nimbus? (AC 00-6)

Cirrus indicates high-altitude clouds (16,500–45,000 feet), alto indicates middle-altitude clouds (6,500–23,000 feet), and nimbus means a rain-producing cloud.

13. What is the significance of virga? (AC 00-6)

Virga is precipitation (drizzle, rain, ice pellets) that evaporates before it reaches the ground. This is often associated with unstable and/or turbulent conditions.

14. What is the significance of towering cumulus clouds? (AC 00-6)

Towering cumulus clouds are indicative of unstable conditions and they potentially can become thunderstorms. Aircraft in these areas can expect a rough ride.

F. Atmospheric Stability, Air Masses, and Fronts

1. What happens to the temperature as air expands? (AC 00-6)

As air expands, temperature decreases.

2. What is meant by the statement, "the atmosphere is unstable"? (AC 00-6)

This means that the temperature at a particular altitude is lower than expected and if a parcel of warm air ascends into air that is much colder, then it will continue to move upwards and very quickly. Therefore, an unstable atmosphere allows an upward disturbance to grow into a vertical or convective current; that is, an unstable atmosphere favors vertical motion.

3. What type of cloud can be expected to form in stable air? In unstable air? (AC 00-6)

In stable air, stratus clouds; in unstable air, cumulus clouds.

4. What is an "air mass"? (AC 00-6)

An air mass is an area of air with similar properties, usually in terms of moisture content and/or temperature.

5. Name four types of air masses and their general characteristics. (AC 00-6)

- Maritime polar: cold, moist
- Continental polar: cold, dry
- Maritime tropical: warm, moist
- Continental tropical: warm, dry

6. What are the characteristics of stable air in terms of cloud type, precipitation type, turbulence, and visibility? (AC 00-6)

- Cloud type: stratiform
- Precipitation: steady
- Turbulence: little or none
- Visibility: poor

7. What are the characteristics of unstable air in terms of cloud type, precipitation type, turbulence, and visibility? (AC 00-6)

- Cloud type: cumuliform
- Precipitation: showery
- Turbulence: rough air
- Visibility: good

8. What is a "front"? (AC 00-6)

A front is a division line between air masses with different attributes. Cold fronts occur when cold air is pushing against warmer air. Warm fronts occur when warm air is pushing against cooler air.

9. A cold front is approaching an airport to which a flight is being dispatched. What can be expected in terms of weather, wind, and wind shear? (AC 00-6)

Cold fronts tend to have steep slopes, which means they usually do not influence weather for long periods of time. Winds will increase as the front approaches, and depending on the strength of the front, poor weather may ensue. After the front passes, weather tends to clear and the wind is strong out of the northwest. Wind shear threats normally exist during and after frontal passage.

10. Which type of front influences weather over a larger geographic area—cold or warm? (AC 00-6)

Warm fronts tend to spread clouds and rain over larger areas than cold fronts.

11. What types of weather are usually associated with occluded fronts? (AC 00-6)

An occluded front can have weather similar to both warm and cold fronts, including embedded thunderstorms.

12. What is a "dry line front"? (AC 00-6)

This is a common occurrence in Texas where dry air from the desert west impinges upon moist air from the Gulf of Mexico. This difference of air masses forms front-like weather, including the possibility for thunderstorms. A simple description is that a dry line front is a division line between air masses that differ in moisture content (as opposed to temperature, like warm and cold fronts)

13. How can you tell if the atmosphere is stable or unstable? (*Turbulence*)

In order to determine the stability of the atmosphere, examine the ambient lapse rate. If the atmosphere is dry and the actual lapse rate is close to the dry adiabatic lapse rate (3°C per 1,000 feet), then the atmospheric stability is considered to be neutral. If the actual lapse rate is more than 3°C, then the atmosphere is considered unstable. If the atmosphere is moist, things work slightly differently. If the actual lapse rate is greater than the moist adiabatic lapse rate (which varies but will be less than the dry lapse rate), then the atmosphere is considered unstable.

14. In general, what direction do weather systems move in the U.S.? (AC 00-6)

In the U.S., weather systems tend to move west to east and follow the flow of the jet stream.

15. What things are expected to change as a front passes? (AC 00-6)

Wind is said to always change during frontal passage, but other common changes are temperature (which gets colder following a cold front passage or warmer after a warm front passes) and pressure (which decreases until front passes, then rises).

16. An approaching low would be associated with winds from the _____ and increasing _____. (AC 00-6)

South/southwest; clouds and wind speeds.

17. An approaching high would be associated with winds from the _____. (AC 00-6)

North.

G. Turbulence and Icing

1. Why is turbulence a concern for flight operations? (AC 00-6)

Most of the time, turbulence is simply an inconvenience. It can also be very uncomfortable for passengers, so it is important that dispatchers recognize where it may form and then plan to avoid it, if possible. However, fuel considerations normally outweigh the concern over turbulence.

2. Name some causes of turbulence. (AC 00-6)

- Convective currents (heating of ground surfaces)
- Mountain waves
- Mechanical (objects on the ground such as trees or buildings)
- Wind shear
- Clouds
- Inversions
- Wake turbulence (from other aircraft)

3. When should dispatchers suspect there is the potential for mountain wave activity? (AC 00-6)

Anytime the winds flow across a mountainous area at 25 knots or more, wave activity may form. When the wind is greater than 40 knots, turbulence associated with the wave activity could become a concern. Generally, the atmosphere must be relatively stable for the waves to propagate. Anytime standing lenticular clouds are present, mountain wave activity is already occurring.

4. What is true about turbulence and flying in the summer? (AC 00-6)

It is common for turbulence to occur during the takeoff and landing phases due to convective activity. Also, there might be a lot of convective activity and associated cumulus clouds, which will also cause an uncomfortable ride for flights.

5. What is "CAT"? (AC 00-6)

Clear air turbulence (CAT) is turbulence that is not associated with clouds. It often occurs at high altitude near the jet stream.

6. Typically, how deep is the turbulent layer associated with strong surface winds? (*Turbulence*)

With surface winds around 30 knots, turbulence from interference with the ground can extend up to 2,000 feet above the ground. Stronger winds can push turbulence up to 5,000 feet above the ground.

7. What type of frontal conditions, in terms of temperature differences ahead and behind the front and speed of movement, are indicative of wind shear/turbulence? (*Turbulence*)

Fronts that involve large temperature changes (over 10°C) and are fast moving (more than 15–20 knots) are more likely to cause shear and turbulent conditions.

8. When is it likely that aircraft will accumulate ice? (AC 00-6)

Anytime there is visible moisture and the temperature is near or below freezing.

9. What are the three types of airframe icing? (AC 00-6)

- Clear
- Rime
- Mixed

10. What determines the type of airframe icing that will form? (AC 00-6)

The type of icing that forms is determined by water droplet size. Rime forms when the droplets are very small, such as in a stratus cloud, while larger droplets that freeze as they flow backwards along a surface form clear ice. Clear ice is common in cumulus clouds.

11. Name some dangers associated with operating in icing conditions. (AC 00-6)

- Disrupts airflow over the wing.
- Increases aircraft weight.
- Reduces thrust (affects airflow over propeller or jet compressor blades).
- Affects probes and associated instrument systems.

12. A flight calls stating they are accumulating ice. They are flying in a stratus layer of clouds. What is the best advice for how to get out of the icing? (AC 00-6)

In stratus layers, lateral deviations are unlikely to produce results. It would be wise to try to find out the location of the cloud tops and freezing level and then determine the best strategy to escape (by climbing or descending).

13. A flight calls, stating they are accumulating ice. They are flying in and out of cumulus clouds. What is the best advice for how to get out of the icing? (AC 00-6)

When dealing with cumulus clouds, vertical deviations are unlikely to produce results. It would be wise to avoid the clouds with lateral deviations.

14. Describe the threat of icing to large, transport jet aircraft. (AC 00-6)

For large transport jets, icing is usually less of a concern than it is for smaller aircraft. This is because they have excellent ice protection systems, they operate in phases of flight where ice formation is critical for shorter time periods, and normally have exceptional performance capabilities. This is not to say that icing is not a concern; it is just unlikely that flight planning will consider large deviations or cancellations simply because icing conditions exist.

15. Describe the locations along a warm front boundary where an aircraft might be likely to encounter icing. (AC 00-6)

As the warm air of the front rises above the cold air it is overtaking, it forms clouds and sometimes precipitation. The area where moisture and cold air meet ahead of the front is a possible location of ice accumulation. This tends to occur over a wide geographic area ahead of the front.

16. Describe the locations along a cold front boundary where an aircraft might be likely to encounter icing. (AC 00-6)

As the front's cold air pushes up against the warm air it is overtaking, this tends to cause the formation of clouds and precipitation in which it is possible for ice accumulation to occur. This tends to occur close to the frontal boundary.

17. How do mountains affect the chance of encountering ice? (AC 00-6)

Air currents being forced up the sides of mountains tend to provide ideal conditions for ice formation. This "danger zone" is frequent near mountaintops and extends upwards 5,000 feet or more above the ridgelines.

18. Why is frost a problem for aircraft? (AC 00-6)

Frost can prevent smooth airflow over critical surfaces, preventing the aircraft from being able to takeoff.

19. A crew calls stating they have frost on the underside of the wing. Will they need to be deiced?

It depends on the aircraft, the amount of accumulation, and the location of the frost. Some aircraft are permitted to have a limited amount of frost on the underside of wings and on the fuselage.

20. A flight is being dispatched to a humid tropical destination. The flight is two and a half hours long. What might be a concern upon arrival?

It is not unusual for fuel to become very cold during high-altitude flight. When the aircraft descends into moist air, the cold-soaked wing can actually accumulate frost even though ambient temperatures are much higher than freezing.

21. What effect might snowfall have on the dispatch of a flight that is still on the ground?

Aircraft cannot depart with any snow, frost, or ice on its critical surfaces. Therefore, the aircraft will have to be deiced. This is likely to cause delays. Check with airport operations to determine how long it is expected to take.

H. Thunderstorms

1. Where are thunderstorms most likely to occur: northeast New Mexico, southern California, New York, or Minnesota? (AC 00-6)

Northeast New Mexico. There are certain places where thunderstorms are more common than others. Thunderstorms are most prevalent in the south, particularly in the Gulf of Mexico region. The most likely place to find thunderstorms is in central Florida.

2. What ingredients and conditions are needed for thunderstorms to occur? (AC 00-6)

- Moisture
- Lifting force
- Unstable air

3. Name some examples of lifting forces needed to create thunderstorms. (AC 00-6)

- Fronts
- Convective currents
- Mountains
- Converging air masses (such as sea breezes that meet in the center of the state of Florida)

4. What are the stages of a thunderstorm? (AC 00-6)

- Cumulus (building)
- Mature
- Dissipating

5. What hazards do thunderstorms pose to aircraft? (AC 00-6)

- Wind shear
- Lightning
- Reduced visibility
- Turbulence
- Icing
- Tornados
- Hail

6. What is true about the relationship between thunderstorm tops and the intensity of the storm? (AC 00-6)

The higher the tops, the more intense the storm.

7. What is true about the relationship between the frequency of lightning and the intensity of the storm? (AC 00-6)

The more frequent the lightning, the more intense the storm.

8. What is a "squall line"? (AC 00-6)

A squall line is a line of severe thunderstorms that typically forms ahead of a fast-moving cold front.

9. If thunderstorms are predicted to occur at the estimated time of a flight's arrival, what should the dispatcher controlling the flight do? (AC 00-6)

Additional fuel should be added in case the aircraft cannot immediately land, or preferably, an alternate airport should be included in the flight planning. Aircraft simply cannot risk taking off or landing in or near thunderstorms.

10. If dispatching a flight in or near thunderstorms, what are realistic expectations as to how far an aircraft must deviate around or above a storm in order to stay safe? (AC 00-6)

Aircraft should avoid storm activity by at least 20 NM laterally, and at least 1,000 feet per 10 knots of wind above the cloud tops. (Remember, this means the cloud top, not the top of the precipitation.)

11. When planning a flight around thunderstorms, should a dispatcher plan a route that is upwind or downwind of storms, and why?

Dispatchers should utilize the upwind route. This is so the storms won't be "chasing" crews as they deviate and will ensure that the aircraft is not exposed to the storm anvils and the potential precipitation and/or hail that may be blown downwind from the storm.

12. What is a "microburst"? (*Turbulence*)

A microburst is a concentrated area of wind shear that flows downward and outward from a strong thunderstorm. Microbursts should be avoided by aircraft at all times.

13. What kind of turbulence can be expected when encountering the various colors of precipitation shown on weather radar? (*Turbulence*)

- Green: Light to moderate
- Yellow: Moderate to severe
- Red: Likely severe

14. What is a low-level jet stream?

This is a strong, elongated area of wind at low altitude (from above the surface to 5,000 feet above the ground) that can, if it interacts with low-pressure systems, cause the potential for severe weather. An example of this would be the low-pressure jet streams that often form along eastern Texas. As a low-pressure system approaches, the jet stream feeds moisture into the frontal region east of the low, causing the potential for severe weather.

I. Fog

1. Name six common types of fog. (AC 00-6)

- Radiation
- Advection
- Upslope
- Precipitation-induced (evaporation)
- Ice
- Steam

2. What type of fog is common on calm, clear, cool nights? (AC 00-6)

Radiation fog. Clear conditions allow heat to escape, cooling the surface. A cold surface cools the air adjacent to it to a point of saturation. Calm conditions are needed so the fog does not blow away.

3. What might occur if warm air is blown over a cold surface, particularly in coastal regions? (AC 00-6)

Advection fog may occur. This is common in the San Francisco area and along the Gulf of Mexico coast (in the fall).

4. How might an inversion affect visibility? (AC 00-6)

Inversions create a capping effect, trapping in haze, fog, or smog near the surface, which obviously will affect visibility.

5. What is an "obscuration"? (AC 00-6)

An obscuration is when the sky is not visible due to smoke, haze, or fog. It is difficult to determine a cloud height per se in such conditions. Instead of reporting a ceiling in such cases, a vertical visibility is measured.

6. When should a dispatcher suspect the possibility of fog formation when reading weather reports? (AC 00-6)

Dispatchers should be aware of the possibility of fog formation whenever the temperature-dew point spread is 3°C or less, particularly if the trend is for the spread to reduce.

7. Which is more concerning in terms of the possibility of fog formation: a small temperature-dew point spread in the evening or a small spread in the morning? (AC 00-6)

The situation in the evening, as the temperature is likely to reduce and bring the dew point spread even lower.

8. Fog is likely to persist if _____ cloud cover exists or _____ is forecast to continue to fall. (AC 00-6)

Overcast; precipitation

9. How might fog affect flight operations?

Fog can affect flight operations to a varying degree. If the fog only slightly reduces visibility, it might simply slow flight operations. This still is a concern to dispatchers, as some contingency fuel may need to be added to deal with the minor delays. If the reduction in visibility caused by fog is significant, it may prevent departures or arrivals and flights might need to be delayed, cancelled, or diverted. Appropriate fuel planning is essential when dealing with such conditions.

J. High-Altitude Weather

1. What is the "tropopause"? (AC 00-6)

This is the division between the troposphere and the stratosphere. It is marked by a dramatic lapse rate change or reversal (temperature stops reducing with an increase in altitude).

2. What is the "jet stream"? (AC 00-6)

The jet stream is a narrow band of strong wind, in excess of 50 knots, that occurs in the upper atmosphere.

3. What is the difference in location and strength of the jet stream in the winter compared to the summer? (AC 00-6)

In the winter, the jet stream tends to move further south and is stronger than in the summer.

4. Where should a dispatcher be suspect of turbulence in relation to the jet stream? (AC 00-6)

Anytime the jet stream core is near the tropopause, turbulence might appear on the polar side of upper-level troughs and in the northeast quadrant of a low where the jet stream crosses this region. Also, turbulence may occur at any location where the jet stream has a rapid change of direction or speed.

5. Vertical wind shear of _____ knots per 1,000 feet is indicative of problematic turbulence. (AC 00-6)

6 knots.

6. Horizontal shear of _____ knots per 150 NM is indicative of problematic turbulence. (AC 00-6)

40 knots.

7. Jet stream winds in excess of _____ knots are likely produce clear air turbulence. (*Turbulence*)

100 knots

8. What is the "tropopause break"? (AC 00-6)

This is where the tropopause changes altitude dramatically over a short distance. This often occurs at mid-latitudes and is a common location of the jet stream. Turbulence is also common in this location.

9. What is the difference between the polar and subtropical jet streams?

The polar jet stream is normally stronger, further north and located around 30,000 feet. The subtropical jet stream is further south and slightly higher (40,000 feet).

10. When describing the jet stream, what is "confluence"? (*Turbulence*)

This is where two or more jet streams join together. These areas tend to be turbulent. Also, an area where a jet stream splits into two (or more) jets also has a high potential for turbulence.

11. When looking at upper-level troughs, what shape is indicative of turbulence? (*Turbulence*)

Deep bends or deep trough lines.

12. If two jet stream cores are within about _____ NM of one another, turbulence is likely to occur between them. (*Turbulence*)

300 NM.

13. What four conditions are indicative of moderate or worse turbulence near the tropopause? (*Turbulence*)

- Colder than standard temperatures.
- Strong winds.
- Inversion exists above the tropopause.
- Jet core is at or above 34,000 feet.

14. Is icing typically a concern at high altitudes? (AC 00-6)

No, because clouds tend to be made of ice crystals in the upper levels of the atmosphere.

K. Miscellaneous Weather

1. Characterize the weather common on tropical islands. (AC 00-6)

Weather on tropical islands tends to be good, with winds consistently coming from the same direction and minimal cloudiness. If such islands have mountains, it is not uncommon for precipitation to build from upslope conditions.

2. What is the "ITCZ"? (AC 00-6)

The intertropical convergence zone is a region near the equator characterized by converging airflows that lead to a steady supply of convective activity with tops to 40,000 feet or higher.

3. What is a "monsoon"? (AC 00-6)

Monsoons are intense, long-term precipitation events that occur in various parts of the world. They typically cause challenging conditions for flight operations. Contingency fuel and alternate planning are important when planning flights to areas affected by these conditions.

4. What is a "tropical wave"? (AC 00-6)

A tropical wave is an area of disturbed weather that includes clouds, thunderstorms, and rain. These are often antecedents to cyclonic activity.

5. What are the wind speeds associated with a tropical depression? A tropical storm? A hurricane? (AC 00-6)

- Tropical depression: up to 34 knots
- Tropical storm: 35–64 knots
- Hurricane (or typhoon): 65+ knots

6. What hazards to flight operations exist as a result of cyclonic activity? (AC 00-6)

Cyclones can cause high winds, thunderstorms, and heavy rain. The more severe types of cyclonic activity must be avoided. Cancelling flights is a smart choice. No flights should be planned to or from airports that are being affected by these systems. It is wise for dispatchers to ensure that aircraft located at airports in the path of a cyclone are flown out of the area prior to the storm's arrival to avoid being damaged. Lastly, aircraft should not be expected to fly through or near such systems, as thunderstorms associated with cyclones can be severe with tops above 50,000 feet, and strong turbulence can occur due to wind shear conditions aloft.

5

Weather Reports and Charts

A. Surface Weather Reports

1. How can a dispatcher know if the weather information they are accessing is legal for use in the dispatch of an air carrier flight?

Weather information has to be from an approved provider as outlined in Ops Specs. Additionally, this weather must come from a secure source. In the case of a web-based system, the site from which the weather is accessed must have an "https" URL indicating that it is secure. This security can also be identified by a small padlock symbol in the lower corner of the browser window.

2. What is a "METAR"? (AC 00-45)

A METAR is an aviation routine weather report. These are the staple regular surface weather reports used by aviation operations. Observations are made by computer systems or human observers at National Weather Service facilities, in control towers, or at flight service stations.

3. What is "ASOS"? (NWS website)

Automated Surface Observing System (ASOS) is a computerized weather observation system used by the National Weather Service, the FAA, and the Department of Defense. These can provide METARs. If they are not augmented by human input, the METAR will include AUTO in the beginning of the observation. ASOS observations are authorized for use for dispatch (per Ops Specs).

4. What is "AWOS"? (NWS website)

Automated Weather Observations System (AWOS) is similar to ASOS in that it is a computer system that reports surface weather. Not all AWOS locations have the ability to detect current weather and precipitation. AWOS locations may or may not be federal facilities. Federal AWOS are approved for use in dispatch (per Ops Specs).

5. What is a "SPECI"? (AC 00-45)

A SPECI is a special METAR report that indicates major changes in the weather since the last report.

6. When must the current weather be reported on a METAR? (AC 00-45)

Whenever the visibility is less than 7 SM (if the station is capable of reporting this function).

7. Decode the following METAR: (AC 00-45)

KAAF 281753Z AUTO 19006KT 10SM -RA CLR 29/24 A2994 RMK AO2 LTG DSNT NW TSB09E21RAB45 SLP139 P0000 60000 T02890239 10328 20278 $

This is a METAR for Apalachicola Regional Airport in Florida. The observation was taken on the 28th at 1753 Zulu. This is an automated report (no human corrections were made). Winds were 190 at 6 knots. Visibility was 10 SM in light rain. Sky was clear (no clouds below 12,000 feet). Temperature was 29°C and dew point was 24°C. The altimeter setting was 29.94" Hg. Remarks are: there is a precipitation discriminator (AO2); there was lightning distant (beyond 10 NM) northwest; thunderstorm began at 1709 Zulu and it ended at 1721 Zulu; rain began at 1745 Zulu; sea level pressure was 1013.9 mb; no rain accumulated in the last hour (P0000); there was no precipitation accumulation over the last six hours (60000); the temperature was 28.9°C and the dew point was 23.9°C; six-hour maximum temperature was 32.8°C (10328) and the six-hour minimum temperature was 27.8°C (20278); some data may be inaccurate as the system needs maintenance ($).

8. **Decode the following METAR:** (AC 00-45)

KFVE 291503Z AUTO 13006KT 1 1/2SM BR OVC004 14/14 A2971 RMK AO2 RAE1459 CIG 001V007 P0000

This is a METAR for Northern Aroostook Regional in Frenchville, Maine. The observation was taken on the 29th at 1503 Zulu. It is an automated report. Winds were 130 at 6 knots. The visibility was 1½ SM in mist. The ceiling was overcast at 400 feet. The temperature and dew point were both 14°C (notice the air is saturated and mist is present). The altimeter setting was 29.71" Hg and the station has a precipitation discriminator (AO2). Remarks were that the ceiling was variable between 100 and 700 feet, and there was trace precipitation in the last hour (P0000).

9. **Decode the following METAR:** (AC 00-45)

KIDA 291453Z 35004KT 10SM SCT110 19/12 A3003 RMK AO1 SLP118 VIRGA DSNT S-SW MOV N

This is a METAR for Idaho Falls Regional airport in Idaho. This METAR station has a human present to correct or augment the report (there is no "AUTO" note). The observation was made on the 29th at 1453 Zulu. The winds were 350 at 4 knots and the visibility was 10 SM. Clouds were scattered at 11,000 feet with a temperature of 19°C and dew point of 12°C. The altimeter setting was 30.03" Hg. Remarks were that this station does not have a precipitation discriminator, the sea level pressure was 1011.8 mb and there was virga beyond 10 SM in the sky to the south clockwise to the southwest and it was moving north.

10. **A METAR includes "MIFG". What does this mean?** (AC 00-45)

Shallow (less than 6-feet deep) fog.

11. **A METAR includes "BCFG". What does this mean?** (AC 00-45)

Patchy (little depth and random placement) fog.

12. **A METAR includes "DRSN". What does this mean?** (AC 00-45)

Drifting snow with a depth less than 6 feet.

13. **A METAR includes "BLPY". What does this mean?** (AC 00-45)

Blowing spray of a depth less than 6 feet.

14. **A METAR includes "TSRA". What does this mean? What about –TSRA? And +TSRA?** (AC 00-45)

- TSRA means thunderstorm with moderate rain. (Note that the description of intensity applies to the precipitation, not the thunderstorm.)
- –TSRA means thunderstorm and light rain.
- +TSRA means thunderstorm and heavy rain.

15. **A METAR includes "GR". What does this mean?** (AC 00-45)

Hail of ¼ inch in diameter or larger is present. Smaller hail is indicated by GS.

16. **A METAR includes "FG". What does this mean and how does it differ from "BR"?** (AC 00-45)

FG is fog and is used to describe visible moisture when the visibility is ½ SM or less. BR is used to describe the same phenomenon when the visibility is more than ½ SM.

17. A METAR includes "FC". What does this mean? (AC 00-45)

FC is a funnel cloud. If it touches the ground, it becomes a tornado and will be noted by +FC.

18. A METAR includes "PL". What does this mean? (AC 00-45)

Ice pellets are falling. This likely means that there is freezing rain aloft.

19. A METAR includes "VA". What does this mean? (AC 00-45)

Volcanic ash is present. Aircraft operations should be ceased until it has cleared.

20. A METAR includes "VV". What does this mean? (AC 00-45)

An obscured sky exists and the vertical visibility is reported in lieu of a ceiling. Also known as an indefinite ceiling.

21. A METAR includes "CLR". What does this mean? (AC 00-45)

No clouds are detected or present below 12,000 feet (at an automated station).

22. A METAR includes "BKN///". What does this mean? (AC 00-45)

A broken layer exists below airport elevation (the airport is in the mountains, the clouds are below in a valley).

23. A METAR includes "CBMAM". What does this mean? (AC 00-45)

Cumulonimbus mammatus clouds are observed. These are bulbous cumulus clouds that indicate severe weather.

24. A METAR includes "ACSL". What does this mean? (AC 00-45)

Altocumulus Standing Lenticular clouds are observed. These indicate mountain wave activity and turbulence.

25. A METAR includes "PRESRR" or "PRESFR". What does this mean? (AC 00-45)

- PRESRR: pressure is rising rapidly (weather is likely to start to improve).
- PRESFR: pressure is falling rapidly (poor weather is probably approaching the station).

26. A METAR includes "R18/2400FT". What does this mean? (AC 00-45)

Runway 18 runway visual range is 2,400 feet.

27. A METAR includes "PWINO". What does this mean? (AC 00-45)

The precipitation identifier at this station is inoperative.

28. A METAR includes "TSNO". What does this mean? (AC 00-45)

The thunderstorm detection at this station is inoperative.

29. A METAR includes "VISNO". What does this mean? (AC 00-45)

Visibility detection is unavailable at this station.

30. A METAR includes "CHINO". What does this mean? (AC 00-45)

Cloud height detection is unavailable at this station.

B. Pilot Reports

1. What is a "PIREP"? (AC 00-45)

A PIREP is a pilot report and is identified by the letters UA. A PIREP containing immediately critical information (such as a tornado) is indicated as an urgent PIREP with the letters UUA.

2. What is an "AIREP"? (FAA Order 7110.10)

An AIREP is a position report or PIREP-like report that is conveyed in a standardized ICAO format and is indicated by the letters ARP.

3. While planning a flight, there are no PIREPs available for turbulence. What does this mean?

It could mean that there is no turbulence; however, it could also mean that no pilots have submitted PIREPs. Be cautious and don't assume that the absence of PIREPs means no icing, turbulence or other negative weather condition are present.

4. Decode the following PIREP: (AC 00-45)

ACK UA /OV ACK045010/TM 1020/FL020/TP C402/WX FV07SM HZ/RM VMC CLOUD DECK COVERS 1/2 ISLAND

This is a PIREP given by an aircraft located on the 045 radial and 10 DME fix from Nantucket. The report was made at 1020 Zulu while flying at 2,000 feet in a Cessna 402. The weather was 7 SM flight visibility in haze. Remarks were that there were visual meteorological conditions, but a cloud deck covered half of Nantucket Island.

5. Decode the following PIREP: (AC 00-45)

BWI UA /OV BAL110040/TM 1436/FL230/TP CRJ2/TA M14/IC LGT RIME

This is a PIREP given by an aircraft located on the 110 radial and 40 DME fix from Baltimore. The report was made at 1436 Zulu while flying at 23,000 feet in a CRJ-200. The temperature aloft was minus 14°C. The aircraft was accumulating light rime ice.

6. Why is it important to consider the type of aircraft that has made a PIREP?

Aircraft react differently to conditions, particularly large aircraft versus small aircraft. For example, a PIREP from a Cessna 172 concerning moderate turbulence would be less of a concern to a Boeing 737 pilot versus a PIREP of the same conditions that was made by a Boeing 747. Unfavorable conditions reported by large aircraft tend to be very significant.

7. Decode the following PIREP: (FAA Order 7110.10)

ARP UAL300 4031N 10718W 1600 F370 MS51 255/012KT TB SMOOTH

This is actually an AIREP given by a United Airlines aircraft that was located 40 degrees 31' North latitude and 107 degrees 18' West longitude. The report was made at 1600 Zulu while flying at 37,000 feet. The temperature aloft was minus 51°C. The wind was 255 degrees at 12 knots. The aircraft was in smooth conditions (no turbulence).

8. What type of icing requires an immediate deviation and cannot be managed by deicing or anti-icing systems? (AC 00-45)

Severe.

9. **What type of turbulence may cause the aircraft to be momentarily out of control, but not cause structural damage?** (AC 00-45)

Severe.

10. **A PIREP contains the remark LLWS +/- 20KT. What does this mean and how may it affect dispatch?** (AC 00-45)

Low-level wind shear has been reported with airspeed fluctuations of 20 knots. A cautionary message should be conveyed to flights being conducted in the area. Diversion is unlikely, but should not be ruled out as an option.

11. **A PIREP contains the remark "DURD". What does this mean?** (AC 00-45)

Something in the PIREP was encountered during the descent. If it occurred during climbout, it would read DURC.

C. Radar Weather Reports

1. **Decode the following radar weather report (SD):** (AC 00-45)

   TBW 1535 AREA 3RW++ 54/98 105/91 22W

   CELL RW+ 182/114 D4

   AREA 5R 302/118 270/124 23W

   AUTO

   This SD was prepared at 1535 Zulu for Tampa Bay, Florida. There was an area of very heavy (++) rain showers (RW) with 3/10 coverage (3) located at azimuth 54 degrees (northeast) and 98 NM to azimuth 105 (east-southeast) and 91 NM and was 22 NM wide. A cell of heavy (+) rain showers was located at azimuth 182 degrees (south) and 112 NM and was 4 NM in diameter. Another area of moderate rain (R) was located from 302 degrees (northwest) and 118 NM to 270 degrees (west) at 124 NM and was 23 NM wide. The report was generated by an automated system.

2. **An SD report includes "PPINE". What does this mean?** (AC 00-45)

   No echoes (precipitation) were detected.

3. **An SD report includes "PPINA". What does this mean?** (AC 00-45)

   No radar information is available at this time.

4. **An SD report includes "PPIOM". What does this mean?** (AC 00-45)

   This radar is out for maintenance or is out of service.

5. **An SD report includes "MT at 50/75". What does this mean?** (AC 00-45)

   The maximum precipitation top is detected at an azimuth of 50 degrees (northeast) and 75 NM from the radar station.

6. **An SD report includes "C18030". What does this mean?** (AC 00-45)

   Weather cells are moving from 180 degrees (i.e., the weather is moving north) at 30 knots.

D. Satellite Imagery

1. What is a weakness of visible satellite imagery in comparison to infrared? (Aviation Weather Center)

Visible satellite images can only be used during daylight hours.

2. When viewing a visible satellite image, what does the appearance of bright white, rippled/puffy clouds indicate? (Aviation Weather Center)

This is indicative of cumulus clouds with high tops, which most likely means that thunderstorms are present, but at the very least that turbulent conditions likely exist.

3. Can visible satellite images detect snow-covered mountains? If so, how does an observer distinguish them from clouds? (Aviation Weather Center)

Yes, visible satellite images can and do detect snow-covered surfaces. They can be distinguished from clouds because clouds move and mountains do not.

For questions 4–6, refer to the visible satellite image of Florida shown in Figure 5-1.

Figure 5-1. Visible satellite image of Florida

4. When was this image captured? (Aviation Weather Center)

1640 Zulu on June 29, 2010.

5. What kind of weather could be expected in the "arm pit" of the west side of the state (where the land turns south)? (Aviation Weather Center)

There is a large area of clouds with a rugged appearance. It also appears the winds aloft are blowing an anvil-like cloud to the south. This image is indicative of thunderstorm activity.

6. **What type of weather could be expected in central Florida just east of the Tampa Bay area (about halfway down the west side of state)?** (Aviation Weather Center)

   Fair weather cumulus clouds appear to be building in this area.

For questions 7–8, refer to the visible satellite image for California and Nevada shown in Figure 5-2.

Figure 5-2. Visible satellite image for California and Nevada

7. **What type of weather could be expected to the south of the San Francisco area (the inlet halfway down the California coast)?** (Aviation Weather Center)

   There appears to be low-lying clouds (fog) that has formed offshore and extends inland.

8. **What type of weather could be expected throughout Nevada?** (Aviation Weather Center)

   Scattered (probably) cumulus clouds without any organized weather.

9. **What does infrared satellite imagery indicate to observers?** (Aviation Weather Center)

   This type of imagery shows relative temperatures. Cooler temperatures translate into higher cloud tops and higher cloud tops indicate more severe weather.

For questions 10–11, view the black-and-white infrared satellite image of the mid-Atlantic region shown in Figure 5-3.

Figure 5-3. Infrared satellite image of the mid-Atlantic region

10. What type of weather can be expected in West Virginia? (Aviation Weather Center)

Scattered (probably) cumulus clouds without any organized weather. Tops do not appear to be very high as the infrared temperature is "warm."

11. What type of weather is occurring off of the coast of South Carolina?
(Aviation Weather Center)

Just off the coast, there are widespread low- to mid-range cloud layers. Further off of the coast, an area of high-topped clouds indicates of an area of thunderstorms (or precipitation).

12. Why is it important to view satellite images and then view them as animations (loops)? (Aviation Weather Center)

This will allow you to observe the direction and speed of movement of weather systems. This can help identify organized areas of weather, storm formation, and storm dissipation.

13. What does a water vapor image indicate to observers? (Aviation Weather Center)

A water vapor image shows the relative moisture content of the mid-altitude range of the atmosphere (around 12,000 to 30,000 feet). "Warmer" colors (reds) indicate dry conditions, while "cooler" colors (greens and blues) indicate high moisture content. High-altitude weather systems and sometimes jet stream locations can also be identified on this chart.

14. What is the scale for measurement of cloud cover in visible satellite images?

Reflectivity (albedo) of the clouds.

15. What is the scale for measurement of cloud cover in infrared satellite images?

Temperature of the cloud in degrees Celsius.

E. Aviation Weather Forecasts

1. What is a "TAF"? (AC 00-45)

A TAF is an aviation terminal forecast and covers an area within a 5 SM radius of the reporting station.

2. Decode the following TAF: (AC 00-45)

KBIL 291724Z 2918/3018 24006KT P6SM FEW080 SCT120 FM292100 22014KT P6SM VCTS SCT120CB FM300400 24010KT P6SM BKN120

This is a TAF for Billings-Logan International in Montana. It was issued at 1724 Zulu on the 29th of the month and is valid from 1800 Zulu on the 29th until 1800 Zulu on the 30th. At 1800 Zulu on the 29th, winds were expected to be 240 at 6 knots, visibility better than 6 SM and the clouds to be few at 8,000 feet and scattered at 12,000 feet. From 2100 Zulu on the 29th, the weather was expected to be winds 220 at 14 knots, better than 6 SM visibility with thunderstorms in the vicinity of the airport (within 5 to 10 SM) and clouds at 12,000 feet with cumulonimbus possible. From 0400 Zulu on the 30th, winds were expected to be 240 at 10 knots, better than 6 SM visibility, and a ceiling of 12,000 feet, broken.

3. A TAF includes "WS010/24040KT". What does this mean? (AC 00-45)

Wind shear is expected at 1,000 feet above the ground with winds 240 at 40 knots.

4. A TAF includes "BECMG". What does this mean? (AC 00-45)

A gradual change in conditions is expected to occur within a 2-hour period.

5. A TAF includes "TEMPO". What does this mean? (AC 00-45)

TEMPO refers to temporary fluctuations in the forecast conditions that will last for one hour or less in each instance. Changes listed under TEMPO have a given time period, within which altogether they will cover less than half that period. TEMPO periods cannot last longer than 4 hours.

6. A TAF includes "PROB30". What does this mean? (AC 00-45)

The probability of the weather outlined is 30 to less than 40 percent.

7. What is an "FA"? (AC 00-45)

An FA is an area forecast which is an aviation weather product covering multi-state geographic areas.

8. How often are FAs issued? (AC 00-45)

FAs are issued three times a day.

9. For how long is an FA valid? (AC 00-45)

The synopsis is valid for 24 hours. The clouds and weather are valid for 18 hours, with a categorical outlook valid for an additional six hours.

10. An FA includes information about weather in the Lower Arkansas Valley. If you are not familiar with this geographic area, where will you need to look to identify its location? (AC 00-45)

You will need to reference the geographical area designator map in AC 00-45. The Lower Arkansas Valley is actually in Colorado, not Arkansas.

11. Decode the following FA excerpt: (AC 00-45)

SYNOPSIS...CDFNT 18Z WRN ME-ERN MA-XTRM SERN VA WL MOV SLOLY SEWD INTO ERN NEW ENG CSTL WTRS-VA CSTL WTRS BY 06Z.

This excerpt is the synopsis portion of the FA. A cold front at 1800 Zulu that extends from western Maine to eastern Massachusetts to extreme southeastern Virginia will move slowly southeastward into eastern New England coastal waters to Virginia coastal waters by 0600 Zulu.

12. Decode the following FA excerpt: (AC 00-45)

ME

NRN...SCT020 BKN050. TOPS 120. WDLY SCT -SHRA. ISOL -TSRA. CB TOPS FL320. 02Z SCT020 SCT120. OTLK...VFR.

This FA excerpt is for Maine, specifically the northern portion of the state. The forecast is for scattered clouds at 2,000 feet and broken clouds at 5,000 feet with tops at 12,000 feet. Widely scattered light rain showers are expected with isolated thunderstorms with light rain, cumulonimbus tops to 32,000 feet. At 0200 Zulu, clouds will be 2,000 ft scattered, 12,000 ft scattered. The six-hour outlook is for VFR weather (better than 3,000-foot ceilings and 5 SM).

13. Are cloud heights in FAs AGL (above the ground) or MSL (in reference to mean sea level)? (AC 00-45)

AGL cloud heights are noted as "AGL" or as ceilings by "CIG." All other cloud height references are MSL.

14. An FA includes the text "WDLY SCT". What does this mean? (AC 00-45)

The weather associated with this statement is predicted to be widely scattered; that is, it will affect less than 25% of the forecast area.

15. An FA includes the text "SCT". What does this mean? (AC 00-45)

The weather associated with this statement is predicted to be scattered; that is, it will affect 25% to 54 % of the forecast area.

16. An FA includes the text "NMRS or WDSPRD". What does this mean? (AC 00-45)

The weather associated with this statement is predicted to be numerous or widespread; that is, it will affect more than 55% of the forecast area.

17. What is a "WS"? (AC 00-45)

This is a SIGMET, which is a special report of significant meteorological conditions for all aircraft.

18. What type of weather will be included in a WS? (AC 00-45)

- Severe icing (non convective)
- Severe or worse turbulence (non convective)
- Clear air turbulence (CAT)
- Dust or sand storms (reducing visibility to less than 3 SM)
- Volcanic ash

19. What is the maximum length of time for which a WS will be valid? (AC 00-45)

Four hours.

20. What is a "WA"? (AC 00-45)

This is an AIRMET, which is a special report of unfavorable weather. AIRMETs tend to focus on threats to smaller aircraft.

21. What are the three types of WAs? (AC 00-45)

- AIRMET Sierra for IFR conditions and mountain obscurations.
- AIRMET Tango for turbulence, sustained winds of 30 knots or more on the surface, and low-level wind shear not associated with convective activity.
- AIRMET Zulu for icing.

22. What is the maximum length of time a WA will be valid? (AC 00-45)

Six hours.

23. Decode the following WA: (AC 00-45)

AIRMET TANGO UPDT 3 FOR TURB VALID UNTIL 300300

AIRMET TURB...NV CA

FROM 60WSW REO TO 20SSE OAL TO 40WSW TRM TO 40ESE SAC MOD TURB BLW 140. CONDS DVLPG 21-00Z. CONDS CONTG BYD 03Z ENDG 03-06Z.

This is an AIRMET Tango (turbulence) report that is valid until 0300 Zulu on the 30th for Nevada and California. From 60 NM west-southwest of Rome, OR, to 20 NM south-southeast of Coaldale, CA, to 40 NM west-southwest of Thermal, CA to 40 NM east-southeast of Sacramento, CA, moderate turbulence below 14,000 feet. Conditions developing from 2100 Zulu to 0000 Zulu with conditions continuing beyond 0300 Zulu but ending between 0300 and 0600 Zulu.

24. What is a "WST"? (AC 00-45)

This is a convective SIGMET, which warns of widespread convective (thunderstorms, funnel clouds and tornadoes) activity.

25. When will a WST be issued? (AC 00-45)

Anytime the following exists:
- Severe thunderstorms
  - Surface winds 50+ knots
  - Hail ¾-inch diameter or larger
  - Tornados
- Embedded thunderstorms
- Lines of thunderstorms
- Thunderstorms producing heavy precipitation covering 40% or more of a given area (3,000 square miles)

26. What is a "G-AIRMET"? (AC 00-45)

This is a Graphical AIRMET. This product outlines the locations of AIRMETs on a map, which allows for easy identification of the geographical areas affected by adverse weather conditions.

27. What is a "FB"? (AC 00-45)

This is a winds and temperature aloft forecast.

28. How often are FBs issued? (AC 00-45)

Twice a day, at 0000 Zulu and 1200 Zulu.

29. Decode the following FB excerpts: (AC 00-45)
9900

303024

855033

859928

- 9900: light and variable.
- 303024: 300 degrees at 30 knots, temperature minus 24.
- 855033: 350 degrees (winds in excess of 100 knots are indicated by adding 50 to the wind direction, so to decode, subtract this value: 85-50 = 35) at 150 knots, temperature minus 33.
- 859928: winds of 199 knots or greater are indicated by "99" as the speed; therefore, the winds are 350 degrees at 199+ and the temperature is minus 28°C.

30. What is an "MIS"? (AC 00-45)

A meteorological impact statement (MIS) details the future potential for unscheduled air traffic control flow control issues. These are valid for two to twelve hours. Traffic traversing the impacted area(s) should expect re-routes and/or deviations.

31. What adjustments to flight planning should dispatchers make in response to the issuance of an MIS?

They should coordinate any appropriate route changes and plan on including contingency fuel for deviations or delays.

32. Decode the following MIS: (Aviation Weather Center)

ZHU MIS 01 VALID 301300-010100
...FOR ATC PLANNING PURPOSES ONLY...
ZHU INCLDG GLFMEX: AREAS WDLY SCT/SCT TS MORE NMRS S TX AND GLFMEX.
TS WITH MOD-EXTRM PCPN. MOV FM 05020-30KTS W
PTRN AND 16015-20KTS EAST. TOPS FL400+.

This is an MIS issued for Houston Center airspace (ZHU). It is the first MIS issuance and is valid on the 30th from 1300 to 0100 Zulu. For Houston Center airspace including the Gulf of Mexico, there are areas of widely scattered to scattered thunderstorms. More numerous storms are expected in south Texas and the Gulf of Mexico. Thunderstorms with moderate to extreme precipitation moving from 050 degrees at 20 to 30 knots (moving southwest) in the western portion of the impacted area and from 160 degrees at 15 to 20 knots (moving north-northwest) in the eastern portion. Storm tops are above 40,000 feet.

33. What is a "CWA"? (AC 00-45)

A Center Weather Advisory (CWA) is a statement of current impacts on traffic flow in the terminal and enroute environments. These tend to focus on short-term (within two hours) influences on flight operations.

34. Decode the following CWA: (AC 00-45)

ZMA CWA 301 VALID UNTIL 301705
FROM 85E ZFP TO 65SSE ZQA TO 90SW ZQA TO ZFP AREA OF WDLY SCT TS MOV
LTL. MAX TOPS EST NR FL380. EXP LTL CHG THRU 1705Z.

This is a CWA issued for Miami Center airspace. It covers the third phenomenon affecting the region, but this is the first CWA issued for this phenomenon. This CWA is valid until 1705 Zulu on the 30th. From 85 NM east of Freeport, Bahamas to 65 NM south-southeast of Nassau, Bahamas to 90 NM southwest of Nassau to Freeport, an area of widely scattered thunderstorms is moving little. Maximum precipitation tops are estimated to be near 38,000 feet. Expect little change through 1705 Zulu.

35. What is a "WH"? (AC 00-45)

A WH is a hurricane advisory. This is a plain language product that conveys information concerning tropical systems.

36. What is an "AC"? (AC 00-45)

An AC is a convective outlook that comes in two parts. The first part looks ahead 24 hours, and the second part looks ahead an additional 24 hours beyond the first. The risk for severe thunderstorm activity is described as slight, moderate, or high.

F. Aviation Weather Charts

1. What is indicated on surface analysis charts? (AC 00-45)

These charts include the location of isobars, fronts, and pressure systems. Also, these charts indicate station weather conditions.

For questions 2–5, refer to the surface analysis chart of the southwest USA shown in Figure 5-4. (National Weather Service)

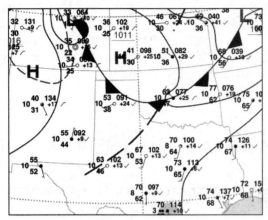

Figure 5-4. Surface analysis chart excerpt

2. What kind of front is depicted in Oklahoma? (AC 00-45)

A cold front.

3. What is the surface pressure reading in western Kansas? (AC 00-45)

1011 mb, which is also the location of a surface high.

4. What are the weather conditions for the station in southeastern New Mexico? (AC 00-45)

There are overcast skies, visibility 10 miles, temperature 55°F, dewpoint 44°F, the sea-level pressure is 1009.2 mb (as indicated by 092), the pressure has increased 0.9 mb in the last three hours (+9) and the pressure trend is downwards then upwards (checkmark-like symbol). Winds are out of the north at 5 knots (small tick on the wind barb).

5. What is the dashed line that extends across northern Texas? (AC 00-45)

This is a trough (an elongated area of low pressure).

6. What types of items are included on weather depiction charts? (AC 00-45)

A weather depiction chart is a map product that is based upon METAR observations. General station conditions and front locations are displayed. This map shows areas of marginal VFR (3 to 5 SM and ceilings 1,000–3,000 feet) in a contoured region while IFR conditions (less than 3 SM and 1,000 feet) are indicated by shading.

For questions 7–10, refer to the weather depiction chart for the California region shown in Figure 5-5. (National Weather Service)

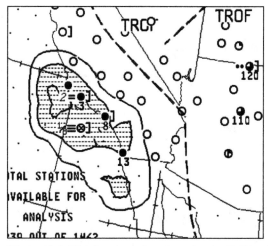

Figure 5-5. Weather depiction chart for the California region

7. **What are the conditions being reported at the airport with the "3" at the bottom of the station location in south central California?** (AC 00-45)

The airport is reporting overcast skies (solid dot), 2 SM in light/shallow fog (2 =) and the ceiling is at 300 feet. The bracket on the right side of the station indicates that the observation was automated.

8. **What sky conditions exist at the station with an "X" in the location marker (in southern California)?** (AC 00-45)

The sky is obscured.

9. **What type of weather event is occurring in extreme northern Arizona?** (AC 00-45)

The station is reporting 12,000 broken in continuous light rain (two dots). This was an automated report.

10. **Where is the weather indicated to be IFR?** (AC 00-45)

The weather is IFR along the central and southern California coast as indicated by the shaded area. Also, IFR conditions exist in a limited area of Baja California.

11. Decode the weather depiction symbol shown in figure at right. (AC 00-45)

Sky conditions are scattered at 25,000 feet.

12. Decode the weather depiction symbol shown in figure at right. (AC 00-45)

Thunderstorm with rain showers.

13. Decode the weather depiction symbol shown in figure at right. (AC 00-45)

Freezing rain.

14. Decode the weather depiction symbol shown in figure at right. (AC 00-45)

Continuous heavy snow.

15. Decode the weather depiction symbol shown in figure at right. (AC 00-45)

Rain showers.

16. Decode the weather depiction symbol shown in figure at right. (AC 00-45)

A building warm front (frontogenesis).

17. Decode the weather depiction symbol shown in figure at right. (AC 00-45)

A squall line.

18. Decode the weather depiction symbol shown in figure at right. (AC 00-45)

A dying stationary front (frontolysis).

19. Decode the weather depiction symbol shown in figure at right. (AC 00-45)

A tropical storm.

20. Decode the weather depiction symbol shown in figure at right. (AC 00-45)

Ice pellets/sleet.

21. Decode the weather depiction symbol shown in figure at right. (AC 00-45)

Haze.

22. What is a radar summary chart?

This is a chart created from radar data (SDs) to give pilots and dispatchers a visual representation of the location of precipitation through use of three contours. The first represents level 1 or 2 storms, the second represents level 3 to 4 storms, and the third represents level 5 to 6 storms. This chart may also indicate the altitude of the tops of the precipitation and the relative movement of the storms.

For questions 23–26, refer to the radar summary chart of the southwest U.S. shown in Figure 5-6.

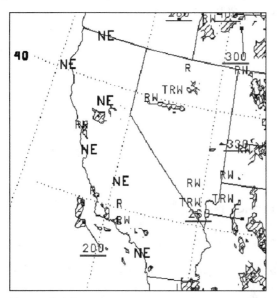

Figure 5-6. Radar summary chart of the southwest U.S.

23. What is the top of the cloud just offshore of Los Angeles? (AC 00-45)

The radar summary chart does not indicate cloud height; however, the top of the precipitation is 20,000. It should be assumed the top of the cloud is higher than this altitude.

24. What type of precipitation is falling in northern Nevada? (AC 00-45)

There is an area of rain showers (RW) and an area of thunderstorms with rain showers (TRW).

25. What is going on along the California-Oregon border? (AC 00-45)

No echoes (NE) are being detected in this location; i.e., there is no precipitation.

26. What do the letters "SLD" mean when depicted on a radar summary chart? (AC 00-45)

This indicates a solid area with 80% or more coverage.

27. What is a "constant pressure analysis chart"?

This is a chart created from information collected mostly from radiosondes (weather balloons). They are released twice a day and indicate the height of a pressure contour in meters. Essentially, areas that are lower than expected are associated with low-pressure systems aloft, while those that are higher than expected indicate a high-pressure system aloft.

28. What is an "isotherm"? (AC 00-45)

An isotherm is a line connecting areas of equal temperature aloft.

29. What is an "isotach"? (AC 00-45)

An isotach is a line connecting areas of equal wind speed aloft.

30. With what altitudes are the following mb pressure heights normally associated? (AC 00-45)

850 mb, 700 mb, 500 mb, 300 mb, 250 mb, 200 mb

850: 5,000
700: 10,000
500: 18,000
300: 30,000
250: 34,000
200: 39,000

31. What is the normal height (in meters) of the 500 mb level? (AC 00-45)

5,500 meters.

32. At what pressure level are isotachs included? (AC 00-45)

At and above 300 mb.

For questions 33–36, refer to the 500 mb chart for the midwest and northern Rockies regions shown in Figure 5-7.

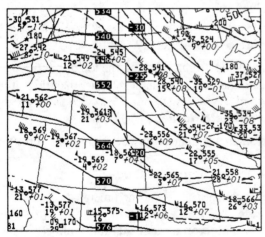

Figure 5-7. 500 mb chart excerpt

33. What does the star symbol station in northern Wisconsin mean? (AC 00-45)

This wind observation was made via satellite estimate.

34. Why are some stations depicted with a solid black circle while others have an open (white) circle? (AC 00-45)

The black circle indicates that the temperature/dew point spread is 5°C or less.

35. What are the current conditions at the station in western Nebraska? (AC 00-45)

Winds are from the west-northwest at 55 knots. The temperature is -23°C and the temperature/dewpoint spread is 6°C. The 500 mb pressure level is at 5,560 meters (approximately the normal height of this pressure level). The height change is +90 meters.

36. What is the -30 in the black box at the top of the chart? (AC 00-45)

This is the -30°C isotherm.

37. What is meant by the term "divergence"? (AC 00-6)

A divergence is an area where isobars expand away from one another. This indicates the potential for air underneath the region being pulled upwards. Upward motion of air is de-stabilizing. Areas of divergence (at the 500+ mb levels) should be cautiously observed for strengthening of surface low-pressure systems or weakening of surface high-pressure systems below.

38. What is meant by the term "convergence"? (AC 00-6)

A convergence is an area where isobars close in towards one another. This indicates that there is potential for air to be pushed downwards. Downward motion of air is stabilizing. Areas of convergence (at the 500+ mb levels) should be assumed to strengthen surface high-pressure systems or weaken low-pressure systems below.

39. How is a trough identified on a constant pressure chart? (AC 00-45)

Troughs are identified by contours that bend downwards (towards the south) and then curve back upwards (towards the north). The lowest point in the curve indicates the center of the trough.

40. Where might you expect poor weather in relationship to a trough? (AC 00-6)

Typically, poor weather occurs just east of the trough, particularly if there is divergence occurring in this region.

41. If an area of divergence aloft is located above a low-pressure system, what can be expected to happen to this surface low? (AC 00-6)

Depending upon the amount of divergence, the low can be expected to strengthen (the pressure will drop). Weather is likely to deteriorate.

For questions 42–46, refer to the 500 mb chart of New England shown in Figure 5-8.

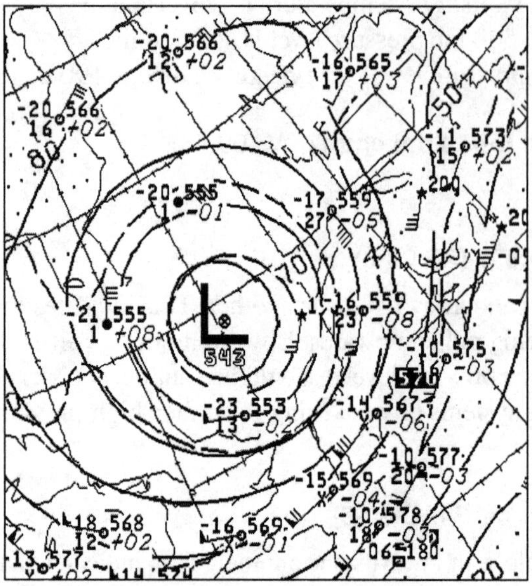

Figure 5-8. 500 mb chart of New England

42. What is the height of the 500 mb pressure level in the center of low? (AC 00-45)

5,430 meters, which is below what is expected (5,500 meters).

43. Where is convergence occurring around the low?

Isobars are converging together from the south to east of the low.

44. Where is divergence occurring around the low?

Isobars are moving away from one another from the east to the northeast of the system.

45. What is the significance of the fact that the height contours completely encircle the low? (AC 00-45)

This is what is referred to as a closed low, which is indicative of a strong low-pressure system.

46. What are the winds aloft just to the west of the low? (AC 00-45)

Winds are from the north at 35 knots.

For questions 47–50, refer to the 200 mb chart shown in Figure 5-9.

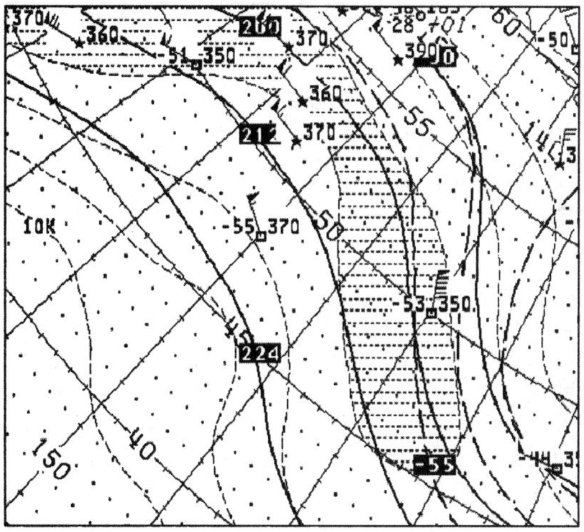

Figure 5-9.

47. What are the conditions associated with the box plot in the center of the chart and what type of report is this? (AC 00-45)

Winds at 37,000 feet were north-northwest at 60 knots and the temperature was -55°C. An aircraft made this report.

48. What is the significance of the dashed line with "10K" on the left side of the chart? (AC 00-45)

This is the 10-knot isotach.

49. What is the significance of the "224" in the black box in the middle of the chart? (AC 00-45)

This is the 12,240-meter height contour.

50. What is the significance of the shaded area? (AC 00-45)

This indicates where the wind is 70 knots or more. Above this speed, shading is alternated with non-shaded areas at 40-knot intervals.

For questions 51–53, refer to the Pacific surface analysis chart shown in Figure 5-10.

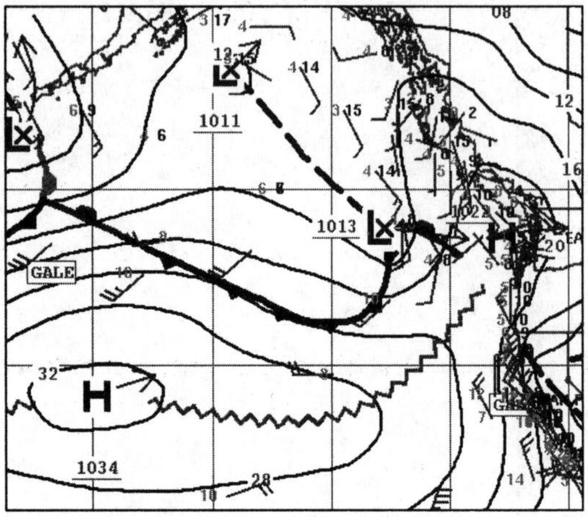

Figure 5-10. Pacific surface analysis chart

51. **What is the meaning of the arrows pointing from the high- and low-pressure systems towards the east?** (AC 00-45)

This is the predicted 24-hour movement of the system.

52. **What is the zigzag line extending from the high in the mid-Pacific to the west coast of the U.S.?** (AC 00-45)

This is a ridge (an elongated area of high pressure).

53. **What is the meaning of the boxed term "GALE" on the left side of the chart?** (AC 00-45)

Winds of 34–47 knots are expected in this area.

54. **When viewing the 500 mb chart, what is the significance of isotherms that curve downwards toward the south?** (AC 00-45)

This indicates cold air advection; that is, cold air is moving in from the north. This tends to be de-stabilizing, as cold air has a tendency to augment the convection of warmer air from below.

55. **What is the significance of cold air advection coupled with a solid station identifier at the 500 mb level?** (AC 00-45)

Recall that the station identifier "dot" is solid when the temperature-dew point spread is 5°C or less, meaning there is a high moisture content. If this is coupled with cold air advection, which has a tendency to de-stabilize the atmosphere, it is likely to lead to cloudy/moist conditions and possible convective activity.

56. **What is the significance of cold air advection at the 850 mb level?** (AC 00-45)

Cold air convection closer to the surface has the opposite effect as cold air advection aloft. Because the 850 mb is so close to the surface, cold air spilling in at this level tends to be stabilizing.

57. **The Aviation Weather Center provides an alternative view of the 500 mb level that includes color coding of vorticity. What is vorticity?** (Aviation Weather Center)

Positive vorticity is the counterclockwise (cyclonic) flow of air. This tends to be associated with divergence and rising air, thus areas of positive vorticity often indicate potential areas of destabilization.

58. **Where can one typically expect positive vorticity?**

This counterclockwise motion of air is typical to the south and east of low-pressure systems and as air moves through troughs.

59. **On the 500 mb chart, an area of height contours that bend southward and then back toward the north is referred to as a _____.** (AC 00-45)

Trough.

60. **On the 500 mb chart, an area of height contours that bend northward and then back toward the south is referred to as a _____.** (AC 00-45)

Ridge.

61. **What is true about troughs that extend far south, have closely spaced height contours, and strong winds?**

These are indicative of strong weather systems and will likely have robust levels of positive vorticity, and thus are prone to produce destabilization and/or poor weather.

For questions 62–64, refer to the stability panel of the composite moisture stability chart shown in Figure 5-11. (Aviation Weather Center)

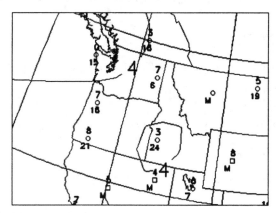

Figure 5-11. Composite moisture stability chart

62. **What is the K index for the station near Portland, OR?** (AC 00-45)

The K index at this location is 16. That is considered to be low (less than +20).

63. **What is the lifted index for the station near Portland, OR?** (AC 00-45)

The lifted index is +7, which indicates positive stability.

64. **In general, what type of weather might be expected in southern Oregon?** (AC 00-45)

Partly cloudy skies with little vertical development.

65. What does the K index convey to the observer? (AC 00-45)

The K index is an indication of stability and moisture of the atmosphere at the 700 to 850 mb levels. A value less than +20 indicates dry, stable air. A value of more than +20 indicates moist, unstable conditions.

66. What is considered a highly unstable lifted index? (AC 00-45)

Anything -6 or less is considered highly unstable.

67. What is considered a highly stable lifted index? (AC 00-45)

Anything +8 or higher is considered highly stable.

68. What K index is equated to a near 0% chance of thunderstorm development? (AC 00-45)

Any K index less than 15.

69. What K index almost guarantees thunderstorm activity (if enough moisture is present)? (AC 00-45)

Any K index more than 40 is likely to be associated with thunderstorm production.

70. What does the precipitable water panel convey to the observer? (AC 00-45)

This panel indicates the amount of moisture from the surface to the 500 mb level. Simply, if all the water vapor was condensed above the reporting station, this would be the amount of liquid water measured.

For questions 71–72, refer to the precipitable moisture chart for the four corners region shown in Figure 5-12. (Aviation Weather Center)

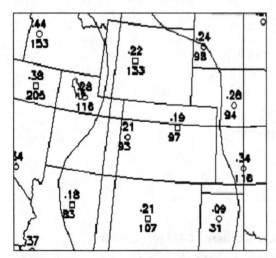

Figure 5-12. Precipitable moisture chart for the four corners region

71. How much precipitable water is present in Wyoming? (AC 00-45)

There is 0.22 inches of water present above this station.

72. Is the amount of moisture in Wyoming normal for the month? (AC 00-45)

No, the value is currently 133% of normal; that is, the moisture content is above average for the month.

For questions 73–74, refer to the freezing level panel for the southwest U.S., shown in Figure 5-13. (Aviation Weather Center)

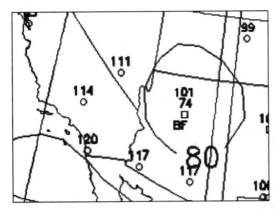

Figure 5-13. Freezing level panel for the southwest U.S.

73. What is the freezing level in southern Nevada? (AC 00-45)

The freezing level near Las Vegas is 11,100 feet MSL.

74. What is the freezing level in northern Arizona? (AC 00-45)

The station is reporting temperatures below freezing at the surface, above freezing from 7,400 MSL to 10,100 MSL, and below freezing above 10,100 MSL.

75. What does an average relative humidity panel convey to observers? (AC 00-45)

This chart indicates the average relative humidity from the surface to the 500 mb level.

For questions 76–77, refer to the average humidity panel for the central U.S. shown in Figure 5-14. (Aviation Weather Center)

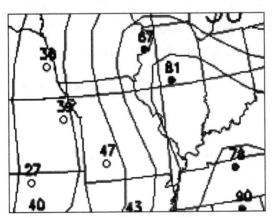

Figure 5-14. Average humidity panel for the central U.S.

76. What is the relative humidity for southwest Missouri? (AC 00-45)

47 percent.

77. What relative humidity is generally indicative of precipitation in stable air? Unstable air? (AC 00-45)

70 percent in stable air; 50 percent in unstable air.

For questions 78–80, refer to the winds aloft chart for the northern Rockies shown in Figure 5-15.
(Aviation Weather Center)

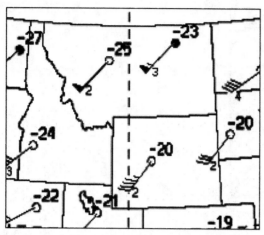

Figure 5-15. Winds aloft chart for the northern Rockies

78. What are the current winds in western Montana? (AC 00-45)

The winds are from 220 at 50 knots (thus the wind is blowing *towards* the northeast).
To determine the wind direction, the observer must estimate the general direction from
which the wind is flowing—in this case from the southwest, which would have a heading
beginning with "2." Then the number adjacent to the tail of the wind barb is used to convey
the second number of the wind direction. Lastly, add a zero, so "2" and "2" and "0" results
in 220.

79. What is the temperature aloft in central Wyoming? (AC 00-45)

-20°C.

**80. Why is the station in western Montana indicated with an open circle, while the one
in eastern Montana is indicated with a darkened circle?** (AC 00-45)

The temperature-dew point spread is 5°C or less at stations with a darkened circle.

**81. Low-level (surface) significant weather prognostic charts cover what altitude
range?** (AC 00-45)

The surface to 24,000 feet (400 mb).

82. What types of things are indicated on the "surface prognosis panel"? (AC 00-45)

A surface prognosis panel shows surface pressure systems, fronts, and precipitation.

83. What types of things are indicated on the "significant weather panel"? (AC 00-45)

A significant weather panel shows weather flying categories (VFR, MVFR, IFR), freezing
levels, and turbulence.

84. What should dispatchers observe prior to using any aviation weather chart?
(AC 00-45)

Dispatchers should check the valid time and date prior to use to ensure that the chart is
applicable to the operation in question.

For questions 85–87, refer to the significant weather prognostic chart shown in Figure 5-16. (Aviation Weather Center)

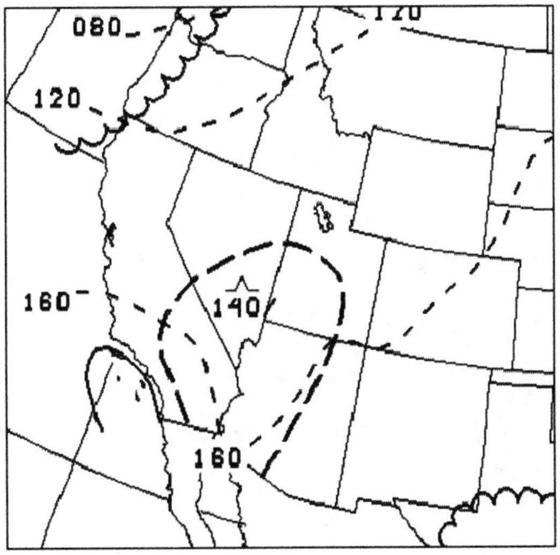

Figure 5-16. Significant weather prognostic chart

85. What is the meaning of the short dashed lines? (AC 00-45)

These lines mark the freezing level. At the end of each dashed line is a number that indicates the freezing level along that line. For example, 160 indicates that the freezing level along the corresponding line is 16,000 feet.

86. What is the meaning of the long dashed lines looping from California northward into Nevada and then back into Arizona? (AC 00-45)

These lines mark an area of moderate turbulence at 14,000 feet and below.

87. What is the meaning of the scalloped lines along the Oregon coast and in Texas? (AC 00-45)

These lines indicate areas of marginal VFR (3–5 SM and ceilings between 1,000 and 3,000 feet).

88. How is an area of IFR conditions depicted on the significant weather prognostic chart? (AC 00-45)

An area of IFR conditions is indicated by a solid, straight line contour inside the MVFR scalloped line.

For questions 89–92, refer to the surface prognostic chart for the southeast U.S. shown in Figure 5-17. (Aviation Weather Center)

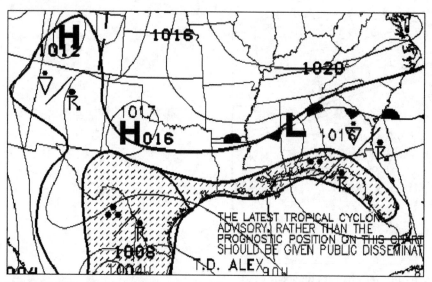

Figure 5-17. Surface prognostic chart for the southeast U.S.

89. What type of weather is occurring in southern Texas? (AC 00-45)

Continuous moderate rain and thunderstorms with rain showers over more than half the contoured area.

90. What is the difference between precipitation that occurs in a shaded region versus a region simply outlined by a contouring line? (AC 00-45)

In the shaded regions, the precipitation is expected to be more widespread, covering more than half the area. In the non-shaded regions, it is expected to cover less than half the area.

91. What type of front is present in the southeast U.S.? (AC 00-45)

A stationary front extends from Louisiana to the Atlantic coast.

92. What is the significance of the line with "1020" in Kentucky? (AC 00-45)

This is an isobar connecting areas with a pressure of 1020 mb.

93. What altitude range does a high-level significant weather prognostic chart cover? (AC 00-45)

This chart covers FL250 (25,000 feet) to FL600 (60,000 feet).

94. What types of weather phenomenon are depicted on a high-level significant weather prognostic chart? (AC 00-45)

This chart shows jet streams, cumulonimbus, turbulence, tropopause heights, surface fronts, tropical systems, squall lines, sand/dust storms, and volcanic eruptions.

For questions 95–99, refer to the high-level significant prognostic chart for the northeast U.S. shown in Figure 5-18. (Aviation Weather Center)

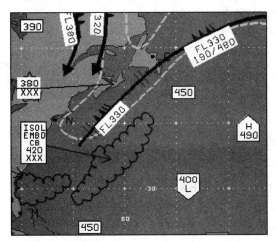

Figure 5-18. High-level significant prognostic chart for the northeast U.S.

95. What is the altitude of the core of the jet stream just off the coast of New England? (AC 00-45)

33,000 feet (FL330).

96. What is the speed of the jet stream off the coast of New England? (AC 00-45)

120 knots. (Big barbs are 50 knots each, thin barbs are 10 knots each.)

97. What is the significance of the dashed lines enclosing Nova Scotia? (AC 00-45)

Moderate turbulence exists from the bottom of the chart's altitude range, which is 25,000 feet (marked by XXX), to 38,000 feet.

98. What is the significance of the scalloped enclosure in the Atlantic? (AC 00-45)

Isolated embedded thunderstorms (cumulonimbus) exist from 42,000 feet down to (and probably below) the bottom of the chart's altitude range (25,000 feet).

99. What is the significant of the "400 L" in the Atlantic? (AC 00-45)

This is a low point in the tropopause. In this location, it is located at 40,000 feet.

100. What is "NEXRAD"? (NWS website)

NEXRAD stands for Next Generation Radar and is the latest radar product that is available from the National Weather Service. This is a Doppler weather radar system with dramatic improvements over previous radar systems, including the enhanced abilities to track relative movements of storms and the contents within an individual storm.

101. What is "WSR-88D"? (NWS website)

Weather Surveillance Radar (WSR) — 88 Doppler (D) is the latest weather radar system used by the National Weather Service (also referred to as NEXRAD).

102. What does NEXRAD indicate to the observer? (NWS website)

NEXRAD can detect precipitation or other objects of appreciable density. It is not unusual for the radar to show flocks of migrating birds. Under certain conditions, it can also show ground clutter (objects on the ground), anomalous precipitation (false returns due to strong atmospheric stability), and returns from wave activity out at sea. This system can also indicate relative velocities of objects in terms of how fast they are moving towards or away from the radar site.

103. What is the range of NEXRAD? (NWS website)

For light precipitation, expect to see returns out to 80 NM, but for stronger returns this distance can be 140 NM or more.

104. In general, what is the maximum tilt angle a NEXRAD can scan overhead? (NWS website)

The maximum tilt angle is 19.5 degrees, which limits the detection of precipitation directly overhead the radar station.

105. What do the colors of a NEXRAD image indicate to the observer? (NWS website)

The amount of reflectivity (energy that reflects off of an object and returns to the radar station), in decibels (dBZ) is indicated in a range of colors. Essentially, green represents light to moderate precipitation, yellow represents moderate to intense precipitation, and red/orange indicates intense to extreme precipitation.

106. What is the difference between the tilt angle(s) of the radar in a base reflectivity image versus a composite reflectivity image? (NWS website)

A base image shows what is detected when the radar is tilted 0.5 degrees above the horizon. In a composite image, the entire range of tilt of the antenna is scanned.

107. What is clear air mode? (NWS website)

This is the most sensitive detection mode of NEXRAD in which the radar rotates at a slow rate and takes multiple scans at different tilt angles. This mode is used when no significant precipitation exists, and it is sensitive enough to detect particulates (such as dust) in the atmosphere. Images are updated approximately every 10 minutes.

108. What is "precipitation mode"? (NWS website)

This NEXRAD mode is used when precipitation is present in the area. The radar antenna will move faster for increased update rates and will scan a wider range of tilt angles to form better images of the entire storm structure. Images are updated approximately every 6 minutes.

109. What type(s) of precipitation has the highest reflectivity (i.e., it shows up the best) on NEXRAD? What type(s) has the lowest? (NWS website)

The more intense and the "wetter" precipitation is, the more likely it will show up on NEXRAD. Thus, a severe downpour from a thunderstorm will reflect a lot of energy; dry snow will not. Likewise, light drizzle will not show up as well as very intense snow showers. Wet hail and wet snow are typically well detected by NEXRAD.

110. What does the relative velocity image radar show? (NWS website)

Through a color-coding scheme, this image indicates the relative speed that clouds and precipitation are moving in relation to the radar station. An isolated area of movement to and from the station shows rotation within a storm, which is indicative of an intense event. Such indications are often associated with storms that produce severe weather such as wind shear and tornados. The location of tornados can often be detected with Doppler radar.

111. When viewing a radar image, what considerations should a dispatcher make depending upon the location of the radar station and the time of year the image is taken?

Not all radar images are created equal. If an image is taken in southern Florida in mid-morning in July, a yellow return is likely indicative of a building cumulus cloud that is well on its way to becoming a thunderstorm later in the day. However, a yellow return that appears on an image in mid-January in Idaho is likely to be an area of strong snow. The former would likely be more turbulent than the latter.

112. On radar imagery, what is the relationship between contouring (the different colors and how closely spaced the borders are between color changes) and the intensity of the weather?

A thin area of green surrounding a larger area of yellow, which has a big area of red immediately within it, is indicative of a strong storm. In contrast, a large area of green with patches of yellow scattered within it is indicative of an area of light-to-moderate rain with a much lower intensity (and concern for dispatch) compared to the previous example.

113. Why is it important to loop radar images?

Looping puts things in motion so the dispatcher can see how the precipitation is moving and the speed at which it is moving.

114. Why is it important to view tops derived from radar reports?

The top of precipitation within a storm cell is an important piece of information to determine the potential intensity of an area of weather: the higher the top, the stronger the cell.

For questions 115–116, view the radar coded message composite image with tops shown in Figure 5-19. (Aviation Weather Center)

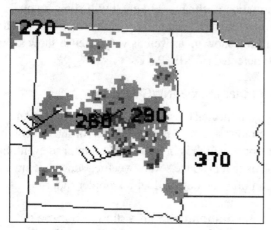

Figure 5-19. Radar coded message composite image

115. What is the top of the storm in southeast South Dakota (bottom right)? (AC 00-45)

The top of the precipitation is 37,000 feet. The cloud top is likely to be several thousand feet higher.

116. Which direction are the storms along the North/South Dakota border moving and at what speed? (AC 00-45)

These storms are moving east-northeast at 35–40 knots.

117. How will the NEXRAD imagery viewed by dispatchers vary from the airborne weather radar imagery seen by flight crews while flying through weather?

Because national and regional NEXRAD imagery are mosaics (i.e., they take images from multiple locations and overlay them on top of one another), these tend to be somewhat overstated; that is, they often show a picture that is worse than what flight crews see on their radars as they approach a storm area.

118. Why is volcanic ash a concern to aircraft?

Volcanic ash can clog probe and air inlets, damage engines, reduce visibility, damage windshields, and cause respiratory irritation to crew and passengers.

119. Where can dispatchers view volcanic ash advisories? (Aviation Weather Center)

Volcanic ash advisories are available from their weather provider, the National Weather Service International Flight Folder Program, or directly from the appropriate Volcanic Ash Advisory Center (VAAC).

120. What type(s) of information accompanies volcanic ash forecasts?
(Aviation Weather Center)

These forecasts, issued by various Volcanic Ash Advisory Centers (VAACs) scattered across the globe, give the location of expected ash clouds and their movement. Graphical products are also typically available.

121. When looking at winds aloft forecasts, where might clear air turbulence be the most likely?

Clear air turbulence will be most likely in areas of shear, such as a rapid change in wind speed or direction in a short distance/small area.

For question 122, see the winds aloft graphic for FL240 shown in Figure 5-20.

122. In the view shown in Figure 5-20, where might you expect to find turbulence?

You might expect turbulence near the jet over Wyoming, North Dakota, and the Minnesota/Canada border region where there is a strong shear (wind speed difference) between the inside of the jet and the areas bordering the core. In addition, the area north of the Chicago area is suspect due to the rapid change in wind speed from slow to fast. Also, the curve in wind direction in eastern Washington is likely to produce some turbulence. The area of slower wind speeds between the jet flowing north into Canada and the wind north of the low-pressure system over Delaware is likely to be problematic. See the actual NWS turbulence prediction model shown in Figure 5-21.

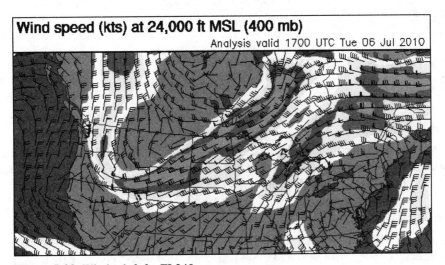

Figure 5-20. Winds aloft for FL240

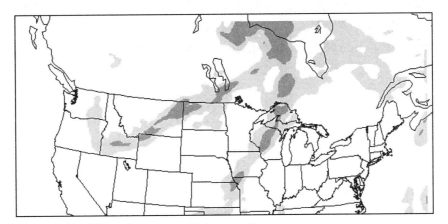

Figure 5-21. NWS turbulence prediction model

123. What are some sources that dispatchers should check to determine the possibility for turbulence?

Dispatchers should check PIREPs, winds aloft forecasts/images, radar imagery (for convective activity), high altitude prognostic charts, AIRMETs/SIGMETs, and turbulence prediction models.

124. What are some sources that dispatchers should check to determine the possibility for icing?

Dispatchers should check PIREPs, winds aloft forecasts, satellite imagery, AIRMETs/SIGMETs, and icing prediction models.

125. What supplementary icing products are available from NWS (or similar providers)? (Aviation Weather Center)

The current icing product (CIP) shows the threat of icing and supercooled water droplets for various altitudes. Threat is conveyed as icing intensity (trace, light, moderate, severe, heavy). Future problems with icing are conveyed as the forecast icing potential (FIP), which indicates the possibility of encountering ice at various altitudes as the percent chance of developing ice.

G. Notices to Airmen (NOTAMs)

1. What is a "NOTAM"? (AIM)

A Notice to Airmen (NOTAM) provides aviation stakeholders with critical information related to the safety of flight. NOTAMs are issued to inform users of things such as inoperative NAVAIDs, airport construction, closed runways, or changes to charts/procedures. NOTAM information is classified into four categories: NOTAM (D) or distant; Flight Data Center (FDC) NOTAMs; pointer NOTAMs; and military NOTAMs.

2. What is a "D NOTAM"? (AIM)

There is no longer a difference between distant (D) NOTAMs and local (L) NOTAMs. The FAA recently changed the NOTAM system so items that used to be classified as L NOTAMs, such a taxiway closure, are disseminated to all sources as D NOTAMs.

3. What is a "FDC NOTAM"? (AIM)

A Flight Data Center (FDC) NOTAM is regulatory in nature and conveys information about changes to instrument procedures/charts.

4. What are the different designations that are included in NOTAMs to convey the type of hazards or situations that exists to operators? (FAA)

- AD—aerodrome means that the NOTAM applies to operations within 5 SM of an airport.
- AIRSPACE—refers to specific activities happening in that airspace, such as parachute jumping, balloons, or aerial refueling.
- APRON or RAMP—applies to issues related to ramp operations.
- COM—communications-related issues, such as inoperative remote communication outlets or frequencies.
- NAV—issues related to VORs, ILS's, GPS, etc.
- O—operational information that is from a reliable source, but that does not meet the aeronautical nature typical of NOTAM requirements.
- OBST—obstruction related issues, such as inoperative warning lights.
- RWY—runway-related concerns, such as closures or inoperative lights.
- SVC—changes to services, such as fuel, available at a particular location.
- TWY—taxiway-related issues, such as inoperative lights or closures.
- U—unverified NOTAM data.
- PAEW—Personnel and Equipment Working, i.e., construction.

6 Aircraft Systems, Performance, and Limitations

This chapter is designed to prepare an aircraft dispatcher for the specific systems knowledge necessary to pass the ADX practical exam. Unless otherwise noted, the system information provided in this section refers to the Boeing 737-800 and/or next generation (NG) models. While this book uses the Boeing 737 NG for systems analysis, you can use the provided questions to guide your studies for other aircraft you may be required to be familiar with for your practical exam. Furthermore, the Boeing 737 provides a good model of most large, transport jet aircraft in terms of general system construction and operation. Unless otherwise noted, the source for the questions in this chapter is The Boeing Company.

A. Airplane, General Equipment, and Doors

1. What is the length and wingspan of the aircraft (-800 model)?

The B737-800 is 129' 6" long and has a 117' 5" wingspan (to the tips of the winglets).

2. Describe the external lighting that is available for viewing the runway during takeoff and landing.

There are two (left/right) retractable landing lights that extend from the belly of the aircraft. To avoid an odd light effect, the light housing can be extended via a switch position in the cockpit prior to illuminating the light. There are also two (left/right) fixed landing lights located in the wing leading edge near the fuselage. In addition, two runway turnoff lights assist in exiting a runway at night. The taxi light is fixed to the nose gear and moves along with the tires when the rudder pedals are moved or the steering tiller is utilized.

3. What other external lights are available?

- *Position lights:* Steady red (left) and green (right) wing-tip lights. Steady white lights face backwards on the wing tips.
- *Strobe lights:* Bright, flashing white lights on the wing tips and tail.
- *Anti-collision:* Flashing red beacons on the upper and lower fuselage
- *Wheel well:* White lights used to illuminate the main and nose landing gear wells for inspection.
- *Logo:* Steady white lights that illuminate the tail. (Lights are on the sides of the vertical stabilizer.)

4. What are emergency lights? When do they illuminate?

Emergency lights are a series of internal and external lights designed to guide occupants from the aircraft during an evacuation. They are independent of aircraft electrical power (they have their own battery power) and will illuminate with the failure of either DC bus 1 or AC power. Some aircraft are equipped with photoluminescent strips on their internal floors that glow in the dark and are used in lieu of actual lights.

5. What are the different entry and exit doors on the B737?

If facing forward, the left front door is termed the forward entry door (1L). This is normally used for boarding at the gate. The front right door is the forward service door (1R). There are four overwing exit doors (two on each side). The aft left door is termed the aft entry door (2L). The aft right door is the aft service door (2R). Earlier 737 models have only two overwing emergency exits.

6. How many cargo doors are installed on the B737? On what side of the aircraft are they?

The B737 has two cargo doors, one forward of the wing and one aft of the wing. They are both located on the right side.

7. When do the passenger overhead oxygen masks automatically deploy?

They will deploy if the cabin altitude reaches 14,000 feet (or if manually deployed by the flight crew).

8. What provides oxygen to the passenger overhead masks?

Chemical oxygen generators. No oxygen bottles are installed for the passenger overhead masks.

9. What is the maximum pressure available from the flight crew oxygen system?

1,850 psi. A chart is available to the flight crew that translates pressure into oxygen capacity in terms of time available based on how many individuals are seated in the cockpit.

10. What is a "PBE"?

A PBE, or portable protective breathing equipment, is a mask-like device that can protect an individual from smoke inhalation for a brief period of time. The device chemically generates its own oxygen supply and seals the user's head, preventing exposure to smoke.

11. What fire category are the lower cargo compartments on the B737-800?

The lower cargo compartments are FAA category C, which means they should be able to keep fire contained without causing aircraft structural or system failures that threaten the safety of the occupants.

12. Describe how the overwing emergency locking system works.

The overwing emergency exits are locked when all of the following conditions exist:
- Three out of four entry doors are closed.
- Engine(s) are in operation.
- The aircraft is in the air or the thrust levers are pushed forward.
- DC power is available.

13. Describe the potable water system.

There is a tank for potable water aft of the rear cargo compartment. This supplies both the galleys and the lavatories with potable water. The system is pressurized with bleed air. Water heaters are installed within the lavatory sinks. Waste water from the system drains from two heated masts on the underside of the aircraft. Servicing is accomplished from a panel on the rear right side of the aircraft.

B. Air Systems

1. What are the two sources of bleed air for the aircraft air systems? When is each available to the air systems?

Bleed air is tapped from the fifth and ninth stages of the compressor section of the engines. The air from the fifth stage is always available (there is only a check valve, not a shutoff valve, in the line from this stage) and as long as the engine bleed valve is open that air is delivered to the rest of the bleed air system. Air from the ninth stage is used when pressure from the fifth stage is inadequate, such as in low thrust scenarios or on the ground. The ninth stage air is controlled through a modulating valve.

2. What is the purpose of the bleed air valves?

These valves, located between the fifth and ninth stage lines and the rest of the air systems, act as pressure modulators and shut offs for bleed air from the engine.

3. What are the uses of bleed air on the aircraft?

- Air conditioning/heat
- Pressurization
- Engine starts
- Hydraulic system reservoir pressurization
- Potable water reservoir pressurization
- Engine cowl and wing thermal ice protection
- TAT probe

4. What sources can supply bleed air?

- Engines
- APU
- External air (ground only)

5. What happens if the temperature or pressure of the bleed air system becomes excessive?

An automatic bleed air trip protection will activate, closing the respective bleed valve.

6. What is the purpose of the isolation valve?

The isolation valve allows for the connection or isolation of one side of the bleed system from the other.

7. Under normal conditions, how is the air system configured?

Normally, the left engine supplies air to the left side of the air system and the right engine supplies air to the right side of the air system.

8. What side of the isolation valve is the APU bleed air line?

The APU feeds the left side of the air system. Therefore, the isolation valve must be opened to supply APU air to the right side of the system (e.g., when starting the right engine).

9. What side of the isolation valve is the external air input?

The external air feeds the right side of the air system. Therefore, the isolation valve must be opened to supply external air to the left side of the system (e.g., when starting the left engine).

10. You are attempting to dispatch an aircraft with an inoperative APU. Describe any special considerations for this condition.

You would want to ensure that the airports to which the aircraft was to be operated have external air capabilities (a high-pressure bleed air cart). You would also want to verify that the isolation valve is operational so that the left engine can be started. The inoperative APU would need to be noted, per MEL instructions, on the dispatch release. In cold or hot weather operations, you will want to ensure that climate control capabilities exist at the gate, as the APU will not be available to supply bleed air for air conditioning or heat.

11. What sources are available for air conditioning and heat for the aircraft?

The aircraft bleed air can be used to run two pneumatic air conditioning kits (PACKs) that then supply the cabin with cool or warm air. PACKs can run off engine or APU bleed air. The aircraft can also be connected to a low-pressure ground air supply (not to be confused with ground pneumatic air, which is a much higher pressure) for cooling or heating. Lastly, a pneumatic ground cart (high pressure) can be connected to the bleed air system to run one or both PACKs.

12. What is the purpose of the ram air inlets on the underside of the aircraft?

These supply cooling air to heat exchangers that are part of the air conditioning system. Fans ensure proper airflow during ground operations. These openings have modulating doors to control airflow and protect the inlets from ingesting foreign object.

13. Describe the cooling cycle of the PACK.

Bleed air is fed to the PACK from the respective bleed air line whenever the PACK valve (shutoff) is open. This air first passes through a heat exchanger to pre-cool it. Next, the air passes through a compressor and then an expansion turbine (air cycle machine), which drastically cools it. This air is then mixed with warm air that bypassed the air cycle machine. Water is removed via a water separator. The resultant air is then sent to a mix manifold where it is distributed to the outlets in the aircraft.

14. Are there any operational limitations if one PACK is inoperative?

The aircraft is limited to operations at or below FL250 whenever a PACK is inoperative.

15. Are there any operational limitations if one bleed shutoff valve is inoperative?

Aircraft limitations prohibit a single bleed from feeding both packs. Therefore, depending upon which bleed is inoperative, flights may be limited to FL250, as the APU is only capable of supplying air to one PACK in flight. In addition, the APU cannot be connected to an engine bleed air source when it is above idle thrust to ensure bleed air does not backflow into the APU. Limitations to operations in icing conditions also may exist.

16. What is the purpose of the recirculation fans?

There are two recirculation fans installed on the aircraft (left and right). These assist in airflow supply by augmenting the output of the PACKs/bleed air.

17. What is the certified ceiling for the aircraft?

41,000 feet.

18. What is the approximate cabin altitude of the aircraft at its certified ceiling?

8,000 feet.

19. How does the pressurization system work?

Bleed air is supplied by the engines (or APU) to the cabin. An outflow valve modulates to maintain the necessary pressure/cabin altitude. This is normally done automatically, but can also be manually conducted by the flight crew.

20. What type(s) of relief valves are available to prevent aircraft damage from the pressurization system?

The positive pressure relief valve vents pressures in excess of 9.1 psi. A negative pressure relief valve also is installed to prevent a cabin pressure that is lower than outside air pressure.

21. What is the purpose of the outflow valve?

The outflow valve modulates to maintain the desired cabin pressure. The outflow valve is located on the underside of the aircraft near the tail.

22. Which cargo compartments are pressurized?

All cargo areas are pressurized.

23. Which cargo compartments are heated?

Cargo areas have no fresh air circulation supply and are heated through exhausted cabin air that is allowed to flow around the holds. Additional heat is available to the forward cargo compartment from the avionics bay.

24. Which is the recommended cargo hold to use for carrying live animals?

The forward hold has better temperature control (heat) and therefore it is the preferred location for live cargo.

C. Ice and Rain Protection

1. What surfaces/locations are protected from ice accumulation?
- Wing (except for portion of leading edge closest to the wing tip)
- Engine cowl inlets
- Flight deck windows
- Probes/sensors (Pitot, TAT, and Angle of Attack vanes)

2. What is used for rain removal on the aircraft?

Windshield wipers are installed on the left and right primary flight crew windows.

3. How might an inoperative ice protection component affect dispatch of an aircraft?

The operation will be restricted to avoid icing conditions. Very few high-altitude and IFR operations can be conducted under such restrictions. It would be advisable to have the problem fixed or swap to another aircraft.

4. How might an inoperative rain protection component affect dispatch of an aircraft?

The operation will be restricted to avoid precipitation that is in the vicinity of the airports of operation.

5. Are the aircraft static ports heated for ice protection?

No.

6. Where does bleed air for cowl anti-ice protection come from?

Bleed air from the 5th stage is always available for cowl anti-ice. Additional air from the 9th stage is fed as needed. A cowl anti-ice valve controls the supply of both 5th and 9th stage air to the engine inlet surface.

7. Where does bleed air for wing anti-ice protection come from?

Bleed air from the fifth and ninth stages are fed to the bleed air system on the respective side of the aircraft. A wing anti-ice control valve installed on each side of the bleed air system controls the operation of the system. The inboard leading edge flaps and the outermost leading edge slat do not receive thermal protection.

8. Does the horizontal stabilizer have thermal ice protection?

No. This surface is not protected.

9. Does the vertical stabilizer have thermal ice protection?

No. This surface is not protected.

10. Windshield heat is not used only for ice protection. What is another use of this system?

A heated windshield is more flexible and therefore provides improved protection from a bird strike (as the windshield will flex rather than shatter). Airspeed limits apply when flying with an inoperative windshield heat system. See the MEL for more details.

D. Autoflight

1. What are the wind limitations for autoland operations?

- Headwind: 25 knots
- Crosswind: 20 knots
- Tailwind: 10 knots (typical restriction)

2. How many autopilot channels are there?

Two.

3. How might an inoperative autopilot affect dispatch?

Typical air carrier operations dictate the use of an autopilot for safe operations. Dispatch may be permitted without the autoflight system if the flight crew is willing to accept such a condition. In addition, the weather must be good enough that the use of the autopilot (for landing) is not required.

4. What is a "yaw damper"?

This is a system that suppresses yaw (left/right movement of the nose) to augment aircraft stability and to avoid a phenomenon known as Dutch roll. The yaw damper system can be inoperative, per the MEL.

5. What is "Mach trim"?

Mach trim is a system that suppresses negative controllability effects from high-speed flight by adjusting stabilizer trim. This can be inoperative per the MEL and if proper procedures are used by the flight crew.

E. Communications

1. How many very high frequency (VHF) radios are installed?

Most operators have three: VHF-1, VHF-2, and VHF-3. The VHF-1 radio antenna is on the top of the fuselage, while VHF-2 and VHF-3 antennae are on the belly of the aircraft.

2. What is an HF radio?

A high frequency (HF) radio is used for long-range communication when aircraft are beyond VHF radio range. Not all operators have HF radios installed.

3. What is "SELCAL"?

Selective calling (SELCAL) is a means to "page" individual aircraft so that they are aware that ATC or dispatch is trying to reach them without having to constantly monitor a specific frequency. SELCAL can be linked to either VHF or HF radios (or both).

4. What is "ACARS"?

Aircraft communications addressing and reporting system (ACARS) is a text-based communication system that can be used by dispatch to communicate with flight crew (and vice versa) to relay information such as weather updates, performance information, questions, etc. Following a transmission, flight crews receive a printout in the cockpit and can answer ACARS messages with a keyboard in the cockpit (usually as part of the flight management computer system).

F. Engines and Auxiliary Power Unit

1. What engines are installed on the aircraft?

The B737-800 has two CFM56-7 turbojet engines.

2. What is the N1 compressor?

This is the low-speed compressor, also referred to as the fan. The N1 compressor is the large bladed component that can be seen from the front of the engine inlet.

3. What is the EEC?

Electronic engine control (EEC) is a two-channel computer system that manages the fuel control to the engine. It can be equated to a sophisticated form of electronic fuel injection. The EEC has protective features that prevent engine damage during starts and in flight. The EEC also ensures proper engine idling.

4. What is an "autothrottle"?

An autothrottle is a subcomponent of the autoflight system that automatically sets engine thrust. It is typically used along with the autopilot to maintain speed, climb, descend, and land. It also sets takeoff thrust under normal conditions.

5. What are some things that operate off of the engine accessory drive?

The rotation of the engine is used to drive a variety of accessories. The following are run off of this engine accessory drive:
• Oil pump
• Fuel pumps
• Integrated drive generator (IDG)
• Starter
• Hydraulic pump

6. How are the engines started?

The CFM56-7 uses an air starter that utilizes bleed air to spin it, which in turn spins the N2 (high-pressure) compressor. Once the engine reaches a minimal speed (as N1 begins to rotate), fuel is introduced to complete the start cycle.

7. How is the engine oil cooled?

A fuel/oil heat exchanger is used to cool oil and at the same time heat fuel.

8. What are thrust reversers and what purposes do they serve?

Thrust reversers are a means to direct some of the engine thrust forward rather than aft. This creates a force to decelerate the aircraft. Thrust reversers on this aircraft are hydraulically actuated. Translating sleeves on the sides of the engine cowls move aft to expose ducts that direct airflow forward. Blocker doors direct air to flow out of these reverser ducts. Thrust reversers are used to slow the aircraft during rejected takeoffs and landings.

9. What is the maximum operating altitude of the auxiliary power unit (APU)?

The same as the operating ceiling of the aircraft: 41,000 feet.

10. How is fuel delivered to the APU?

The APU receives fuel from a line linked to the left side of the fuel system. A DC fuel pump assists during start and an AC pump takes over once electrical power is available from the APU itself. Fuel can be suction fed (without the assistance of the pumps) if necessary. Fuel is heated to prevent icing whenever the APU is running.

11. How is the APU supplied with cooling and combustion air?

Air supply is made available via an automatic inlet door on the right rear of the fuselage. This door closes when the APU is not in use.

12. What is the APU "ECU"?

The electronic control unit (ECU) is the system that controls fuel flow to the APU. The ECU has protective features to prevent APU damage from abnormal operation such as overspeed, overtemperature, and fire.

13. How does the APU assist in aircraft operations?

- Bleed air for:
  - Air conditioning/heat
  - Pressurization
  - Engine start
- Electrical power during:
  - Ground operations
  - Emergency operations

14. How can the use of the APU assist in improving takeoff performance?

An operational APU allows the use of its bleed air for pressurization/PACK use so that bleed air is not needed from the engines during takeoff. This allows more thrust to be available for acceleration and climb, thus improving takeoff performance.

15. Is ground/external electrical power required to start the APU?

No, the APU can be started with onboard battery power.

G. Fire Protection

1. How many fire bottles are installed on the aircraft?

Three: two for the engines and one for the APU.

2. How many fire detection loops are installed on the aircraft?

Six: two for each engine, one in the main wheel well, and one for the APU.

3. How does the fire detection system work?

The fire detection system is comprised of closed loops of metal tubing that are sealed with a gas inside. Excessive temperatures cause an elevation of gas pressure in the line, which trips a fire warning.

4. Can the left fire bottle be used on the number two (right) engine?

Yes. The engine fire bottles can be used for either engine. Both bottles can also be used on only one engine.

5. Can the APU fire bottle be used for extinguishing an engine fire?

No, the APU fire bottle can only be used to extinguish an APU fire, and the engine fire bottles can only be used to extinguish engine fires.

6. How is fire detected in the cargo compartments?

The forward and aft cargo compartments have smoke detectors. Two smoke detection loops exist and both must detect smoke to trigger a fire warning.

7. How might an inoperative engine fire detection loop affect dispatch of an aircraft?

Per the MEL, one may be inoperative as long as the aircraft is not operated beyond ETOPS 120 minutes.

8. If a problem exists with the APU fire detection system, what operational restriction might you expect?

Most failures associated with this system result in the prohibition of APU use, which affects dispatch in terms of necessitating ground equipment to service and start the aircraft.

9. What type of fire protection is available in the wheel well area?

There is no fire protection in the wheel well area, but fire detection is available. Crews should lower the landing gear, declare an emergency, and land if a wheel well fire occurs.

10. What kind of fire protection is available in the aircraft lavatories?

The lavatories have smoke detectors and an automatic fire extinguishing system that discharges into the trash bin and area underneath the sink.

11. What types of portable fire extinguishers are in the cabin of the aircraft?

Both Halon and water fire extinguishers are available. Halon is used for electrical and liquid fires. Water is used for other types of fires. Extinguishers are installed at each galley and in other locations throughout the cabin.

H. Flight Controls

1. Describe the operation of the primary flight controls.

The ailerons (roll), rudder (yaw), and elevators (pitch) are hydraulically actuated under normal conditions. Either of the two primary hydraulic systems can power the flight controls. In case of a hydraulic system failure, the ailerons and elevators can be controlled via mechanical link (cables) and the rudder can be actuated via the stand-by hydraulic system.

2. What is the purpose of spoilers/speed brakes?

Flight spoilers consist of eight panels on the upper surface of the wing that rise to disrupt airflow. These are used in flight to slow the aircraft down and to increase its rate of descent. They also extend to assist in banking the aircraft. On the ground, four more panels raise to assist in slowing the aircraft on landing or during an aborted takeoff. This system normally automatically actuates upon touchdown.

3. How might inoperative auto-speed brakes (spoilers) affect dispatch?

Because of their positive effects on landing performance (and aborted takeoff performance) this will likely affect the maximum landing and takeoff weights that will be available for flight.

4. What is "speed trim"?

Speed trim is a system that assists pilots in maintaining pitch control in light weight and high thrust setting conditions. It relies on an automatic actuation of stabilizer trim.

5. What is a "yaw damper"?

This is a system that suppresses yaw (left/right movement of the nose) to augment aircraft stability and to avoid a phenomenon known as Dutch roll. The yaw damper system can be inoperative, per the MEL.

6. What is "Mach trim"?

Mach trim is a system that suppresses negative controllability effects from high-speed flight (Mach 0.615) by adjusting stabilizer trim. This can be inoperative per the MEL and if proper procedures are used by the flight crew.

7. What is a "Krueger flap"?

A Krueger flap is a leading-edge flap that augments lift during takeoff and landing. This is the type of leading edge device that is installed on the most inboard portion of the wing.

8. What is a "slat"?

A slat is a leading edge device that augments lift during takeoff and landing. There are eight slat panels on the 737NG.

9. How are the leading edge devices normally extended?

Leading edge devices are extended by hydraulic system B, but system A can extend them in an emergency.

10. What are "trailing edge flaps"?

Trailing edge flaps are panels installed on the trailing edges of the wings and that move down and aft to augment lift during takeoff and landing.

11. What flap settings are available for takeoff?

Flaps 1, 2, 5, 10, 15, and 25.

12. What flap settings are available for landing?

Any flap setting can be used for landing, but normally flaps 30 or 40 are used.

13. How are trailing edge flaps normally extended?

Trailing edge flaps are normally extended by hydraulic system B. They can be extended electrically in emergency situations (alternate flaps).

14. Can the trailing edge flaps be extended following hydraulic system failure?

Yes, through the use of the electrically driven alternate flap system.

I. Flight Instruments

1. What is the "PFD"?

The primary flight display (PFD) provides the pilots with their attitude and heading information, their altitude and airspeed, and navigation and autopilot information.

2. What is the "ND"?

The navigation display (ND) provides the pilots with supplementary information such as map and navigation information.

3. What is "TCAS"?

Traffic alert and collision avoidance system (TCAS) is an avionics component that notifies the flight crew of proximate air traffic. TCAS also displays the location of this traffic, warns of potential conflicts, and gives collision avoidance procedures. In some references, TCAS stands for traffic collision avoidance system.

4. What is "GPWS"?

Ground proximity warning system (GPWS) is an avionics component that notifies the flight crew of an impending impact with the ground. The system uses a radar altimeter to determine the height of the aircraft above the ground and the closure rate with terrain. Enhanced GPWS (EGPWS) visually displays the location of terrain on the ND and its relative height in relation to aircraft altitude.

5. What is "PWS"?

Predictive wind shear system (PWS) is an avionics component that notifies flight crew of a dangerous wind shear event occurring in front of the aircraft.

6. What is a "HUD"?

The heads-up display (HUD) is device that is a transparent screen installed in the pilot's field of view that displays flight guidance information such as attitude, airspeed, altitude, and navigation data. This allows the pilot to look outside while still receiving critical flight information. HUDs assist in landing in poor weather conditions, but can also be used at any time deemed necessary by the flight crew.

7. What is "EFIS"?

Electronic flight information system (EFIS) is the term for the various electronic screens and displays in a "glass" cockpit. EFIS includes the PFDs, NDs, and supplementary displays (such as those for messages and engine indications).

8. What provides the air data, attitude, and heading information to the cockpit?

This information is provided by the air data inertial reference system (ADIRS).

9. What type of dispatch restriction might be expected if an IRS is inoperative?

One IRS may be inoperative if the flight is conducted in visual meteorological conditions. See the MEL for specific details and restrictions.

J. Flight Management and Navigation

1. What types of navigation sources are available in this aircraft?

- Flight management system (FMS)
- Global positioning system (GPS)
- Air data inertial reference system (ADIRS)
- Radio navigation (ILS, VOR, DME)

2. What are the components of the flight management system (FMS)?

- Flight management computer system (FMCS)
- Autopilot (AFDS)
- Flight director
- Autothrottle
- Inertial reference system (IRS)
- Global positioning system (GPS)

3. What is the "CDU"?

The control display unit (CDU) enables pilots to interface with the FMCS. This is the screen and keyboard commonly referred to as the FMC or FMS.

4. If GPS is unavailable, what does the aircraft use to locate its position?

The aircraft will revert to radio navigation or inertial navigation for location data.

5. How many GPS receivers are installed on the aircraft?

Two: one on each the left and the right.

6. How many inertial reference system (IRS) units are installed on the aircraft?

Two.

7. What type of gyros does the IRS utilize?

Each IRS has three ring laser gyros.

8. What do the IRS units provide?

The IRS units are the source for attitude and heading information provided to the PFDs.

9. What type(s) of weather avoidance equipment is installed on the aircraft?

The aircraft has a weather radar installed in the nose that provides pilots with the intensity of precipitation ahead of the aircraft. A turbulence detection mode is also available out to 40 NM.

10. What is the difference between the FMC and the FMS?

The flight management computer (FMC) does much of the calculation or "work" of the larger system, which is termed the flight management system (FMS).

11. How many FMCs are installed on the aircraft?

There are two FMCs as well as two CDUs through which the pilots interface with the FMCs.

12. When there are no external position sources (GPS or radio), what does the FMC use for position data?

In this circumstance, the FMC uses IRS position data.

13. What are some uses of the FMS?

- Performance management
- Thrust management
- Fuel management
- Flight deck display
- Lateral navigation (LNAV)
- Vertical navigation (VNAV)
- Route selection/entry
- Approach selection/entry
- Auto-tuning of radio navigation
- Flight plan data (time enroute/time of arrival)

14. What is the priority of navigation sources used for position updates?

The following priority, in order, is used for position data:
- GPS
- DME stations (two or more)
- VOR/DME or VORTAC
- Localizer and DME
- Localizer

15. What is "ANP"?

Actual navigation performance (ANP) is the estimated quality of the calculated aircraft position at a 95% confidence level.

16. What is "RNP"?

Required navigation performance (RNP) is the minimum navigation performance value required for phases of flight (terminal, enroute, approach) and/or for specific airspace operations. RNP is stated in terms of nautical miles. For example, RNP 1.0 requires that 95% of the time, the aircraft must be within 1 NM of where it "thinks" it is, and must be within 2 x RNP (or 2 NM in this example) 99% of the time. If the ANP exceeds RNP, the crew will receive the message "UNABLE REQUIRED NAVIGATION PERFORMANCE."

17. What is the "FDR"?

The flight data recorder (FDR) details critical flight information, which can be accessed for analysis following a flight event or accident.

18. What is a "CVR"?

A cockpit voice recorder (CVR) is a device that records voices and sounds via microphones in the cockpit. This information is typically only accessed after an aircraft accident.

19. What type of dispatch restrictions might be expected if a GPS receiver is inoperative?

No specific restrictions typically exist for domestic/class I navigation operations. However there may be restrictions to international/class II navigation flights. See MEL for specific details and restrictions.

20. What type of dispatch restrictions might be expected if an FMC is inoperative?

No restrictions typically exist, other than that navigation must be conducted through the use of ground-based navigation aids, and an operational inertial reference system must be available. See the MEL for specific details.

21. What type of dispatch restrictions might be expected if an FMC database is not current?

The database can be used if the crew verifies database information with current maps and charts. See the MEL for specific details.

K. Fuel

1. How many fuel tanks are installed in the aircraft?

Three: The number one (left wing), the number two (right wing), and the center.

2. How many pounds of fuel can each tank carry (at a fuel density of 7.1 pounds per gallon)?

- Tanks number one and two: 9,144 pounds each
- Center tank: 30,522 pounds
- Total: 48,810 pounds

3. Describe how fuel is normally distributed to the engines.

Fuel is normally fed from the center tank first, then from the wing tanks.

4. How many electric fuel pumps are in the aircraft?

The aircraft has a total of seven electric pumps. There are two AC fuel pumps in each of tanks one, two, and center. One DC fuel pump feeds the APU.

5. Can fuel from tank number one (left) be used to feed the number two engine (right)?

Yes, via the cross-feed valve.

6. Fuel from the center tank can be used by which engine(s)?

Two pumps exist in the center tank: one feeds the fuel system on the left side of the cross-feed valve while the other feeds the right side.

7. From which tank does the APU pump siphon fuel?

The number one tank.

8. Is it possible to run the APU using fuel from the center tank?

Yes. The left center tank can be used to feed the APU. Alternatively, the cross-feed can be opened and the right center tank can be used to feed the APU.

9. If all of the electric fuel pumps are on, how is fuel distributed in the system?

The center pumps have a higher pressure output than the main tank pumps. Therefore, fuel is fed from the center tank first.

10. Between the fuel tanks and the engine, how many shutoff valves are installed?

Two shutoff valves for each engine: the spar fuel shutoff valve located near the main fuel tank, and the engine fuel shutoff valve in the engine.

11. What is the difference in output rates between the center tank pumps and the main tank pumps?

The center tank pumps have a minimum output of 23 psi while the main pumps have a minimum output of 10 psi. Therefore, anytime the center pumps are running and fuel is available, fuel will be delivered from the center tank even if the main tank pumps are on.

12. What is the center tank scavenge pump?

This is a jet pump (one that works with existing fuel pressure in the system) that transfers approximately 177 lbs per hour from the center tank to the number one fuel (left) tank when the number one fuel tank is approximately half full, and the forward electric fuel pump in the number one tank is on.

13. What type of restrictions might be expected if the main tank fuel quantity indicator is inoperative?

Crews will be required to verify fuel quantity prior to each flight. This may take more time, thus affecting turnaround/scheduling times. Also, all pumps in the respective tank as well as the fuel flow indicator associated with the affected side of the fuel system must be operational. See the MEL for detailed instructions.

14. How do crews verify fuel quantity if the associated tank gauge is inoperative?

There are sticks that drop from the underside of the wing that can be used to determine quantity. At the end of each stick is a magnet. In the tank, there is a floating magnet. Where the stick magnet meets the tank magnet determines the length of the stick that is exposed to the flight crew. The value read from the exposed stick is used to determine fuel quantity.

L. Electrical

1. How many generators are onboard the aircraft?

Three: one on each engine and one on the APU.

2. What is the power output of the AC electrical system?

The two integrated drive generators (IDGs) and the APU generator each supply 115-volt, 400 cycle (Hz) AC power.

3. What is the power output of the DC electrical system?

28 volts.

4. How many batteries are installed on the aircraft?

Two: the main and the auxiliary.

5. What kind of batteries are installed on the aircraft?

24-volt, nickel-cadmium batteries.

6. How much power (time) is available from the batteries in an emergency?

Approximately 60 minutes.

7. What supplies DC electricity for use onboard the aircraft?

DC power is made available through transformer rectifiers and the two aircraft batteries.

8. In an emergency, can the batteries supply AC and DC power?

Yes, the DC power comes directly from the batteries, while DC power is converted to AC via an inverter. Thus both AC and DC power are provided to the stand-by power system.

9. What is an "IDG"?

An integrated drive generator (IDG) is installed on each engine. The integrated drive keeps the generator at a constant speed regardless of engine speed to ensure constant and stable AC power output. In case of an emergency, such as during an overheat situation, the integrated drive can be disconnected from the engine accessory drive.

10. What are the options for providing electrical power to the aircraft when it is on the ground without the engines running?

Ground power can be connected to the AC external power receptacle located on the lower right side of the aircraft nose. The APU can also be run to provide aircraft power.

11. What is an "electrical bus"?

An electrical bus is a means of distributing electricity to other system components. Usually, a power source is connected to a bus (essentially, an electrically conductive material), which is then connected to other electrical components and power delivered to the bus is distributed to other power lines for other components/systems.

12. How is AC power distributed from its source to the aircraft components?

Only one AC power source can be connected to an individual transfer bus. Therefore, external power, an IDG, or the APU generator can be connected to a transfer bus at any given time. Once a new AC source is connected to a transfer bus, the previous source is removed. The transfer bus then distributes AC power to certain heavy electrical draw components (such as electric hydraulic pumps) as well as other buses such as the galley and main buses. In addition, each transfer bus powers one or two transformer rectifiers that convert AC to DC power.

13. How is DC power distributed from its source to the aircraft components?

DC power comes from the three transformer rectifiers (TRs). TR1 is normally connected to AC transfer bus 1; TR2 is normally connected to AC transfer bus 2; and TR3 is normally connected to AC transfer bus 2, but can be connected to AC transfer bus 1. DC power is distributed to DC bus 1, DC bus 2, and the DC standby bus via a cross bus. TR3 also provides DC power to the battery bus. The main battery provides DC power to the hot battery bus and the switched hot battery bus. In emergency (standby power) scenarios, it can also supply power to the battery bus, DC standby bus, and (via an inverter) the AC standby bus. The auxiliary battery is normally isolated from the rest of the DC system, but is paralleled with the main battery during emergency (standby power) operations.

14. **External AC power is connected to the airplane. The APU is then started. Describe what happens if the crew wants to instead use the APU generator to supply power.**

    The crew would select the appropriate transfer bus(es) that they would like the APU generator to supply with AC power. This would remove the external power from that bus and replace it with APU power.

15. **How many transformer rectifiers (TRs) are installed on the aircraft?**

    Five: three TRs connect the AC system to the DC buses, the DC standby bus, and the battery bus. Two TRs act as battery chargers for the main and auxiliary batteries.

16. **How many inverters are installed on the aircraft?**

    One. It connects the DC system to the AC standby bus and is used in emergencies so that the DC system can power the AC system.

17. **Describe how AC power is distributed from the APU to the primary electrical system.**

    The APU generator connects to a central line in between the two transfer buses. The crew can then individually connect the APU to either or both transfer bus 1 and transfer bus 2.

18. **What happens if each IDG is connected to its respective transfer bus, but one IDG fails?**

    The transfer bus associated with the failed IDG will be connected to the remaining IDG as long as the bus transfer switch is in the AUTO position.

19. **A crew calls stating that they have an inoperative engine-driven generator. What type of effect might be expected on dispatch?**

    The APU generator must be used throughout the flight. See the MEL for detailed instructions.

M. Hydraulics

1. **How many hydraulic systems are installed on the aircraft?**

    There are three hydraulic systems: system A, system B, and the standby system.

2. **Which hydraulic system(s) can power the flight control systems?**

    Either hydraulic system A or B. Neither system provides any operational advantage over the other.

3. **How many hydraulic pumps are installed in the aircraft?**

    Five hydraulic pumps are installed. There is one engine-driven hydraulic pump for each engine and one electric hydraulic pump in each system (A, B, and standby).

4. **How many pumps are installed in each hydraulic system?**

    System A and system B each have two: an engine-driven pump and an electrically driven pump. The standby system has one: an electrically driven pump.

5. **If a leak exists in the system A engine-driven hydraulic pump or associated lines, what will happen to the fluid level in the system A reservoir?**

Following a leak in this component of the system, approximately 20% of the fluid will remain to be utilized by the electric hydraulic pump.

6. **Does a leak in hydraulic system B endanger the usability of the standby system?**

No. A fluid leak from system B should not affect the standby system.

7. **If a leak exists in hydraulic system B, what will happen to the fluid level in the system B reservoir?**

A leak in the system itself will likely drain the fluid down to the top of the stand-pipe, which is designed so there will be enough residual fluid to still utilize the power transfer unit (PTU).

8. **Which system normally powers the landing gear?**

System A.

9. **What is the approximate difference in fluid volume pumping capabilities of the electric vs. the engine-driven hydraulic pumps?**

The engine-driven pumps have four times the volume flow compared to the electric pumps.

10. **What is used to cool the hydraulic fluid?**

Some hydraulic fluid is sent through a heat exchanger in the fuel tanks (system A uses tank 1; system B uses tank 2).

11. **What is a "PTU"?**

A power transfer unit (PTU) is a hydraulically actuated pump that is used to transfer pressure from one hydraulic system to another without having to exchange fluid.

12. **Does a backup capability exist for hydraulic system B in case both pumps fail in that system?**

A power transfer unit (PTU) uses system A pressure to drive a turbine that is connected to a pump-like device in system B, which pressurizes the fluid in that system.

13. **Can the landing gear be retracted if the hydraulic system that actuates the gear fails?**

Yes, normally system A actuates the landing gear, but the landing gear transfer unit allows system B to operate the landing gear, although at a slower rate.

14. **What does the standby hydraulic system power?**

- Thrust reversers
- Rudder
- Leading edge flaps/slats
- Standby yaw damper

15. **Can the standby system retract the leading edge flaps/slats?**

No, the system allows for extension only.

16. Will a leak in the standby hydraulic system affect either system A or B?

Yes, since the standby system receives its fluid supply from system B, a leak in the standby system will drain the system B reservoir to approximately the 72% level.

17. What is a "hydraulic fuse"?

A hydraulic fuse is a device installed in a hydraulic line that prevents a leak in the line downstream of the fuse from consuming all of the remaining fluid in the system.

18. What is the normal hydraulic system pressure?

3000 psi.

19. How might an inoperative hydraulic quantity gauge affect dispatch?

The hydraulic fluid quantity will need to be verified prior to each flight. This may cause minor delays. This requires maintenance action, so each station must have maintenance available and they must be informed to meet the aircraft. See the MEL for detailed instructions.

20. Can the landing gear be extended following a complete hydraulic failure?

Yes, no hydraulic pressure is required to extend the gear.

N. Landing Gear

1. What normally actuates the landing gear?

Hydraulic system A normally operates the landing gear, but system B can take over in case system A fails.

2. What normally actuates the nose wheel steering?

Hydraulic system A normally operates nose wheel steering, but an alternate steering system is available from system B.

3. What normally actuates the brake system?

Hydraulic system B normally operates the brakes, but they can alternatively be operated by system A.

4. What is an anti-skid system?

This is an anti-lock brake system that improves braking performance during landing and rejected takeoffs.

5. Is anti-skid capability lost if the primary hydraulic source for the brake system is lost?

No. Normally system B operates the brakes, but even if this system fails, anti-skid would be available.

6. What happens if one of the main tires is damaged during gear retraction?

There is a sensor that detects a damaged tire and will prevent retraction into the wheel well so that the tire cannot damage sensitive components.

7. Can the landing gear be retracted if the primary hydraulic system that powers the gear fails?

Yes. Normally system A powers retraction, but the landing gear transfer unit allows system B to retract the gear.

8. How is the landing gear held up?

There are mechanical uplocks that hold the gear. During extension, these release to allow the gear to extend.

9. How is the landing gear extended following a hydraulic failure?

Manual extension occurs by pulling levers in the cockpit that manually release the mechanical uplocks for each gear (left main, right main, and nose).

10. How is nose wheel steering accomplished?

A limited amount of steering is available through the rudder pedals that are linked to the nose wheel. For large turns and maneuvering, there is a nose wheel tiller located on the captain's side of the cockpit. This "steering wheel" allows the pilot more precise steering control. During ground operations, nose wheel steering can be disabled through the insertion of a pin in the towing level.

11. What happens to the brakes when the hydraulic system that normally actuates them fails?

The brakes are normally powered by system B; however, if system B fails the alternate brakes powered by system A will supply the necessary pressure to actuate the brakes.

12. What happens to the brakes if all hydraulic systems fail?

There is a brake accumulator pressurized by system B that stores enough pressure to provide several actuations of the brake system.

13. What protections does the anti-skid system provide?

- Skid protection
- Locked wheel protection
- Touchdown (spin-up) protection
- Hydroplaning protection

14. What does the autobrake system provide?

The autobrake allows for an automatic actuation of the brake system during a rejected takeoff or during landing. The autobrakes use hydraulic pressure from system B.

15. What provides the hydraulic pressure to set the parking brake?

Pressure can be provided from system A, B, or the system B accumulator.

16. What is the air/ground system?

The air/ground system provides data to various systems on whether the aircraft is on the ground or in the air.

17. How does the air/ground system work?

The air/ground system uses six sensors, two on each landing gear, that indicate if the weight of the aircraft is being applied to the landing gear, indicating the aircraft is on the ground. The system also receives inputs from the thrust lever position, engine operation, wheel speed/spin-up, and parking brake.

18. How might inoperative anti-skid affect dispatch of the aircraft?

The maximum allowable takeoff and landing weights will be reduced. Severe limitations may exist when operating without anti-skid if the runway is wet, slippery, or contaminated. Reduced thrust operations are generally prohibited when anti-skid is inoperative, which will affect performance calculations for both the dispatcher and flight crew.

O. Warning Systems

1. What is the purpose of the master fire warning lights?

These lights illuminate to draw the attention of the flight crew to warning and/or fire conditions. The lights remain illuminated until the condition is rectified. The lights are on the glare shield in the direct view of the flight crew.

2. What is the purpose of the master caution lights?

These lights illuminate to draw the attention of the flight crew to any caution condition. The lights remain illuminated until the condition is rectified. The lights are on the glare shield in the direct view of the flight crew.

3. What is the purpose of the takeoff configuration warning?

This warning announces when the flight crew attempts to takeoff when the aircraft is not properly configured for departure. Issues that may sound this alarm include:
- Flaps not in takeoff position
- Leading edge devices not in takeoff position
- Speed brake lever not stowed
- Spoilers not down/stowed
- Parking brake set
- Stabilizer trim not set for takeoff

4. What is the "PSEU"?

The proximity switch electronic unit (PSEU) is a computer that manages warnings based on aircraft configuration. These include:
- Takeoff configuration warnings
- Landing configuration warnings
- Landing gear position
- Air/ground sensing

5. What is "GPWS"?

Ground proximity warning system (GPWS) is an avionics component that notifies the flight crew of an impending impact with the ground. The system uses a radar altimeter to determine the height of the aircraft above the ground and the closure rate with terrain. Enhanced GPWS (EGPWS) visually displays the location of terrain on the ND and its relative height in relation to aircraft altitude.

6. What is look-ahead terrain alerting?

This is a component of GPWS (often referred to as "enhanced GPWS"). This system has a terrain database which is compared to aircraft location and altitude. If a conflict is predicted, a warning is issued to the flight crew. Pilots can also select to view a color-coded pictorial display of nearby terrain.

7. What types of wind shear warnings are available on this aircraft?

The GPWS has a wind shear warning component that warns pilots once they have encountered conditions that match a wind shear computer model. There is also a predictive wind shear system that uses the airborne weather radar to look ahead of the aircraft for suspect wind shear conditions. This warning sounds prior to the aircraft encountering the wind shear.

8. What is "TCAS"?

Traffic alert and collision avoidance system (TCAS) is an avionics component that notifies the flight crew of proximate air traffic. TCAS also displays the location of this traffic, warns of potential conflicts, and gives collision avoidance procedures. In some references, TCAS stands for traffic collision avoidance system.

9. What is the purpose of the tail skid?

The tail skid protects the tail of the aircraft from a tail strike. It also has physical indicators to tell flight, ground, and maintenance crews that a tail strike has occurred.

10. What effects might an inoperative APU fire warning system have on dispatch?

The APU will not be able to be started or used. Therefore, a means to air condition/heat the aircraft, provide ground power, and start the engines must exist at each station of operation.

P. Performance

1. What is "accelerate/stop distance"? (14 CFR §25.109)

This is the total distance an aircraft will travel from the initiation of the takeoff roll to accelerate to V_1 and then abort the takeoff. The maximum accelerate/stop distance cannot exceed the length of the runway plus the stopway (if one exists). A two-second delay in reaction at V_1 is allowed.

2. What is "accelerate/go distance"?

This is the total distance an aircraft will travel from the initiation of the takeoff roll to accelerate to V_1, continue a takeoff following an engine failure, and climb to 35 feet by the end of the takeoff surface (which can include the clearway).

3. What is "balanced field length"?

Balanced field length is a condition where an aircraft is at a weight at which the accelerate/stop distance equals the accelerate/go distance.

4. What is the definition of "takeoff run" for a dry runway? (14 CFR §25.113)

Takeoff run is the distance an aircraft uses to accelerate and become airborne to a point halfway between reaching liftoff speed and climbing to 35 feet above the ground.

5. What is the definition of "takeoff distance" for a dry runway? (14 CFR §25.113)

Takeoff distance is typically the distance from the initiation of the takeoff roll to a point at which the aircraft reaches 35 feet above the ground.

6. The takeoff run can never exceed the length of the _____.

Runway.

7. Accelerate/stop distance can never exceed the length of the _____.

Runway plus the stopway.

8. Takeoff distance can never exceed the length of the _____.

Runway plus the clearway.

9. What aircraft weight limits must a dispatcher consider during takeoff performance calculations?

- Structural weight (aircraft manufacturer maximum takeoff weight)
- Runway limit weight (based on field length and ambient conditions)
- Climb limit weight (based on obstacle/terrain and ambient conditions)
- Of course, the aircraft must be at a weight that complies with enroute and/or landing weight limits

10. What things might affect the runway limit weight?

- Runway length
- Field conditions (wet, slippery, or contaminated)
- Temperature
- Flap setting
- Runway slope
- Wind
- Barometric pressure
- Engine bleed configuration
- Anti-ice system use
- Inoperative systems (such as anti-skid)

11. Explain how each of the aforementioned issues would affect takeoff performance in terms of runway limit weight.

- Runway length:
  - Longer runways will yield higher maximum weights.
- Field conditions (wet, slippery, or contaminated):
  - Non-dry runway conditions will yield lower maximum weights.
- Temperature:
  - High temperatures decrease the maximum takeoff weight.
  - Low temperatures increase the maximum takeoff weight.
- Flap setting:
  - Typically, the larger the flap setting, the more the aircraft can weigh during takeoff. Therefore, when facing a low runway weight limit, dispatchers should see if using a higher flap setting will allow for a higher weight departure. Conversely, the larger the flap setting, the lower the climb limit weight may be. Therefore, it is often necessary to balance the benefits of using a particular flap setting in terms of the runway limit versus the climb limit.
- Runway slope:
  - A downslope typically will improve takeoff performance, but it does slightly hinder rejected takeoff performance.
- Wind:
  - Headwinds will result in increased takeoff weight limits.
  - Tailwinds will result in decreased takeoff weight limits.
- Barometric pressure:
  - High barometric pressure (altimeter settings) will result in increased takeoff weight limits.
  - Low barometric pressure will result in decreased takeoff weight limits.
- Engine bleed configuration:
  - When engine bleeds are used for takeoff, this reduces the takeoff weight limit.
  - If extra performance is needed for takeoff (i.e., a higher weight is needed for departure) consider using a bleeds off (sometimes referred to as an air conditioning off) takeoff. This will add significant weight to the takeoff limit. Since this is not necessarily a normal procedure, be sure to tell flight crews that takeoff performance was based on a bleeds off condition (usually this is conveyed as a note on the dispatch release).
- Anti-ice system use:
  - Anti-ice system use will degrade takeoff weight limits.
- Inoperative systems (such as anti-skid):
  - Inoperative anti-skid will degrade takeoff weight limits. The performance hit taken with an inoperative anti-skid is usually fairly significant, particularly with wet or contaminated conditions. Dispatchers might consider fixing the problem or trying to swap aircraft, if possible.

12. If an aircraft is operated at or below the climb limit weight, what will this guarantee the flight crew?

The aircraft will clear obstacles from 35 feet above the runway to 1,500 feet above the runway (or other higher altitudes depending upon local terrain and obstacles).

13. What are some things that may affect the climb limit weight?

- High terrain or obstacles close to the airport
- Engine bleed configuration
- Anti-ice system usage
- Flap setting

14. Which typically results in a higher climb weight limit: a flaps 1 takeoff or a flaps 25 takeoff?

A flaps 1 takeoff would likely yield a higher climb weight limit. Normally, the larger the flap setting, the lower the climb limit (more flaps creates more drag, reducing climb performance). Therefore, if a dispatcher needs more leeway in weight to meet the requirements of a climb weight limit, it is usually beneficial to use a lower flap setting.

15. During takeoff, when must the aircraft reach V$_2$? (14 CFR §25.111)

No later than at 35 feet above the ground.

16. What is the minimum net takeoff flight path of a transport category aircraft? (14 CFR §25.111)

It must always be positive. Specifically, from 400 feet above the surface it must be 1.2 percent for a two-engine aircraft, 1.5 percent for a three-engine aircraft, and 1.7 percent for a four-engine aircraft.

17. Are flight crews permitted to raise the landing gear and flaps during a takeoff following an engine failure? (14 CFR §25.111)

Pilots can only raise the landing gear and feather the propeller (if applicable) prior to reaching 400 feet. No other configuration changes are permitted.

18. Transport category aircraft takeoffs and departures are divided into different parts. What are these called?

These are referred to as "segments." There are four segments of a climb/departure.

19. Are transport aircraft authorized to be banked (turned) below 50 feet above the ground?

No, and segment climb performance is based upon this restriction.

20. When is an aircraft considered to be in first-segment climb?

First-segment climb begins at brake release on takeoff and ends at a point when the aircraft has reached V$_2$ and the landing gear has been retracted. The aircraft is generally above 35 feet.

21. When is an aircraft considered to be in second-segment climb?

Second-segment climb begins at the end of the first-segment climb and ends at 400 feet, which is often referred to as acceleration altitude. Some operators or airports require a higher acceleration altitude.

22. What minimum climb gradient is required for a two-engine aircraft during the second-segment climb?

2.4 percent.

23. When is an aircraft considered to be in third-segment climb?

Third-segment climb begins at the end of the second segment and ends once the aircraft is in clean/climb configuration and at clean/climb airspeed.

24. What is the minimum climb gradient required for a two-engine aircraft during the third-segment climb?

1.2 percent.

25. When is an aircraft considered to be in fourth-segment climb?

Fourth-segment climb begins at the end of the third-segment climb and ends once the aircraft reaches 1,500 feet above the ground.

26. What is the minimum climb gradient required for a two-engine aircraft during the fourth-segment climb?

1.2 percent.

27. Net takeoff flight paths of transport category aircraft must be calculated to take into account a safety factor of _____ percent. (14 CFR §25.115)

0.8 for two-engine aircraft, 0.9 for three-engine aircraft, and 1.0 for four-engine aircraft.

28. In general, what is the limit to how far an aircraft can fly from an "adequate airport"? (14 CFR §121.161)

For aircraft with two engines, 60 minutes; for those with more than two engines, 180 minutes. To go beyond these maximums, the operator must be certified for extended range/ETOPS.

29. While enroute, the aircraft cannot exceed a weight that will prevent the aircraft from maintaining terrain clearance in case of engine failure. What two standards can be used to determine if the aircraft is able to fly a route based on enroute weight restrictions? (14 CFR §121.191)

The aircraft must comply with one of the following:

- The aircraft must be able to maintain a positive slope (be able to maintain altitude and climb) at an altitude no lower than 1,000 feet above the highest obstacle within 5 SM of the intended route. Also, the aircraft must be able to maintain a positive slope at 1,500 feet above the diversionary airport.

- The aircraft must be able to drift down from cruise altitude clearing terrain and obstacles within 5 SM on either side of the route by not less than 2,000 feet during this altitude loss. Also, the aircraft must maintain a positive slope at 1,500 feet above the diversionary airport.

30. What environmental and/or aircraft factors affect the net level-off weight (driftdown altitude)?

- Temperature
- Desired net level-off altitude
- Engine anti-ice use
- Wing anti-ice use

31. How do the aforementioned environmental and/or aircraft factors affect the net level-off weight (driftdown altitude)?

- *Temperature:* Increases in temperatures aloft decrease the net level-off weight.
- *Desired net level-off altitude:* The higher the desired or necessary net level-off altitude, the lower the net level-off weight.
- *Engine anti-ice use:* Use of this system reduces net level-off weight.
- *Wing anti-ice use:* Use of this system reduces net level-off weight.

32. How can the dispatcher determine if a particular route is legally compliant with driftdown requirements?

First, the dispatcher must determine the driftdown altitude for the estimated weight of the aircraft when it is overflying critical terrain/obstructions. Alternately, the dispatcher can work backwards from a known minimum altitude to determine the maximum weight the aircraft can be at a particular point enroute.

33. While dispatch planning, it is determined that the desired route will take the aircraft over terrain that limits the weight of the aircraft due to driftdown requirements. What are some options that the dispatcher can use to avoid having to remove weight from the aircraft?

- Re-route the aircraft around the critical terrain.
- Use an alternate method of driftdown calculation. (Use the 1,000 feet of separation rule versus the driftdown with 2,000 feet of separation rule.)
- Check the minimum IFR altitudes on different charts (low-altitude versus high-altitude charts).
- Check the actual location of terrain and its height on a sectional chart and determine if the aircraft will fly within 5 SM of critical point(s).
- Fly at a higher cruise altitude to allow for more room/time to driftdown.
- Have a contingency plan for flight crews to avoid the terrain in an emergency.

34. Other than driftdown weight limits, what else must dispatchers consider when evaluating possible cruise altitudes to use?

- Maximum cruise thrust limit altitude.
- Maximum maneuvering limit altitude (also referred to as "margin to initial buffet G" load/bank angle altitude).
- Optimum (best fuel economy) altitude.

35. What performance factors will affect the rate of fuel consumption at cruise altitude?

- Temperature
- Aircraft weight
- Bleed configuration/anti-ice use

36. How does wind affect fuel consumption in climb, cruise, and descent?

The fuel required to climb to a cruise altitude does not change with wind. It takes the same amount of fuel to climb from sea level to FL350 whether the aircraft has a tailwind or a headwind. The distance this climb takes will change decreasing with a headwind and increasing with a tailwind. Cruise fuel consumption will increase with a headwind, as it will take longer to go from point A to point B. The amount of fuel needed to descend is independent of wind. The distance, of course, is not.

37. As a general rule of thumb, what fuel consumption rate can be used to estimate the fuel necessary for a flight?

The Boeing 737-800 uses an average of 5,500 lbs per hour, though this varies with weight and cruise altitude. Some operators use the rule of thumb of 6,000 lbs for the first hour of flight and 5,000 lbs per hour for each hour thereafter. Alternatively, for every 500 miles, one can expect to burn approximately 6,000 lbs.

38. What is the minimum climb gradient for a landing configuration climb (go around)? (14 CFR §25.119)

3.2 percent.

39. Can an aircraft be dispatched at a weight that will cause it to be above a maximum landing weight?

No.

40. What weight restrictions exist for landing aircraft?

Three weight restrictions are factors. The first is a structural weight limit—the maximum landing weight published by the aircraft manufacturer. The second is a maximum landing field weight, which is dependent upon the runway length and conditions. Lastly, the landing climb (go around) weight limit is to ensure the aircraft can successfully clear obstacles in case of a balked landing or missed approach. The aircraft cannot be dispatched if the aircraft is expected to exceed any of these weights.

41. What might affect the maximum landing field weight?

- Runway length
- Runway slope
- Runway conditions (wet, slippery, or contaminated)
- Flap setting
- Wind
- Anti-skid
- Auto-spoilers

42. How do the aforementioned factors affect maximum landing field weight?

- *Runway length:* Longer runways increase maximum landing field weight.
- *Runway slope:*
  ◦ Normally, an upsloping runway would increase maximum landing field weight.
  ◦ Normally, a downsloping runway would decrease maximum landing field weight.
- *Runway conditions (wet, slippery, or contaminated):* Unfavorable pavement conditions reduce the maximum landing field weight.
- *Flap setting:* Larger flap settings tend to increase the maximum landing field weight but often reduce the landing climb (go-around) limit weight.
- *Wind:*
  ◦ Headwinds increase maximum landing field weights.
  ◦ Tailwinds (to a maximum of 10 knots) reduce maximum landing field weights. This is usually a large hit and it would be advisable to avoid landing with a tailwind, especially when pavement conditions are other than dry.
- *Anti-skid:* When anti-skid is inoperative, it can dramatically decrease the maximum landing field weight. This is especially problematic when the pavement conditions are other than dry.
- *Auto-spoilers:* When auto-spoilers are inoperative, the maximum landing field weight is reduced.

43. What factors affect the maximum landing and approach climb, and go-around weight?

- Temperature (higher temperatures reduce maximum weight)
- Engine anti-ice use (reduces maximum weight)
- Wing anti-ice use (reduces maximum weight)
- Air conditioning (bleed) use (reduces maximum weight)
- Approach flap setting (larger flap settings reduce maximum weight)

44. An aircraft is determined to have a takeoff field limit weight of 127,000 lbs, a climb limit of 128,000 lbs, no enroute weight limit, a landing field limit of 120,000 lbs, and a landing climb limit of 123,000 lbs. The structural takeoff weight is 130,000 lbs and the structural landing weight is 121,000 lbs. The aircraft is expected to weigh 127,000 lbs at departure and burn 5,000 lbs of fuel enroute. What is the restricting weight limit in this case? Is the aircraft legal to depart?

In this case, the aircraft is landing field weight limited. Because the aircraft is expected to burn 5,000 lbs of fuel, it can safely depart at 125,000 lbs and still arrive at the maximum of 120,000 lbs. Currently, the aircraft is 2,000 lbs too heavy. The dispatcher can check to see if a larger flap setting is available for landing to potentially boost the landing field limit weight.

45. An aircraft is determined to have a takeoff field limit weight of 126,000 lbs, a climb limit of 128,000 lbs, no enroute weight limit, a landing field limit of 120,000 lbs, and a landing climb limit of 123,000 lbs. The structural takeoff weight is 130,000 lbs and the structural landing weight is 121,000 lbs. The aircraft is expected to weigh 127,000 lbs at departure and burn 8,000 lbs of fuel en route. What is the restricting weight limit in this case? Is the aircraft legal to depart?

The aircraft is takeoff field weight limited. The aircraft is not legal to depart because it can only weigh 126,000 lbs but currently weighs 127,000 lbs. The dispatcher should check to see if a larger flap setting will allow for a higher field limit weight.

46. An aircraft is determined to have a takeoff field limit weight of 133,000 lbs, a climb limit of 133,000 lbs, no enroute weight limit, a landing field limit of 125,000 lbs, and a landing climb limit of 123,000 lbs. The structural takeoff weight is 130,000 lbs and the structural landing weight is 123,000 lbs. The aircraft is expected to weigh 127,000 lbs at departure and burn 8,000 lbs of fuel en route. What is the restricting weight limit in this case? Is the aircraft legal to depart?

The aircraft is landing climb weight limited. The aircraft is legal to depart because it can only weigh 131,000 lbs on departure (the landing climb weight is 123,000 lbs and it will burn 8,000 lbs en route) but it currently weighs 127,000 lbs.

47. Why is there a quick turnaround limit weight?

This is the maximum weight at which an aircraft can land and be able to immediately turn around for departure. This limit exists to ensure that the brakes will be able to absorb the energy of a rejected takeoff and/or will not melt the wheel thermal fuse plugs. If the aircraft lands above this weight, it must remain on the ground for a minimum of 62 minutes to allow for the brakes to sufficiently cool.

48. When considering cruise altitude, what technique is recommended if the optimum altitude is determined to be FL330?

Boeing recommends using a cruise altitude 2,000 feet above optimum, if maneuver and thrust limits allow it, so as the aircraft loses weight (from burning fuel), the optimum altitude will rise to meet cruise altitude.

49. What is the best holding altitude range?

Boeing recommends 25,000 to 30,000 feet for the 737-800.

50. What effect does the use of engine anti-ice have on fuel consumption?

The use of this system increases fuel flow rates by approximately 220 lbs per hour per engine. When dispatching a flight in icing conditions over large portions of a route, dispatchers should take this into account for fuel consumption calculations.

51. What effect does the use of wing anti-ice have on fuel consumption?

The use of this system increases fuel flow rates by approximately 660 lbs per hour per engine. When dispatching a flight in icing conditions over large portions of a route, dispatchers should take this into account for fuel consumption calculations.

52. When is the use of a reduced thrust takeoff prohibited?

- EEC inoperative
- Contaminated or wet runway
- Anti-skid inoperative
- Anti-ice use on takeoff
- Wind shear report
- FMC inoperative
- Aircraft has been de-iced

53. Approximately what increase in takeoff weight is possible by doing a bleeds-off takeoff?

5,100 lbs.

54. What, in general, is the cruising Mach number for long range cruise (LRC)?

0.765 Mach.

55. Will an inoperative thrust reverser affect the maximum takeoff weight?

No, reverse thrust is not taken into account for takeoff performance. However, it is used in case of a rejected takeoff, but its contribution to performance is simply a "bonus."

56. What is "fuel tankering"?

Fuel tankering is when extra fuel is carried on a flight so less (or no) fuel is required at the destination airport. This is often used when fuel prices at the destination are significantly higher than those at another airport. This precludes the need to refuel at inflated costs.

57. What factors should be included in the selection of a cruise altitude?

The optimum altitude in terms of economy (fuel consumption), altitude capability of the aircraft (thrust limit, maneuvering limit), winds aloft (for most favorable tailwind or minimal headwind), turbulence (or other weather-related issues), and correct altitude for direction of flight.

58. Ideally, how should cargo be distributed among the cargo areas?

Cargo should be placed in the aft first, then the forward area(s).

59. What are benefits of having an aft CG?

Lower drag, higher speed, and lower fuel consumption.

Q. Limitations

1. What is the maximum runway slope allowed for this aircraft?

Plus or minus 2 percent.

2. What is the maximum operating pressure altitude?

41,000 feet.

3. What is the maximum takeoff and landing pressure altitude?

8,400 feet.

4. What are the maximum G load limits?

Flaps up: +2.5 and -1.0.
Flaps down: +2.0 and 0.0.

5. What is the maximum tailwind component that is allowed?

10 knots.

6. What is the maximum structural taxi weight?

174,700 lbs.

7. What is the maximum structural takeoff weight?

174,200 lbs.

8. What is the maximum structural landing weight?

146,300 lbs.

9. What is the maximum structural zero fuel weight?

138,300 lbs.

10. When must engine anti-ice be used on the ground?

When icing conditions exist.

11. What is Boeing's definition of icing conditions?

Anytime there is visible moisture and the temperature is 10°C or less. Also, anytime the temperature is 10°C or less and there is standing water, slush, snow, or other moisture present when the aircraft is taxiing on the ground.

12. What flap settings can be used with autoland?

Flaps 30 and flaps 40 degrees.

13. What is the maximum altitude at which the APU can be used as bleed and electrical sources?

10,000 feet in flight; 15,000 feet on the ground.

14. What is the maximum altitude at which the APU can be used as a bleed source?

17,000 feet.

15. What are the maximum usable fuel tank quantities (fuel density of 7.1 pounds per gallon)?

- Tanks number one and two: 9,144 pounds each.
- Center tank: 30,522 pounds.
- Total: 48,810 pounds.

16. What is the maximum demonstrated crosswind component?

34 knots (with winglets).

7

Navigation and Aircraft Navigation Systems

A. Navigation, Navigation Chart Symbols, and the National Airspace System

1. How is an NDB depicted on an enroute chart? (*Aeronautical Chart User's Guide;* Jeppesen charts, introduction)

On National Aeronautical Navigation Product charts (FAA), NDBs are normally depicted in brown; on Jeppesen charts they are green.

2. How are airports with instrument approaches depicted on an enroute chart? (*Aeronautical Chart User's Guide;* Jeppesen charts, introduction)

On FAA charts, airports with approaches are shown in green or blue. Blue airports have Department of Defense approaches while green airports do not. Airports with no instrument approaches are shown in brown. Jeppesen depicts airports with approaches in blue and those without approaches in green.

3. How is a civil airport depicted on an enroute chart? (*Aeronautical Chart User's Guide;* Jeppesen charts, introduction)

On both Jeppesen and FAA charts, these are shown as circles with tick marks extending from them.

4. What are the named star-like symbols on enroute charts? (*Aeronautical Chart User's Guide;* Jeppesen charts, introduction)

These are RNAV fixes (waypoints).

5. What is the significance of an airport depicted with a plain circle on an enroute chart? (*Aeronautical Chart User's Guide;* Jeppesen charts, introduction)

This is a military airport.

6. How is a military operations area (MOA) depicted on an enroute chart? (*Aeronautical Chart User's Guide;* Jeppesen charts, introduction)

On FAA charts, MOAs are shown as areas outlined with brown hashed lines. Jeppesen uses a green shaded region to show MOAs.

7. How is a restricted airspace depicted on an enroute chart? (*Aeronautical Chart User's Guide;* Jeppesen charts, introduction)

On FAA charts, a restricted airspace is conveyed as blue hash-marked regions. Jeppesen uses red shading to indicate this type of airspace.

8. On an enroute chart, what is the difference between a solid triangle (intersection) and a hollow triangle? (*Aeronautical Chart User's Guide;* Jeppesen charts, introduction)

The solid triangle (intersection) is a compulsory reporting point. Flight crews must report their position to ATC when passing these points when not in radar contact (such as in remote areas) or when requested by ATC.

9. How are airways depicted on an enroute chart? (*Aeronautical Chart User's Guide;* Jeppesen charts, introduction)

VHF airways are normally shown as black lines on FAA and Jeppesen charts. FAA shows NDB airways in brown and Jeppesen shows them in green.

10. How wide are airways in the U.S.? (FAA-H-8261-1)

Victor and jet airways are 8 NM wide (4 NM either side). Beyond 51 NM from the NAVAID, this width splays outward slightly.

11. Most airways in the U.S. are indicated by "V" or "J." What is the significance of an airway identified by the following: BR, G, NAT, OTR, R, UL? (*Aeronautical Chart User's Guide;* Jeppesen charts, introduction)

- BR: Bahamas route or Canadian Bravo route
- G: Green or Golf route
- NAT: North Atlantic track
- OTR: Oceanic transition route
- R: Red or Romeo route; or if at end of airway designation—RNAV
- UL: Upper Lima— outside the U.S., high altitude airways are often called "upper" to distinguish them from low-altitude airways

12. What is the difference between true and magnetic north? (FAA-H-8261-1)

True north is located at the geographic North Pole. Lines of longitude meet at the North Pole. Magnetic north is located at the magnetic north pole, which is located in extreme north/northeast Canada. The difference between true and magnetic north is called variation and is indicated on aeronautical charts with a dashed line and the amount of variation in degrees. These are called isogonic lines and they extend from the magnetic north and south poles.

13. What is the significance of a "T" next to the radial defining an airway? (*Aeronautical Chart User's Guide;* Jeppesen charts, introduction)

Airways are normally defined by magnetic radials, but in areas with large magnetic variation, they may instead be defined by radials in reference to true north, which will be shown with a "T" adjacent to the defining course.

14. What is the significance of an airway designation box with an arrow shape? (*Aeronautical Chart User's Guide;* Jeppesen charts, introduction)

This means that the airway is unidirectional. If this requirement only exists at certain times of the day, the effective hours are given adjacent to the arrow.

15. What is an "ARTCC"? (FAA-H-8261-1)

An air route traffic control center (ARTCC) is an ATC facility that provides information (for VFR and IFR flights) and separation services (for IFR flights) to aircraft in the U.S. These centers control enroute IFR traffic.

16. Describe what ATC facilities a typical flight would communicate with during a flight between two large airports. (FAA-H-8261-1)

Clearance control, ground control, tower, departure control, centers, approach control, tower, ground. Some large airports also have a ramp control.

17. How many ATC centers are there? (FAA)

There are currently 20.

18. What is an "FIR"? (*Aeronautical Chart User's Guide;* Jeppesen charts, introduction)

A flight information region (FIR) is an area of airspace typically outside the U.S. where flight information and alerting services are provided (similar to ARTCCs in the U.S.).

19. What is a "UIR"? (*Aeronautical Chart User's Guide;* Jeppesen charts, introduction)

An upper information region (UIR) is an area of high-altitude airspace outside the U.S. where flight information and alerting services are provided (similar to ARTCCs in the U.S.).

20. How is a border between center (or FIR/UIR) airspace depicted on enroute charts? (*Aeronautical Chart User's Guide;* Jeppesen charts, introduction)

On FAA charts, this is shown as a zigzag/castle wall line. On Jeppesen charts, this border is depicted as a line with tick marks that extend from alternating, opposite sides.

21 How is an MEA depicted on an enroute chart? (*Aeronautical Chart User's Guide;* Jeppesen charts, introduction)

The MEA is the altitude that is printed above (at the top) of the airway and is usually located in the middle of the section of airway to which it applies.

22. How is a MOCA depicted on an enroute chart? (*Aeronautical Chart User's Guide;* Jeppesen charts, introduction)

A MOCA is depicted as an altitude with a "*" adjacent to it on FAA charts, while on Jeppesen charts it is depicted with a "T" adjacent to the altitude number.

23. What is the significance of a "G" adjacent to an airway altitude on an enroute chart? (*Aeronautical Chart User's Guide;* Jeppesen charts, introduction)

This denotes an MEA that can be utilized by aircraft using GPS.

24. How is an MRA depicted on an enroute chart? (*Aeronautical Chart User's Guide;* Jeppesen charts, introduction)

An MRA is shown on FAA charts with an "R" flag symbol, while on Jeppesen charts it is simply shown as an altitude with "MRA" adjacent to it.

25. How is an MCA depicted on an enroute chart? (*Aeronautical Chart User's Guide;* Jeppesen charts, introduction)

An MCA is shown on FAA charts with an "X" flag symbol, while on Jeppesen charts it is simply shown as an altitude with "MCA" adjacent to it.

26. How is an MAA depicted on an enroute chart? (*Aeronautical Chart User's Guide;* Jeppesen charts, introduction)

On both FAA and Jeppesen charts, an MAA is shown as an altitude with "MAA" adjacent to the number.

27. How is an OROCA depicted on an enroute chart? (FAA-H-8261-1; Jeppesen charts, introduction)

Off-route obstruction clearance altitudes (OROCAs) are only published on FAA charts. These are shown as large brown numbers in each latitude/longitude quadrant. If the number is "124" that means the OROCA for that quadrant is 12,400 feet. These provide 1,000 feet of obstacle clearance (or 2,000 feet in mountainous areas) from the highest point within the applicable quadrant. On Jeppesen charts, OROCAs are instead termed MORAs (minimum off-route altitudes).

28. What is a MORA? (Jeppesen charts, introduction)

A minimum off-route altitude is an altitude published on Jeppesen charts that provides 1,000 feet of obstacle clearance (or 2,000 feet in mountainous areas) from the highest point within the applicable quadrant. MORAs below 14,000 feet are shown in green; at or above 14,000 feet they are shown in red. A "22" means that the MORA for that quadrant is 2,200 feet.

29. Is radar coverage assured while flying at the MEA? (FAA-H-8261-1)

No, flight at or above the MEA only assures NAVAID signal coverage and obstacle clearance.

30. Can an aircraft that is flying using GPS as the primary source of navigation operate at the MOCA at any time? (14 CFR §91.177)

Yes, according to CFR 91.177 only aircraft using VOR navigation are required to comply with the requirement to stay within 22 NM of the NAVAID when flying at the MOCA.

31. How is the total mileage between NAVAIDs defining an airway shown on enroute charts? (*Aeronautical Chart User's Guide;* Jeppesen charts, introduction)

On FAA charts, this is conveyed by the mileage shown enclosed in a box. On Jeppesen charts, the mileage is enclosed in a box with pointed sides.

32. How are airway segment mileages depicted on enroute charts? (*Aeronautical Chart User's Guide;* Jeppesen charts, introduction)

On both FAA and Jeppesen charts, segment mileages are indicated below (on the bottom of) the airway approximately in the middle of the applicable segment.

33. Where can the radial that defines an airway be found? (*Aeronautical Chart User's Guide;* Jeppesen charts, introduction)

The radial defining the airway is the number found adjacent to the NAVAID where the airway moves outward from the facility.

34. While viewing an enroute chart, you see "V80-12." What does this mean? (*Aeronautical Chart User's Guide;* Jeppesen charts, introduction)

Airways are identified by numbers and letters. Low-altitude airways (below 18,000 feet) are Victor airways and are indicated with a "V" and a number. High-altitude airways are identified as jet routes/airways and are indicated by a "J" and a number. In this example, you are viewing Victor 80 and Victor 12. These two airways overlap, but at some point they probably split and go in different directions. When filing a flight plan, pick the number identification for the airway that goes the longest in the desired direction. You cannot file "V80-12"; instead you must pick only one for that segment of the flight.

35. What does the presence of a star/asterisk adjacent to a frequency or airspace typically mean on aeronautical charts? (*Aeronautical Chart User's Guide;* Jeppesen charts, introduction)

The star/asterisk means that the item is operated part-time. For example, a control tower is not open 24 hours a day.

36. How can an airway that bypasses a NAVAID that it appears to overfly/include be identified? (*Aeronautical Chart User's Guide;* Jeppesen charts, introduction)

On FAA charts, this is shown as a curved/loop line that bypasses the NAVAID. On Jeppesen charts, this is indicated by the airway line remaining solid overhead the NAVAID (as opposed to ending at the edge of the NAVAID).

37. What is the significance of a shaded background on enroute charts? (*Aeronautical Chart User's Guide;* Jeppesen charts, introduction)

Brown shading on FAA charts and grey shading on Jeppesen charts indicate uncontrolled airspace.

38. What is a T route? What is a Q route? (FAA-H-8261-1)

T and Q routes are RNAV airways. T is the designation for low-altitude routes while Q is used to denote high-altitude routes.

For questions 39–44, refer to the low-altitude IFR enroute chart excerpt shown in Figure 7-1.

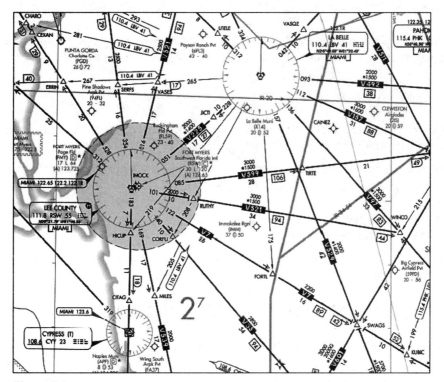

Figure 7-1.

39. What is the MEA on V599 east of RSW VORTAC? (*Aeronautical Chart User's Guide*)

3,000 feet.

40. What is the meaning of the number with the "*" adjacent to it just above the designation box for V599? (*Aeronautical Chart User's Guide*)

This is the MOCA (1,500 feet) for the route.

41. What is the distance from RSW to FORTL intersection on V7? (*Aeronautical Chart User's Guide*)

26 NM.

42. What is the distance from RSW to SWAGS intersection on V7? (*Aeronautical Chart User's Guide*)

42 NM.

43. What is the distance between FORTL and SWAGS on V7? (*Aeronautical Chart User's Guide*)

16 NM.

44. What kind of airspace exists around Fort Myers Southwest Florida Intl? (*Aeronautical Chart User's Guide*)

Class C.

For questions 45–51, refer to the low-altitude IFR enroute chart excerpt shown in Figure 7-2.

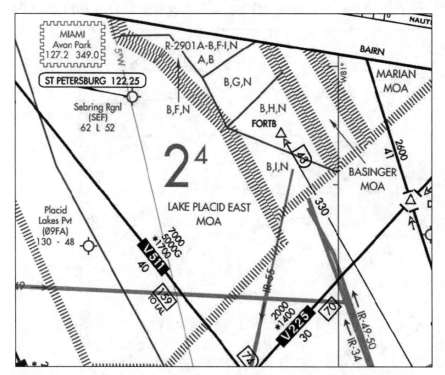

Figure 7-2.

45. If you could not reach a dispatched flight that was cruising along V511, how might you try to communicate with the flight? (*Aeronautical Chart User's Guide*)

You could call Miami Center, as the aircraft is likely to be communicating with them on 127.2 (see box in upper left).

46. How long is the longest runway at Sebring Regional (SEF)? (*Aeronautical Chart User's Guide*)

5,200 feet (add two zeros to the "52").

47. What is the airport elevation at SEF? (*Aeronautical Chart User's Guide*)

62 feet MSL.

48. What kind of special use airspace engulfs SEF? (*Aeronautical Chart User's Guide*)

Lake Placid East MOA.

49. What kind of special use airspace exists just east of SEF? (*Aeronautical Chart User's Guide*)

Restricted airspace (R-2901).

50. What is the significance of the big 2⁴? (*Aeronautical Chart User's Guide*)

This is an off-route obstruction clearance altitude (OROCA) with a particular latitude/longitude grid box. This is the minimum altitude an IFR flight should fly off airway while enroute. This provides 1,000 feet of obstacle clearance (2,000 feet in mountainous areas). This does not ensure navigation or communication reception.

51. What is the significance of the numbers 7,000; 5,000G; and 1,700* adjacent to the V511 box? (*Aeronautical Chart User's Guide*)

7,000 is the MEA, 5,000 is the GPS MEA, and 1,700 is the MOCA for V511.

For questions 52–56, refer to the low-altitude IFR enroute chart excerpt shown in Figure 7-3.

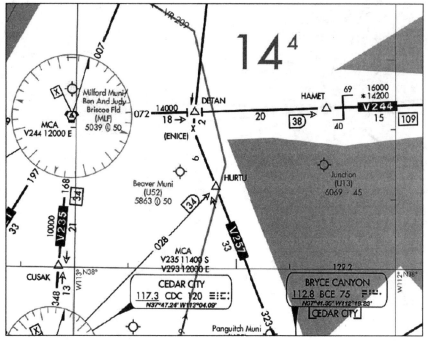

Figure 7-3.

52. Where does the MEA change along V244? (*Aeronautical Chart User's Guide*)

The MEA changes from 14,000 to 16,000 feet at DETAN. This is noted by the vertical lines on either side of the intersection.

53. What is the significance of the flag with an "X" on it at the VORTAC south of Milford? (*Aeronautical Chart User's Guide*)

There is a minimum crossing altitude (MCA) of 12,000 feet for eastbound flights on V244.

54. Why is ENICE marked with an "X" instead of a triangle, like DETAN? (*Aeronautical Chart User's Guide*)

ENICE is a computer navigation fix, not a standard intersection.

55. At what point would an aircraft switch navigation frequencies when flying eastbound on V244?

At the changeover point (COP) marked with zigzag lines just east of HAMET. The COP is 40 DME from the VORTAC to the west and 69 DME from the facility to the east (not shown).

56. What is the significance of the shading east of V257 and south of V244? (*Aeronautical Chart User's Guide*)

This is where class G airspace extends up to 14,500 MSL.

For questions 57–62, refer to the high altitude IFR enroute chart excerpt shown in Figure 7-4.

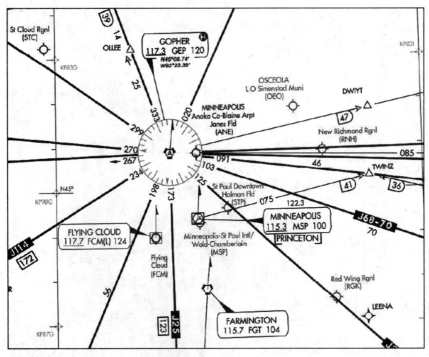

Figure 7-4.

57. What is the MEA for J25? (*Aeronautical Chart User's Guide*)

18,000 feet. On high-altitude enroute charts, MEAs are not published unless higher than 18,000.

58. Why is FCM VOR/DME lighter (grey) than GEP (dark black)? (*Aeronautical Chart User's Guide*)

FCM is only for situational awareness purposes as it is a low-altitude facility and should not be used for flights above 18,000 feet.

59. What is the star-like symbol marked "LEENA" in the lower right corner? (*Aeronautical Chart User's Guide*)

This is an RNAV waypoint.

60. What jet route is DWIYT on? (*Aeronautical Chart User's Guide*)

This intersection is not on an airway; instead, it is identifiable by a radial off of GEP at 47 DME.

61. If a dispatcher wanted a flight to utilize the latitude/longitude intersection just west of GEP (noted with N45), how could this be done using RNAV databases? (*Aeronautical Chart User's Guide*)

The waypoint "KP90C" could be used to designate this point in a flight plan.

62. Jet routes are normally marked in black. What does it mean if a route is marked in blue? (*Aeronautical Chart User's Guide*)

This is an RNAV route. High-altitude RNAV routes are "Q" routes.

For questions 63–66, refer to the high-altitude IFR enroute chart excerpt shown in Figure 7-5.

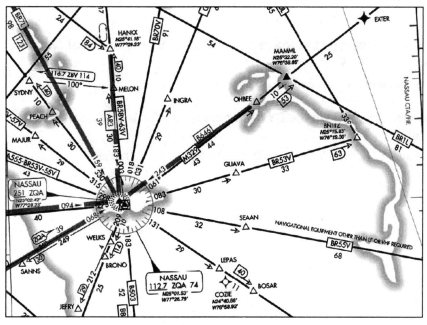

Figure 7-5.

63. What is the difference between BR58V and AR3? (*Aeronautical Chart User's Guide*)

BR58V is a VHF airway that requires the use of ZQA VOR/DME. AR3 is an NDB airway requiring the use of ZQA NDB.

64. What is the significance of MAMML being a shaded triangle versus OHBEE being a non-shaded triangle? (*Aeronautical Chart User's Guide*)

Solid triangles are compulsory reporting points. Aircraft are required to make position reports at these points whenever outside of radar contact.

65. What is the odd-shaped object below BNITZ? (*Aeronautical Chart User's Guide*)

That is an island. This map is in the Bahamas.

66. What is the symbol to the west of HANKX? (*Aeronautical Chart User's Guide*)

That symbol is a published holding pattern. These are published where aircraft may commonly be requested to hold.

For questions 67–68, identify the applicable IFR enroute chart symbols in Figure 7-6.

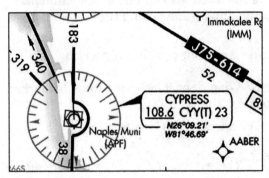

Figure 7-6.

67. Does the airway defined by the 183 radial include CYY? (*Aeronautical Chart User's Guide*)

No, it bypasses it, note the curved line.

68. What is the meaning of (T) in the CYY information box? (*Aeronautical Chart User's Guide*)

This is a terminal VOR usable only within 25 NM and up to 12,000 feet.

69. In Figure 7-7, why does the ZFP NDB frequency have lines over it? (*Aeronautical Chart User's Guide*)

The facility may be out of service; check NOTAMs.

70. What is the meaning of the image shown in Figure 7-8? (*Aeronautical Chart User's Guide*)

This is the border between Jacksonville and Miami air route traffic control centers (ARTCC).

71. What are the meanings of all of the numbers shown in Figure 7-9? (*Aeronautical Chart User's Guide*)

8,000 is the MEA for northbound flights; 5,000 is the MEA for southbound flights; 4,000 is the GPS MEA for all flights; *3,600 is the MOCA for all flights; and 10 is the mileage for this leg along the airway.

Figure 7-7.

Figure 7-8.

Figure 7-9.

72. What is the difference between the airport symbols for PNS and NPA shown in Figure 7-10? (*Aeronautical Chart User's Guide*)

Pensacola Gulf Coast Regional (PNS) is a civilian airport. NPA is a military airfield.

73. Describe the meaning of the airport details shown in Figure 7-11. (*Aeronautical Chart User's Guide*)

This is Chehalis-Centralia airport. Its identifier is CLS, airport elevation is 176 feet MSL, it has pilot-controlled lighting, and the longest runway is 5,000 feet.

74. Why does the airway shown in Figure 7-12 have hash marks on each side? (*Aeronautical Chart User's Guide*)

This airway is impeded by special use airspace (in this case a restricted area).

75. What does the image shown in Figure 7-13 mean? (*Aeronautical Chart User's Guide*)

This is an airport with Class D airspace (D in the box) that is not open 24 hours a day (star).

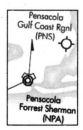

Figure 7-10.

Figure 7-11.

Figure 7-12.

Figure 7-13.

76. What does the image shown in Figure 7-14 mean? (*Aeronautical Chart User's Guide*)

There is a minimum reception altitude (MRA) at SHELA. This applies only to aircraft that must identify SHELA with ground-based navigation systems.

77. What does the image shown in Figure 7-15 mean? (*Aeronautical Chart User's Guide*)

This means that there is a minimum crossing altitude (MCA) at the VORTAC. Aircraft must cross at or above the listed altitude for this point.

78. If an airway has the symbol shown in Figure 7-16 superimposed upon it, what does this mean? (*Aeronautical Chart User's Guide*)

The route is unusable (most likely due to an inoperative NAVAID).

79. What is the meaning of the black box within the NDB symbol shown in Figure 7-17? (*Aeronautical Chart User's Guide*)

This is an NDB with DME.

Figure 7-14.

Figure 7-15.

Figure 7-16.

Figure 7-17.

80. How do you know if an airport has an approach on an FAA enroute chart? (*Aeronautical Chart User's Guide*)

Airports with approaches are blue or green. Those without approaches are brown. Blue airports have Department of Defense (DOD) approaches while green airports only have civilian approaches.

81. What is a "SID"? (FAA-H-8261-1)

A Standard Instrument Departure (SID) is a published departure route typically used at busy airports. When these exist, it is wise to file them as part of the flight plan route.

82. What is "DP"? (FAA-H-8261-1)

A departure procedure (DP) is a set departure route from an airport. There are two types: obstacle departure procedures (ODPs) and SIDs.

83. What two types of SIDs exist? (FAA-H-8261-1; *Aeronautical Chart User's Guide*; Jeppesen charts, introduction)

Pilot navigation and vector SIDs. Dispatchers can (and should) file pilot navigation SIDs as part of the flight plan route. Vector departures will not be accepted by ATC computers as part of a flight plan. Vector SIDs can be identified on Jeppesen charts with the term "VECTOR" next to the title. FAA charts make this harder to identify—typically these departures do not have any specific NAVAID courses to fly, or simply have a picture of a variety of nearby NAVAIDs and only instruct pilots to fly a certain heading and to expect vectors to their assigned route.

84. What is SID transition? (FAA-H-8261-1; *Aeronautical Chart User's Guide;* Jeppesen charts, introduction)

SIDs guide pilots to a specific point (normally the NAVAID or intersection after which the procedure is named). From this location, several sub-routes often span out in different directions; these are termed transitions. On FAA charts, transitions are shown as thin black lines (as opposed to thick lines used to designate the primary SID routing). On Jeppesen charts, the SID is shown as a solid line and transitions are depicted with a dashed line.

85. What is a "climb gradient"? (FAA-H-8261-1)

A climb gradient is a required climb rate, in feet per NM, which must be met to safely depart an airport. Climb gradient requirements vary from airport to airport and even runway to runway.

86. How do you calculate the rate of climb necessary to comply with a climb gradient requirement? (FAA-H-8261-1; *Aeronautical Chart User's Guide;* Jeppesen charts, introduction)

On both FAA and Jeppesen charts, a ground speed to climb rate (feet per minute) conversion is given. Also, you can multiply the ground speed in NM per minute by the climb gradient. For example, 180 knots ground speed is 3 NM per minute. If the climb gradient is 500 feet per NM, the resultant climb rate requirement would be 1,500 feet per minute (3×500).

87. If the destination airport has a VOR/DME approach, what equipment must be available on the aircraft to use this approach? (FAA-H-8261-1)

Both VOR and DME equipment must be onboard and functioning. A GPS can be used in lieu of DME.

88. If the destination has an NDB approach but the aircraft is only equipped with a GPS, can the flight be expected to use this approach? (FAA-H-8261-1)

No, in this case the aircraft would need an ADF. If the approach title was "NDB or GPS", the aircraft could use the procedure with only a GPS unit.

89. What is a "procedure turn"? (FAA-H-8261-1)

A procedure turn is a course reversal procedure used by aircraft to become aligned with an approach course.

90. What is a "holding pattern"? (FAA-H-8261-1)

A holding pattern is a circular flight pattern used to delay aircraft. In some cases these can be used as procedure turns.

91. What is a "missed approach"? (FAA-H-8261-1)

A missed approach is when an aircraft is unsuccessful in a landing/approach attempt. Published route and climb procedures exist for instrument approaches. Missed approaches normally guide aircraft to a holding pattern.

92. What is an "FAF"? (FAA-H-8261-1)

A final approach fix (FAF) is a point along an approach where an aircraft begins its final descent for the runway. This is normally located approximately 5 NM from the runway/airport.

93. What is the difference between a straight-in and a circling approach? (FAA-H-8261-1)

Straight-in approaches are aligned within 30 degrees of the runway heading and involve a normal descent from the approach minimums to the runway. Circling approaches are those that are not aligned within 30 degrees of the runway heading, do not involve a normal descent to land, and/or occur when an approach is conducted to one runway but landing is to occur on a different runway. Straight-in approaches almost always allow for lower approach minimums.

94. Which is controlling in terms of approach weather minimums—ceiling or visibility? (FAA-H-8261-1)

Visibility.

95. What is a "sidestep"? (FAA-H-8261-1)

A sidestep is when an aircraft shoots an approach to one runway and intends to land on a runway adjacent to the approach runway (normally a parallel runway).

96. How might inoperative approach lights affect minimums? (FAA-H-8261-1)

Inoperative lights normally raise visibility requirements. Reference the inoperative table in the front of FAA approach plates, or simply view the minimums section on Jeppesen charts.

97. What is "RVR"? (FAA-H-8261-1)

Runway visual range (RVR) is the distance (in feet in the U.S.; in meters in other countries) pilots can expect to see down the runway when viewed at runway level.

98. What different types of RVRs are available? (FAA-H-8261-1)

Some airports have only touchdown RVR, while others report midfield and rollout RVR measurements.

99. What is an "approach category"? (FAA-H-8261-1)

The approach category is based upon 1.3 times the stall speed of the aircraft in landing configuration. Category A includes aircraft with speeds up to 90 knots; category B 91–120 knots; category C 121–140 knots; and category D 141–165 knots; and category E is for those exceeding 165 knots. The higher the speed, the higher the minimums required to use an approach. The B737 is a category C aircraft. If an aircraft is flying an approach at a speed higher than the category in which it falls, it should use the next higher category to determine appropriate minimums.

100. If both RVR and visibility are reported, which is controlling? (FAA-H-8261-1)

RVR.

101. An approach requires 2,400 RVR but the RVR is out of service. What can be done in order to use this approach? (FAA-H-8261-1)

Convert the RVR to visibility: 2,400 feet RVR is ½ SM.

102. An approach requires 550 m RVR. What is this in feet? (FAA-H-8261-1)

The exact conversion can be done by multiplying the meter value by 3.28. In this case, 550 m is equivalent to approximately 1,800 feet.

103. Some Category I ILS approaches require ½ SM (2,400 RVR) while others require 1,800 RVR. What is the difference between the two? (FAA-H-8261-1)

In order to allow for 1,800 RVR minimums, the runway must have operational centerline lights and touchdown zone lights. Other instances can allow for this reduction, but they are rare.

104. What are the best types of approach light systems to help ensure a successful approach to landing? (FAA-H-8261-1)

ALSF-1 and ALSF-2 provide the best lighting to permit a landing in poor weather conditions.

105. What is a "precision approach"? (FAA-H-8261-1)

This is an approach that provides both lateral (LNAV) and vertical (VNAV) guidance. Examples include ILS, some LDA, LNAV/VNAV GPS, and LPV GPS approaches.

106. What is a "non-precision approach"? (FAA-H-8261-1)

This is an approach that only provides lateral (LNAV) guidance. Examples include VOR, localizer only, SDF, NDB, and LNAV GPS approaches.

107. What is a "MAP"? (FAA-H-8261-1)

A missed approach point (MAP) is the location at which a flight crew must either decide to land or go around. For precision approaches, this is normally about ½ SM from the runway. For non-precision approaches, the location of the MAP varies depending upon the type of approach.

108. Where are approach minimums found? (*Aeronautical Chart User's Guide;* Jeppesen charts, introduction)

Approach minimums are located at the bottom of both FAA and Jeppesen approach plates.

109. What is a "DA"? (FAA-H-8261-1)

Decision altitude (DA) is the altitude (read on the aircraft altimeter) at which a flight crew must make the decision to land or go around when using a precision approach.

110. What is "DH"? (FAA-H-8261-1)

Decision height (DH) is the altitude above the ground (runway/touchdown zone) when the aircraft is at the DA. For example, an airport has a touchdown zone elevation (TDZE) of 500 feet MSL. An approach to this runway has a DH of 200 feet. Therefore the DA would be 700 feet (500 + 200). In this case, the flight crew would decide to land/go missed when their altimeter read 700 feet. At that time they would be 200 feet above TDZE.

111. How are DA and DH identified on an approach plate? (*Aeronautical Chart User's Guide;* Jeppesen charts, introduction)

The DA is located in the minimums section of Jeppesen charts next to the heading "DA." DH is indicated in parentheses adjacent to DA. For example you would see DA (H) 227' (200'). This means DA is 227 feet and DH is 200' above TDZE.

   On FAA charts, DA is located in the precision approach row of the minimums section and is the item (group of numbers) from left to right. DH is the third item from left to right (just right of the visibility). For example, you would see a row indicated S-ILS for the straight-in ILS. In this row you would see 227-3/4 200. The DA in this case is 227 feet, the minimum visibility is ¾ SM and the DH is 200 feet above TDZE.

112. What is a "MDA"? (FAA-H-8261-1)

A minimum decent altitude is the lowest altitude to which an aircraft can descend during a non-precision approach. An aircraft will descend to MDA to arrive at that altitude at or before reaching the MAP. The MDH (minimum descent height) is the altitude above TDZE when the aircraft is operated at the MDA.

113. What is a "STAR"? (FAA-H-8261-1)

A standard terminal arrival route (STAR) is a published arrival route to busy terminal environments. Dispatchers should plan to use these where available.

114. What is a "preferred route"? (FAA-H-8261-1)

A preferred route is one that ATC prefers aircraft to use between particular airport pairs (normally large terminal environments). These are found in the *Airport/Facility Directory* (A/FD) or from the ATC Command Center preferred route database.

115. What is required to use a random or direct RNAV route? (AIM; FAA)

An RNAV equipped aircraft and ATC radar coverage is required. Also, an ICAO flight plan form is now required for flights using RNAV.

116. What is "RAIM"? (AIM; FAA)

Receiver autonomous integrity monitoring (RAIM) is GPS's built-in capability to ensure that its condition for use as primary navigation is sound. Pilots/dispatchers using or planning to use GPS during flight must conduct a RAIM check.

117. What is a service volume in terms of a NAVAID? (AIM)

These provide guidance on the service capability of a NAVAID when used off of published routes. Flights planned off airways should limit the distance flown from a particular NAVAID to remain within the service volume.

118. What is the service volume of a low-altitude VOR? (AIM)

Up to 18,000 feet out to 40 NM.

119. What is the service volume of a high-altitude VOR? (AIM)

Up to 14,500 feet— 40 NM
14,500 to 18,000 feet—100 NM
18,000 to 45,000 feet—130 NM
45,000 to 60,000 feet—100 NM

120. What general requirements exist to conduct category II ILS operations?
(14 CFR §91.189)

- Flight crew must be qualified to perform Cat II.
- Flight crew must be knowledgeable about Cat II procedures.
- Aircraft must be properly equipped to conduct Cat II approaches.

121. In order to land during an approach, what must a flight crew do/see?
(14 CFR §91.189)

- Runway environment.
- Minimum visibility required for approach must exist.
- Aircraft is able to make a normal descent to land.
- Aircraft operated under Part 121 must comply with the appropriate Ops Specs.

122. What equipment must be installed to conduct category II ILS approaches?
(14 CFR Part 91 Appendix A)

Group I.
- Two localizer and glide slope receiving systems.
- A communications system that does not affect the operation of at least one of the ILS systems.
- Marker beacon receiver.
- Two gyroscopic pitch and bank indicating systems.
- Two gyroscopic direction indicating systems.
- Two airspeed indicators.
- Two sensitive altimeters adjustable for barometric pressure.
- Two vertical speed indicators.
- A flight control guidance system that consists of either an automatic approach coupler or a flight director system.
- For Category II operations with decision heights below 150 feet, either a marker beacon receiver providing aural and visual indications of the inner marker or a radio altimeter.

Group II.
- Warning systems for immediate detection by the pilot of system faults in localizer/glide slope, gyroscopic systems and the flight control guidance system of Group I and, if installed for use in Category III operations, the radio altimeter and autothrottle system.
- Dual controls.
- An externally vented static pressure system with an alternate static pressure source.
- A windshield wiper or equivalent means of providing adequate cockpit visibility for a safe visual transition by either pilot to touchdown and rollout.
- A heat source for each airspeed system pitot tube installed or an equivalent means of preventing malfunctioning due to icing of the pitot system.

123. What happens if equipment required for Category II operations is inoperative?

Most likely, Cat II operations will no longer be possible. Check the MEL.

124. What are the flight planning requirements for filing a RNAV direct flight plan? (AIM)

The route should include a SID and a STAR, if appropriate, with direct routing in between defined by either named waypoints or by degree/distance fixes based on NAVAID (within service volumes). A waypoint must be included within each ARTCC airspace. This designated waypoint must be within 200 NM of the boundary of the previous center airspace. The route must avoid conflictive airspace (restricted, prohibited) by 3 NM. Any turns in the route must include a waypoint to mark the location of the turn. In certain cases, latitude/longitude or National Reference Waypoints can be used to define the route.

125. What is meant by the term "controlled airspace"? (AIM)

This is the airspace in which IFR traffic is subject to air traffic control. Controlled airspace includes class A, B, C, D, and E airspace areas.

126. Describe Class A airspace. (AIM)

In the 48 contiguous U.S. states and Alaska, Class A airspace extends from 18,000 feet to FL600 within 12 NM of the coast and in designated international airspace beyond 12 NM. Aircraft must operate under IFR in this airspace. Class A is not indicated on aeronautical charts.

127. Describe Class B airspace. (AIM)

Class B airspace is designated around large, busy airports and surrounding terminal areas. It extends from the surface (close to the primary airport) typically up to 10,000 ft MSL. Other tiers of altitude ranges exist with the floor of Class B rising as distance from the primary airport increases. The appearance of the airspace, if imagined in a three-dimensional image, is often described as an upside-down wedding cake. All aircraft in Class B are subject to Air Traffic Control. IFR flights are required to have a VOR or TACAN receiver. A speed restriction of 250 knots applies with Class B. ATC is supposed to keep turbojet aircraft within the vertical confines of this airspace when within the lateral boundaries.

128. Describe Class C airspace. (AIM)

Class C airspace is designated around medium-density terminal areas. Although the dimensions of this airspace are tailored to individual areas, the general size/shape of Class C is from the surface to 4,000 AGL within 5 NM of the primary airport and from 1,200 ft AGL to 4,000 ft AGL from 5 NM to 10 NM. There is a speed restriction of 200 knots within 4 NM and below 2,500 ft AGL.

129. Describe Class D airspace. (AIM)

Class D airspace is designated around airports with control towers. Although the dimensions of this airspace are tailored to individual areas, the general size/shape of Class D is from the surface to 2,500 ft AGL within 4 NM of the primary airport. There is a speed restriction of 200 knots within 4 NM and below 2,500 ft AGL.

130. Describe Class E airspace. (AIM)

Class E airspace is any controlled airspace not designated as A, B, C, or D. In some areas, Class E begins at 14,500 ft MSL, while in most areas in the U.S. it begins at 1,200 ft AGL. In designated transition areas, located near airports with instrument approaches, class E begins at 700 ft AGL. Class E extends up to but not including 18,000 feet, and then exists above FL600. Federal airways are considered Class E and extend from 1,200 ft AGL up to but not including 18,000 feet.

131. Describe Class G airspace. (AIM)

Class G airspace is uncontrolled airspace. Obviously, this is any airspace not designated class A, B, C, D, or E. Class G normally extends up to but not including 1,200 AGL, but in some cases this limit is 700 ft AGL (in transition areas) and 14,500 ft MSL in remote areas.

132. What is a "military operations area" (MOA)? How might these areas affect dispatch of an aircraft? (AIM)

MOAs are designated areas in which military aircraft can conduct training. This activity is obviously not conducive to the separation of military aircraft from civilian IFR traffic. Therefore, IFR flights are normally prohibited from entering MOAs that are active (sometimes referred to as "hot"). Dispatchers should be aware that routes that traverse MOAs are subject to rerouting or delay if the MOA is hot. It is best to determine if such airspace is available prior to planning routes through MOAs.

133. What is "restricted airspace" and how might this affect dispatch of an aircraft? (AIM)

Restricted airspace is a designated area in which aircraft operations are subject to restriction. IFR flights are normally not authorized to enter restricted airspace that is active. Dispatchers should be aware that routes that traverse restricted areas are not recommended unless it is known that such airspace is not active.

134. What is a "warning area" and how might these areas affect dispatch of aircraft? (AIM)

A warning area contain hazards to flight operations, but cannot be designated as "restricted" or other type because it falls outside of the 3 NM limit from U.S. shorelines. Dispatchers should be aware that routes that traverse such areas are not recommended unless it is known that they are not in use.

135. What is "prohibited airspace" and how might this affect dispatch of an aircraft? (AIM)

Prohibited airspace is a designated area in which aircraft operations are normally prohibited. IFR flights are typically not authorized to enter prohibited airspace. Dispatchers should not plan routes that traverse these areas.

136. What is an "alert area"? (AIM)

These are designated areas of dense traffic concentrations. Pilots should be made aware of routes that traverse or are close to alert areas.

137. What is a "controlled firing area"? (AIM)

In controlled firing areas, the military may conduct operations that are hazardous to non-participating aircraft. These are not marked on aeronautical charts. These areas have designated spotters that suspend hazardous operations if a non-participating aircraft encroaches on the area.

B. Aircraft Navigation Systems

1. What is an "HSI"? (FAA-H-8261-1)

A horizontal situation indicator (HSI) is a cockpit instrument that combines a course deviation indicator (CDI) and a heading indicator.

2. What is an "RMI"? (FAA-H-8261-1)

A radio magnetic indicator (RMI) is a cockpit instrument that combines an automatic direction finder (ADF) and a heading indicator. There may be one or two ADF needles. Some RMIs can also be used so that the needle(s) points to a VOR instead of an NDB.

3. What is a "CDI"? (FAA-H-8261-1)

A course deviation indicator (CDI) is a cockpit instrument that displays deviation from a VOR course.

4. What is an "ADF"? (FAA-H-8261-1)

An automatic direction finder (ADF) is a cockpit instrument that indicates the relationship of an aircraft from an NDB. The needle always points to the station. This indication can be used to determine the bearing on which the aircraft is located.

5. What is an "NDB"? (FAA-H-8261-1)

A nondirectional beacon (NDB) is a navigation aid that requires the use of an ADF to provide positional information.

6. What is a "VSI"? (FAA-H-8261-1)

A vertical speed indicator (VSI) is a cockpit instrument that tells pilots how fast they are climbing or descending in feet per minute.

7. What is a "DG"? (FAA-H-8261-1)

A directional gyro (DG) is a cockpit instrument that indicates the aircraft heading. This instrument is much more reliable and easy to use than a magnetic compass.

8. What is "EFIS"? (FAA-H-8261-1)

Electronic Flight Information System (EFIS) is an electronic display of flight instruments. It is commonly referred to as a "glass cockpit."

9. What is an "ADI"? (FAA-H-8261-1)

An attitude-direction indicator (ADI) is a cockpit instrument that displays aircraft pitch and bank.

10. What is an "EADI"? (FAA-H-8261-1)

An electronic attitude-direction indicator (EADI) is an electronic (TV screen/LCD screen) version of an ADI.

11. What instruments receive inputs from the pitot tube? (FAA-H-8261-1)

The airspeed indicator receives information from the pitot tube (or the air data computer receives this input and then conveys it to the airspeed indicator).

12. What instruments receive inputs from the static port? (FAA-H-8261-1)

The static port is connected to the altimeter, vertical speed indicator, and airspeed indicator (or it is connected to the air data computer, which conveys appropriate data to these instruments).

13. What is a "ring laser gyro" (RLG)? (FAA-H-8261-1)

A ring laser gyro is the most precise gyro system available within an inertial reference/navigation system. RLGs have no moving parts; instead, the changes in frequency within a laser that is beamed in a triangle within the system is used to detect motion. There is a gyro (triangle) for each of the three aircraft axes.

14. What instruments are normally gyroscopic? (FAA-H-8261-1)

In small aircraft, the attitude indicator, heading indicator (or DG), and turn coordinator are gyroscopic. The first two are normally pneumatically operated while the latter is electrically driven. Large aircraft may have an electrically driven gyroscopic HSI and attitude indicator. However, in the B737 there are no such gyroscopic instruments (except perhaps stand-by instruments).

15. What is a radar (or radio) altimeter? (FAA-H-8261-1)

This is a cockpit instrument that displays the height of the aircraft above the ground. It works by bouncing a radio wave from the aircraft off of the ground.

16. What is "DME"? (FAA-H-8261-1)

Distance measuring equipment (DME) is an ultra-high frequency (UHF) system that allows an aircraft to determine its distance from a NAVAID location. This is a required piece of equipment for operations above FL240. GPS can be used in place of DME.

17. How might an inoperative navigation radio or instrument affect the dispatch of a flight?

If the route or airports of use require the use of the affected navigation system, a re-route or alternative plan might be necessary. For example, if the destination airport has only an NDB approach and the ADF onboard the aircraft is malfunctioning, it may be necessary to explore other options, delay the flight for repairs, cancel the flight, or swap to another aircraft.

18. What is an "FMS"? What is an "FMC"?

A flight management system (FMS) is a comprehensive avionics suite that provides performance and navigation calculations and databases for use in flight. An FMS allows for RNAV (direct to) routings. The flight management computer (FMC) is the "guts" of an FMS and is the actually computer (calculator) of the navigation and performance data used by the FMS.

19. What is an "IRS"? What is an "INS"?

An inertial reference system (IRS) provides attitude information for flight instruments. It can also detect accelerations, therefore providing aircraft position, speed, and drift data. An inertial navigation system (INS) takes the concept of an IRS further by providing navigation capabilities, in particular RNAV (direct to) routing capabilities. IRS and INS are completely independent of any outside navigation sources and can be used for long-range (oceanic) navigation. These systems typically use gyros (or ring laser gyros) to detect the forces necessary to provide proper output data.

20. What is an "ADIRU"? (Honeywell)

An Air Data Inertial Reference Unit (ADIRU) is essentially an IRS and an air data sensor combined into one unit. This provides air (pitot/static), attitude, and position data. When coupled with additional features that provide navigation capability, such a system is referred to an ADIRS (Air Data Inertial Reference System).

21. What is "LORAN"? (AIM)

Long range navigation (LORAN) is a navigation system utilizing a variety of stations that transmit radio waves that can propagate over long distances. The system essentially measures the differences in time of receipt of these radio waves to determine the position of the aircraft in relation to ground stations. This system was decommissioned in 2010.

22. What is an "ILS"? (AIM)

An instrument landing system (ILS) is a precision-approach system used to help aircraft land in poor weather. Lateral guidance to the runway is provided by a transmitter called a localizer, which is several times more sensitive than a VOR. Aircraft are guided vertically to the runway by a transmitter called the glide slope. There are three categories of ILS approaches. The most basic is Category I, which normally allows aircraft to fly down to within 200 feet of the runway surface and in visibilities as low as ½ SM (or in some cases 1,800 feet RVR). Category II approaches allow aircraft to fly down to half the Category I values (100 feet and 1,000 to 1,200 RVR). Category III approaches can allow the aircraft to land with no height or visibility requirements (these are referred to as Category IIIc).

23. What is a "transponder"? (AIM)

A transponder is a device that allows for the detection of aircraft position on air traffic control radar. This device "replies" to radar interrogations. Pilots can set a transponder code for easy identification of one aircraft versus another.

24. What is "Mode C"? What is "Mode S"? (AIM)

Mode C is the subcomponent of a transponder that transmits altitude information to air traffic control. Mode S provides altitude information and also allows for datalink (messaging, data transmission, and data receipt) capabilities.

25. What is "GNSS"? (AIM)

Global navigation satellite system (GNSS) is a term that describes all satellite-based navigation systems. An example of GNSS is GPS, the network maintained by the U.S. Other countries may operate their own GNSS.

26. What is "WAAS"? (FAA; European Space Agency)

Wide area augmentation system (WAAS) consists of ground monitoring stations that detect GPS satellite errors. These errors are used to generate a correction message that is transmitted to two WAAS satellites. These satellites in turn transmit the correction message to users (aircraft) who have the appropriate avionics to receive the data (not all GPS units are WAAS enabled). This is also referred to as differential GPS. The European equivalent is called European Geostationary Navigation Overlay Service (EGNOS).

27. What is "LAAS"? (FAA)

Local area augmentation system (LAAS) consists of ground monitoring stations that detect GPS satellite errors. These errors are used to generate a location-specific correction message that is transmitted to aircraft in the immediate geographic area via VHF transmitters.

28. What is "APV"? (FAA; ICAO)

APV is a GPS/GNSS-based approach with vertical guidance. Among ICAO standards, there are two types of APV: one that uses barometric data for the vertical component, and a second that uses augmented (WAAS/EGNOS) satellite transmissions for vertical guidance.

29. What is "LPV"? (FAA)

This is a GPS/GNSS-based approach which has localizer performance with vertical guidance (LPV). An LPV approach is a type of APV. Augmented (WAAS) satellite transmissions are required to conduct this type of approach.

30. What is "LNAV/VNAV"? (FAA)

This is a type of navigation or an approach procedure that provides both lateral navigation guidance (LNAV) and vertical navigation guidance (VNAV), but typically does not allow for minimums as low as normally associated with LPV approaches. Augmented (WAAS) satellite transmissions are required to conduct this type of approach.

31. What is "LNAV"? (FAA)

This is navigation or an approach that provides only lateral navigation (LNAV) guidance.

32. What is "LP"? (FAA)

This is an approach procedure with localizer performance (LP) providing only LNAV. Augmented (WAAS) satellite transmissions are required to conduct this type of approach.

33. What is "ADS-B"? (FAA)

Automatic Dependent Surveillance-Broadcast (ADS-B) is a system that allows for data communication to and from (depending upon avionics capabilities) an aircraft. Examples of its use include the transmission of position to other aircraft and/or air traffic control as well as the receipt of flight data such as weather.

34. What is "RVSM"? (FAA)

Reduced vertical separation minimums (RVSM) is a set of rules and requirements for aircraft to be vertically separated by a minimum of 1,000 feet while enroute. Most of the world (excluding Russia) is now using RVSM.

35. What is "DRVSM"? (FAA)

Domestic RVSM is the RVSM rules/standards that exist in the contiguous U.S, Alaska, the Gulf of Mexico, the Atlantic High Offshore Airspace, and the San Juan FIR. DRVSM applies from FL290 to FL410.

36. What is "ETOPS"? (FAA)

Extended range operation with twin-engine aircraft (ETOPS) allows aircraft with only two engines to operate on long-range flights beyond one-hour flying time (on one engine) from an alternate airport. Special authorizations, training, and equipment are required to conduct such operations.

37. What is "RNAV"? (FAA)

Area navigation (RNAV) is a capability of an aircraft to fly any route including direct, point-to-point paths. This is made possible by a variety of onboard systems such as GPS, DME/DME, or FMS.

38. What is "RNP"? (FAA)

Required navigation performance is RNAV plus the capability to monitor navigation quality to ensure it meets necessary standards to operate in certain airspace or on particular approach procedures. Flight crews receive an indication when the system does not meet RNP standards.

39. What is "ANP"? (FAA)

Actual navigation performance (ANP) is the actual navigation quality being maintained by an aircraft. ANP should be better than RNP. For example, if the RNP is 1.0 NM, the aircraft should have an ANP equal to or less than 1.0 NM in order to comply with RNP mandates. Aircraft typically have a cockpit indication of RNP vs. ANP and have some way of conveying to pilots when ANP exceeds standards.

40. What is "B-RNAV"? (Eurocontrol)

Basic area navigation (B-RNAV) is a term used to describe airspace in which RNP is 5 NM.

41. What is "P-RNAV"? (Eurocontrol)

Precision area navigation (P-RNAV) is a term used to describe airspace in which RNP is 1 NM.

42. What is "GBAS"? (Eurocontrol)

Ground-based augmentation system (GBAS) is a means of improving global navigation satellite system (GNSS) precision to allow for instrument approach procedures similar to an ILS. In the U.S., this is referred to as local area augmentation system (LAAS).

43. What is "SBAS"? (Eurocontrol)

Satellite-based augmentation system (SBAS) is a means of improving GNSS precision to allow for more accurate enroute, terminal, and approach navigation, although it is less precise than GBAS. This is referred to as wide area augmentation system (WAAS) in the U.S. and as European geostationary navigation overlay service (EGNOS) in Europe.

C. Navigation Definitions, Time References, and Location

1. Define longitude.

Lines of longitude connect the north and south poles of the Earth.

2. How is longitude normally expressed on maps or in terms of navigation?

Longitude is expressed in degrees. Within each degree are 60 minutes. Within each minute are 60 seconds. Longitude is designated east or west in reference to the Prime Meridian or 0 degrees longitude which passes through Greenwich, England. Longitude may also be shown as positive (+) or negative (−), which equate to east and west, respectively. There are 180 degrees of east longitude and 180 degrees of west longitude.

3. Where is 180°E longitude?

This line passes through extreme eastern Siberia and the Bering Sea, down to just east of New Zealand.

4. What is the International Date Line?

This zigzagging line generally follows 180°E/W longitude. This serves as the division line in day/date on the planet. To the left of the line (Asia side), the date/day is one date/day ahead of the area on the right (Hawaii side) of the line. For example, if it is Friday on the west side of the IDL, it is Thursday on the east side.

5. Define latitude.

Lines of latitude circle the Earth perpendicular to lines of longitude.

6. How is latitude normally expressed on maps or in terms of navigation?

Latitude is expressed in degrees. Within each degree are 60 minutes. Within each minute are 60 seconds. Latitude is designated north or south in reference to the equator or 0 degrees latitude. Latitude may also be shown as positive (+) or negative (-), which equate to north and south, respectively. There are 90 degrees of north latitude and 90 degrees of south latitude.

7. Where is 90°N latitude?

This is the North Pole.

8. Locate the following latitude and longitude position on the Earth: 33° 56' 33.0800"N / 118° 24' 25.7800"W

This is the KLAX airport near Los Angeles, California.

9. Is there a given distance that equates to a second, minute, and degree of latitude?

Yes, spacing of lines of latitude are equal. A second of latitude is about 100 feet. A minute of latitude is approximately equal to one nautical mile. A degree of latitude is equal to 60 nautical miles.

10. What is a great circle route?

The shortest distance between two points on a sphere (or close to it, as the Earth is not a true sphere) is connected by a curved (circular) path. Such a route is termed "great circle." This type of route can also be referred to as "geodesic."

11. Where is the magnetic north pole? (FAA-H-8083-25)

It is approximately located at 85°N and 132.6°W, but it moves constantly. It is slowly migrating towards the geographic North Pole. This change in magnetic alignment is why runway numbers occasionally change at airports.

12. What is the difference between true and magnetic courses, headings, and references?

True references are in relation to the geographic North Pole; magnetic references are in relation to the magnetic North Pole. Aircraft compasses align with the magnetic North Pole, however latitude and longitude lines on maps are perpendicular to/aligned with (respectively) the geographic North Pole. Aircraft normally navigate in terms of magnetic courses/headings.

13. What is magnetic variation?

This type of variation is the difference between the magnetic and true North Poles at an individual location measured in degrees.

14. How do you convert from true to magnetic?

You subtract easterly variation from true to come up with magnetic, while you add westerly variation to true in order to come up with magnetic.

15. What is the term used to describe a line of equal variation?

Isogonic lines connect areas of equal magnetic variation.

16. What is "magnetic deviation"?

Magnetic deviation is the error to an aircraft compass caused by aircraft equipment such as avionics, heated windshields, engines, etc. A correction to this must be made so that the aircraft flies the correct magnetic heading to align with the desired route.

17. What is meant by the term "track"?

Track is the actual direction the aircraft is travelling. Most navigation systems have the ability to display track. In order to stay on course, the aircraft track should be aligned with the planned track to get to the destination.

18. What is "desired track" (DTK)?

Desired track is a term commonly used in navigation systems to convey the track necessary to fly the planned route. To stay on the route, the actual aircraft track should match the DTK.

19. What is "cross track error"?

Cross track error is the distance that an aircraft has deviated from the DTK. It is usually further noted to convey if the error is to the left or right of DTK.

20. What is "azimuth"?

Azimuth is an angle or direction from an object. An example would be a VOR radial.

21. What is "UTC"?

Universal Coordinated Time (UTC) is the standard time used in aviation applications. This is in reference to the time at the Prime Meridian (Greenwich, England) and is not corrected for daylight savings. It is also referred to as Greenwich Mean Time (GMT) or Zulu time (Z). The correction from local to UTC time can be found in the airport/facility directory.

22. What is "Zulu"?

Zulu time (Z) is the standard time used in aviation applications. This is in reference to the time at the Prime Meridian (Greenwich, England) and is not corrected for daylight savings. It is also referred to as Universal Coordinated Time (UTC) or Greenwich Mean Time (GMT).

23. What is "dead reckoning"?

Dead reckoning is a type of navigation in which an aircraft simply flies a heading for a specified period of time. If the position of the aircraft was known prior to beginning the flight, one could determine the new position by plotting the heading and distance onto a chart.

24. What is a "bearing"?

A bearing is a heading that would take the aircraft directly to a point. For example, if an aircraft was south of a VOR, its bearing to the facility would be 360 degrees (north), meaning it would need to fly due north to fly to the station. The term can also be used to describe a bearing from a point, so in the aforementioned case, the bearing from the VOR would be 180 degrees (south), meaning an aircraft would need to fly a 180-degree heading to fly away from the facility.

25. What is a "fix"?

A fix is a term used to describe any point used for routing or navigation. Fixes can be intersections, RNAV waypoints, NAVAIDs, etc. It can also be used to generically describe a geographic location or the identification of one's position.

26. What is "ephemeris"? (AIM)

Ephemeris is a transmission made by GPS/GNSS satellites that communicate the health/status and exact orbital position of the satellite.

27. What is "pilotage"?

Pilotage is a means of aircraft navigation that uses visual checkpoints located on the ground. These references can be both natural and manmade features.

28. What is a "pseudorange"? (FAA)

A pseudorange is a distance determined by the time a signal takes to travel. Pseudoranges are utilized in GPS navigation.

29. What is a "radar altimeter"? (FAA-H-8261-1)

A radar altimeter is an aircraft system that bounces a signal off of the ground to determine the height of the aircraft above the ground. The results are then displayed to the pilots in digital or analog form on a cockpit instrument. Most radar altimeters work from 0 feet AGL to 2,500 feet AGL.

30. What is a "waypoint"?

A waypoint is a geographic location defined by radials/bearings and distances from NAVAIDs or by latitude and longitude coordinates. It is sometimes used interchangeably with the term "fix."

31. What is a "random RNAV route"? (AIM)

This is any route that is not published that uses RNAV. This typically refers to direct (point-to-point) routes. Air traffic control radar coverage is generally required to fly random routes.

32. What is a "preferred route"? (AIM)

Preferred routes, outlined in the A/FD and available from the Air Traffic Control Command Center website, connect busy terminal areas. ATC prefers that pilots use these routes when filing itineraries through busy airspace. If pilots/dispatchers ignore these routes, ATC will likely assign them anyway, so for flight planning purposes it is best to plan to use these routes where available.

33. What is a "changeover point" (COP)?

A changeover point is the location where an aircraft would switch from using one NAVAID to using another. This is typically done halfway between NAVAIDs on Victor/Jet airways, or at a designated, published point noted on an aeronautical chart.

34. What is a "compulsory reporting point"?

This is a location at which aircraft are required to make a position report whenever outside radar coverage, or if instructed to do so when within radar contact. These are indicated with solid triangles or solid black NAVAID symbols on aeronautical charts.

8 Practical Dispatch Applications

A. Resource Management and Decision Making

This chapter's material is based on a variety of FAA handbooks, ACs, and regulations, for example: the FAA-H-8083-25 Pilot's Handbook of Aeronautical Knowledge; the Practical Test Standards, FAA-H-8083-2 Risk Management Handbook; 14 CFR Part 65, and many more—see "References" on Page viii.

1. How can a dispatcher be sure to conduct flights in the safest and most thorough manner possible?

Dispatchers should utilize all available resources to plan and monitor flights. This philosophy is termed Dispatch Resource Management (DRM).

2. What are some resources that dispatchers can use to ensure they conduct flights in the safest and most thorough manner possible?

Dispatchers should use all available resources, which include fellow dispatchers, management, air traffic control, weather reports/forecasts, weather imagery, computer flight-planning software, computer flight-monitoring equipment, the flight crew, maintenance personnel, airport operations personnel, and all related publications.

3. Aircraft accidents are most often caused by _____.

Human factors. People are the primary cause (normally 70–80%) of all aviation accidents. Extreme caution should be exercised at all times to ensure that no omissions to flight planning or monitoring are made.

4. How can a dispatcher try to ensure that they have positive teamwork in the workplace?

Dispatchers should be helpful and cooperative in the workplace. They need to be proactive and interact freely with their fellow team members. Communication is also essential, and dispatchers need to fully disclose errors and other concerns to colleagues.

5. You are about to go home after a long day of dispatching. Your replacement arrives. What should you do to ensure a viable "handoff"?

Positive information exchange is mandatory in the world of dispatching. You should fully brief your replacement on the current situation relating to the places aircraft have been dispatched. This should include weather status, air traffic control issues, Notices to Airmen (NOTAMs), station details, and so forth. Each flight being handled should also be briefed to include any aircraft malfunctions/maintenance items, crew duty and rest time status, current location, any deviations from the norm, flight plan, fuel status, estimated delays, estimated arrival times, and any special needs.

6. What are some ways to contact a flight once it is airborne under normal conditions?

- Radio (company frequencies)
- Selective calling (SELCAL)
- Aircraft communications addressing and reporting system (ACARS)

7. What are some ways to contact a flight if it cannot be reached by normal means?

- Via other company aircraft.
- Via air traffic control.
- If the aircraft is on the ground, via crew cell phone numbers or via airport operations.

8. **An aircraft you have dispatched is approaching an area of severe weather along its route about 250 NM ahead of its current position. What should you do?**

   It is wise to contact the flight via radio (you will likely need to SELCAL the aircraft). Normally, aircraft weather radar is limited to around 200 NM or less, so they may not be aware of the conditions ahead. Describe the weather, including the width and length of the area, and any holes or gaps that exist in the weather and their location. Offer suggestions as to how to circumvent the weather. If possible, check with the local air traffic control facility or other company aircraft to see if or how aircraft are making it through the weather.

9. **What is aeronautical decision making (ADM)?** (AC 60-22)

   Aeronautical decision making is a systematic approach to decision making and risk assessment in aviation in order to choose the best course of action.

10. **What are the steps in the ADM process?** (AC 60-22)

    - Hazard identification
    - Behavior modification
    - Recognizing and coping with stress
    - Risk assessment
    - Use of all resources (DRM)
    - Evaluating one's DRM skills

11. **ADM relies on the recognition of a problem, and then the dispatcher should evaluate _____ and whether or not to take action.**

    Alternatives. All problems generate alternative responses. Each should be evaluated in terms of appropriateness and risk, and then the best alternative should be selected. Be aware that the best answer may involve no action.

12. **A flight is being planned to the Gulf Coast in the afternoon on a summer day. A humid air mass is presently situated over the destination area. What are some risks and/or hazards associated with such a flight? What might a dispatcher do to mitigate these issues?**

    In the summer, the Gulf of Mexico region typically has towering cumulus and thunderstorm activity in the afternoon, particularly when a considerable amount of moisture is present. While such weather should appear in aviation forecasts, it is wise for dispatchers to do their own cautionary prediction that such weather might occur. This will have the potential to induce flight delays. Further, aircraft may need additional fuel to deviate around the weather, which means planning for an alternate airport even though it is not legally required. In order to minimize effects of this weather, dispatchers should plan more fuel; investigate potential alternate airports (both along the route and for the destination); use strategic flight planning to avoid areas with the highest potential for poor weather; monitor the flight and the weather as long as the aircraft is airborne (with particular attention to the destination airport and surrounding areas as well as any alternate airports); and ensure good communication exists between flight control and the flight crew.

13. A flight is being planned out of an airport in the northeastern U.S. in the winter. Although no precipitation is currently falling, it is mentioned in the TAF and some light snow is starting to appear on the local weather radar. What are some risks and/or hazards to this flight? How can a dispatcher plan ahead to mitigate such issues?

Aircraft are not permitted to depart with any snow or ice adhering to the aircraft wings and control surfaces. Snow and ice can disrupt the airflow over these critical parts, making it impossible for the aircraft to safely takeoff. Anytime frozen precipitation is predicted, it is likely to cause flight delays due to slowed arrivals and departures as well as the need for aircraft deicing. Dispatchers can ensure the station and the flight crew are ready for deicing. Additional fuel should be added for extended ground operations. Snow clearing operations on runways could hinder arrival and departure rates. In some instances they cause temporary runway, taxiway, and ramp closures.

14. A flight is being dispatched to a location that has freezing rain forecast at the time of arrival. What are some risks and/or hazards to this flight? How can a dispatcher plan ahead to mitigate such issues?

Freezing rain is a very dangerous phenomenon to aircraft operations. Depending upon the intensity, it may overwhelm even the most effective aircraft deice/anti-ice systems. Also, ground deice/anti-ice may not be sufficient to allow for a safe departure during such conditions. Refer to the Ops Specs of your air carrier for references regarding what intensity of freezing precipitation is permissible during flight operations. Long flight delays are possible. Also, freezing rain has the potential to coat ground surfaces with ice, precluding airport operations. Therefore, a dispatcher should plan for additional fuel, and planning for an alternate is mandatory even if not legally required.

15. How might runway or taxiway construction affect a flight? Why might this increase the risk of operation at the airport?

Closures of components of an airport always have the potential for increasing flight delays and taxi times. This should be considered during fuel calculations. Such closures also have the risk of causing confusion among flight crews. It is essential that pilots be informed (if not briefed) on such closures and how they may affect operations, including approaches, landings, takeoffs, and taxiing to/from the gate area.

16. What are some support tools and technologies that assist a dispatcher in monitoring a flight?

Many air carriers have aircraft situational displays (or similar systems) that allow dispatchers to see the location of their aircraft in real time, superimposed upon maps that may display other critical data such as weather, warning/watch boxes, airspace, and operational issues. Dispatchers can also monitor aircraft status and fuel loads with a variety of tools and technologies such as ACARS and other automated reporting systems. Dispatchers can also monitor air traffic control delay programs and arrival/departure rates using the tools available through the air traffic control command center. Of course, each air carrier is unique in their capabilities and dispatchers should ensure they are intimately familiar with all available tools, technologies, and procedures.

B. Trip Records

1. What documents are required to be kept following the completion of a flight?
(14 CFR §121.695)

- Load manifest
- Dispatch release
- Flight plan

2. How long must the aforementioned records be kept? (14 CFR §121.695)

Three months.

3. Who is responsible for ensuring that copies of these documents are returned to the company so they may be retained to meet regulatory record-keeping requirements?
(14 CFR §121.695)

The pilot-in-command.

4. What important aircraft limitation calculation information is found on the load manifest?

Weight and balance data can be found on this form.

5. What other types of documents may companies choose to keep?

- Fuel slips
- Crew logs
- Jump seat authorizations
- Autoland records (if applicable)
- Passenger manifests (for charter flights)

6. When might it be important for a copy of a plotting chart, NOTAMs, and/or weather to be retained?

In case of a diversion, an emergency, or any other unexpected occurrence, it may be helpful to retain additional documents to assist in the filing of reports or explaining to supervisors what occurred.

C. Other Records

1. What communications between the company and aircraft must be recorded?
(14 CFR §121.711)

All types of enroute communications should be recorded.

2. How long must radio communications records be kept? (14 CFR §121.711)

30 days.

3. Do telephone lines need to be recorded? (14 CFR §121.711)

Yes, these recordings should include crew scheduling, JetComm phone patches, dispatch, and maintenance.

4. How long must phone records be kept? (14 CFR §121.711)

30 days.

5. Prior to being able to conduct a flight, what maintenance record must be noted in the aircraft logbook? (14 CFR §121.709)

An airworthiness release or other appropriate maintenance logbook entry must exist.

6. How long do copies of maintenance records (such as write-ups/malfunctions) remain on the aircraft until filed?

This may vary by air carrier, but normally 15 days, or long enough for crews to be able to view recent aircraft maintenance histories.

9

Manuals, Handbooks, and Other Written Materials

A. Regulation Sources

1. What part of the CFR can dispatchers reference for guidance on the carriage of hazardous materials?

This can be found in 49 CFR Part 175.

2. What is the maximum amount of hazardous materials acceptable for carriage on a passenger-carrying aircraft that is allowed to be carried on such an aircraft in an inaccessible location? (49 CFR §175.75)

25 kg (55 pounds). However, an additional 75 kg (165 pounds) of non-flammable compressed gas can also be carried.

3. What is the maximum amount of hazardous materials acceptable for carriage on a passenger-carrying aircraft that is allowed to be carried on such an aircraft in an accessible location? (49 CFR §175.75)

There is no set limit to hazmat packages in accessible areas because these are generally restricted from carriage in these areas.

4. What package textual marking would preclude a package from being carried on a passenger aircraft? (49 CFR §175.75)

"Cargo Aircraft Only."

5. How can a dispatcher determine the necessary distances that radioactive materials must be from passengers or crew when carried on passenger aircraft?

This information can be found in 49 CFR §175.701.

6. What is a possible concern about carrying dry ice?

Dry ice is frozen carbon dioxide. Caution should be taken when dry ice is present in cargo areas, as it can be lethal to live cargo.

7. Where can dispatchers look for regulations related to transportation security, such as screening of baggage and cargo?

49 CFR Part 1544.

B. Manuals—General

1. What manual provides dispatchers with the various duties and responsibilities that apply to them? (14 CFR §121.133)

The company operations manual.

2. What is an "AFM"? (14 CFR §121.133)

An aircraft flight manual (AFM) contains all of the data necessary for crews to operate their aircraft, such as checklists and performance information.

3. What is a "CFM"? (14 CFR §121.133)

A company flight manual (CFM) is an AFM that is specifically tailored to the operation needs of a particular company.

4. What is a "GOM"? (14 CFR §121.135)

A general operations manual (GOM) includes all the operational procedures applicable to the entire company, not specific aircraft.

5. What is an "MMEL"? (FSIMS website)

A master minimum equipment list (MMEL) is a document approved and published by the FAA that serves as a guide to operators as they produce their own MELs for aircraft that they operate.

6. What is an "MEL"? (FSIMS website)

A minimum equipment list (MEL) is a listing of items onboard an aircraft that can be inoperative under certain conditions. Examples of items in the MEL would be a flight instrument or a cabin light.

7. What is a "DDG"? (Boeing)

A dispatch deviation guide is a dispatcher-oriented MEL. MELs tend to focus on flight operations procedures and issues that are geared towards pilots. DDGs essentially provide the same data, but are focused on the effects of aircraft defects on the dispatchability of the flight.

8. What is a "CDL"? (FSIMS website)

A configuration deviation list (CDL) is a listing of items on the outside of an aircraft that can be missing or broken under certain conditions. Examples of items in the CDL would be a navigation light lens cover or an antenna.

9. What are operations specifications (Ops Specs)? (FSIMS website)

This document describes how an air carrier is to comply with the various applicable regulations and procedures. This manual must include procedures, authorizations, and limitations related to the operation of all aircraft authorized to be operated by the carrier.

C. Minimum Equipment Lists

1. What is meant by the term "defer" when referring to inoperative equipment? (FSIMS website)

A deferral is a provision permitted by the MEL to placard an inoperative aircraft component and wait until a later date to repair it.

2. What is a placard? (FSIMS website)

A placard is a marking, usually a sticker, which is placed near an inoperative item so that it is obvious that the component is not working.

3. If an inoperative component is allowed to be deferred by the MEL, what actions must a dispatcher take to ensure proper documentation of such a deferral? (FSIMS website)

The dispatcher must coordinate with the flight crew and maintenance to ensure that the MEL requirements are complied with and the dispatcher must add the deferral item to the dispatch release. This requires an amendment to the original release. Notation should be made to include this deferral on all future flights involving the applicable aircraft.

4. How are the systems chapters organized in a MEL? (FSIMS website)

MELs use a standardized organization of chapters based upon the Air Transport Association (ATA). For example, hydraulics will be in the same chapter number regardless of the aircraft type or manufacturer.

5. MELs list two columns that refer to numbers of system components. To what do the numbers in these two columns refer? (FSIMS website)

One column lists the number of components that are actually installed in the aircraft. The second lists the number of components that must be operational for dispatch.

6. A flight crew calls with an inoperative system item. You cannot find it in the MEL. What should you do? (FSIMS website)

It is possible you are looking in the wrong section. It would be advisable to contact maintenance control for assistance. If the item is not printed in the MEL, it cannot be deferred, and therefore the aircraft is grounded until the problem is fixed.

7. Many MEL items require actions on the part of flight crews and/or maintenance personnel. How are these requirements conveyed in the MEL? (FSIMS website)

- Items requiring input from the flight crew will be indicated with "(O)".
- Items requiring input from maintenance personnel will be indicated with a "(M)".
- If both flight crew and maintenance must do something, it will be indicated by "(O)(M)".
- If either the flight crew or maintenance must do something, it will be indicated by "(O) or (M)".

8. MEL items must be repaired within a specific period of time. What are the repair interval categories that are normally printed in MELs? (FSIMS website)

There are four repair categories: A, B, C, and D.

9. By when must a category A MEL item be repaired? (FSIMS website)

Category A items have a specific repair interval that is noted in the remarks section of the item.

10. A Category B MEL item breaks at 1200Z on August 1. By when must this item be repaired? (FSIMS website)

Category B items must be repaired within three consecutive calendar days (72 hours), but the day on which the malfunction occurs does not count. So the item must be repaired by the end of the day on August 4 (midnight).

11. How long can a Category C item be inoperative? (FSIMS website)

Category C items can be inoperative for 10 consecutive calendar days (120 hours).

12. What kinds of items are typically assigned Category D repair intervals and how long is this interval? (FSIMS website)

Non-essential items, such as passenger service items, are assigned Category D repair intervals. These must be repaired within 120 consecutive calendar days (2880 hours).

13. What is meant by the notation "FR" associated with a deferred item?

This means that follow-up action in required. Additional actions/verifications are required in the future. For example, a certain valve must be inspected to ensure that it is closed prior to each flight, or perhaps the flight crew must verify fuel quantity prior to each flight.

14. A particular item has a note stating that extended overwater operations are not permitted when it is inoperative. What is the maximum distance the aircraft can be flown offshore?

This aircraft would be limited to fly no more than 50 NM from shore.

15. When adding a MEL item to a dispatch release, what must the dispatcher include?

The item should be listed verbatim as it is written in the MEL. This includes the chapter, item number, description of the item (as written in the MEL), and the date by which it must be repaired.

16. Most air carriers have a special crew placarding procedure that allows flight crews to defer certain items. If an aircraft is departing a maintenance base and is still parked at the gate, are flight crews allowed to defer malfunctioning item(s)?

No, they must still call maintenance for a deferral.

17. Most air carriers have a special crew placarding procedure that allows flight crews to defer certain items. If an aircraft is departing a maintenance base and has departed the gate, are flight crews allowed to defer malfunctioning item(s)?

Yes, if the MEL indicates that the item is "crew deferrable."

18. Most air carriers have a special crew placarding procedure that allows flight crews to defer certain items. If an aircraft is departing a non-maintenance base and is still parked at the gate, are flight crews allowed to defer malfunctioning item(s)?

Yes, if the MEL indicates that the item is "crew deferrable." This is permitted so that flights are not delayed at stations where no company maintenance is available.

19. If flight crews defer an item, are they still required to comply with (M) and/or (O) restrictions/procedures?

Yes. It is unlikely an (M) item would be crew deferrable; however, if it is, they will need to contact local maintenance.

20. A crew calls that they have an equipment problem that is not crew deferrable (dispatch notification required), but they are at an outstation with no company maintenance. What should the dispatcher do?

The dispatcher should contact maintenance control to garner information about the availability of local contract maintenance. It is not unusual to contract with another airline or operator in these cases. The worst case is if no such capability exists and a company maintenance personnel has to be flown in on a company flight or another carrier's flight.

21. Are CDL items normally crew deferrable?

No, these normally require maintenance to ensure there are no structural issues, but at the very least they require dispatch notification.

D. Inoperative Items—Boeing 737

This section inquires into the possible effects that various inoperative components might have on aircraft operations and dispatching. While these refer specifically to the Boeing 737-800 and are referenced from the Boeing MMEL for this aircraft, use these questions to guide your studies for your specific aircraft and operational procedures. Always refer to the actual MEL for guidance in real-world flight operations.

1. What can be expected if an air conditioning pack is inoperative?

Two packs are installed but only one is required for dispatch. Operation with one inoperative pack is limited to 25,000 feet. This makes long-range flights impractical due to elevated fuel consumption. For long flights, it is recommended that the pack be repaired or the flight be swapped to another aircraft (tail swap).

2. Can an aircraft be dispatched with both packs inoperative?

Technically yes, but this requires the flight to be operated with poor ventilation and no pressurization, thus limiting the aircraft to low altitude (10,000 feet). This is not practical for either passenger comfort or fuel consumption. It would be wise to tail swap or fix the problem.

3. Is it possible to dispatch an aircraft with an inoperative recirculation fan?

Yes, as long as one fan remains operational and certain conditions apply (such as operating the flight pressurized). Flight with both fans inoperative is permitted as long as the temperature does not exceed 38°C.

4. Can a flight be dispatched with an inoperative autopilot?

Yes, as long as the weather minimums do not require its use for landing (such as in cases of very low weather conditions) and/or the crew accepts to perform all flight functions manually. Flight with an inoperative autopilot dramatically increases the workload for flight crews. Therefore, it is advisable to either have the problem fixed, to swap the flight to another aircraft, or to limit the use of the aircraft to only short flight segments.

5. Can a flight be dispatched with an inoperative yaw damper?

Yes, as long as the system switch remains in the off position.

6. The aircraft passenger address (PA) system is inoperative. What effect does this have on the dispatch of the aircraft?

This does not affect dispatch as long as an alternative method of communication is established and the flight attendant alerting system works (both visual and oral).

7. A crew reports a malfunctioning engine generator before pushback. What implications does this have for dispatch?

The APU generator must be operating normally and used continuously during the flight.

8. What type(s) of operations are affected by an inoperative APU generator?

In the case of a malfunctioning APU generator, extended-range (ER) operations are prohibited.

9. A transformer rectifier is determined to be malfunctioning. How might this affect dispatch?

The aircraft is grounded until the problem is fixed, as this issue is not listed in the MEL.

10. A crew reports that a passenger seat is broken. What must be done in order to dispatch the aircraft?

The seat must be examined to ensure that it does not block an emergency exit or the egress of other passengers. It must also be placarded "do not occupy."

11. How might an inoperative lavatory affect operations?

The crew and passengers should be notified prior to the flight to ensure all parties are aware of the problem. Also, all stations that will receive the aircraft should be given special notification. The lavatory should be placarded as inoperative.

12. The wheel well fire warning system is broken on one aircraft that you are responsible for dispatching. Can this aircraft be flown?

Yes, if the brake temperature monitoring system (BTMS) is operating normally or if the brakes are inspected prior to flight and are cool to the touch.

13. One of two APU fire loops is determined to be inoperative. What limits, if any, are placed upon the aircraft?

The aircraft is limited to extended-rage (ER) operations no further than 120 minutes from a diversionary airport.

14. Can a lavatory be used if the smoke detector inside it is broken?

Yes, but it can only be used by crewmembers. The waste receptacle must remain empty and the door must have a placard placed upon it stating "inoperative — do not enter."

15. Maintenance discovers that one aft main tank fuel pump is inoperative. What limitations are imposed on the aircraft?

ER operations are limited to no more than 120 minutes. Also, both forward tank pumps must be operational, the tank fuel quantity at takeoff must be 7,500 lbs or greater, and the quantity cannot be allowed to decrease below 2,500 lbs.

16 Maintenance discovers that one forward main tank fuel pump is inoperative. What limitations are imposed on the aircraft?

ER operations are limited to no more than 120 minutes. Also, both aft tank pumps must be operational, the tank fuel quantity at takeoff must be 4,800 lbs or greater, and the quantity cannot be allowed to decrease below 1,800 lbs.

17. Maintenance discovers that one center tank fuel pump is inoperative. What limitations are imposed on the aircraft?

Dispatchers must ensure that the wing tanks contain enough fuel to reach a diversionary airport in case the remaining center pump fails. Operations should not be limited or weight/balance limits exceeded in case the remaining center pump fails. The fuel quantity and low-pressure indications for the center tank must also be functioning normally.

18. One of the cockpit main tank fuel quantity gauges is not working properly. How does this affect operations?

ER operations are prohibited. All tank pumps must work normally, the fuel flow gauges must work, the center tank indications must be operational, the flight crew needs to calculate fuel consumption and fuel remaining throughout the flight, and the fuel quantity must be confirmed by the crew prior to departure.

19. One of the main (number 1 or 2) cockpit window heat systems is inoperative. What limits are placed on aircraft operations?

The aircraft cannot be operated in known or forecast icing conditions. Otherwise, the aircraft can be flown if the windshield defogging system is working and the airspeed is limited to 250 knots below 10,000 feet. ER operations beyond 120 minutes are also prohibited.

20. A flight crew reports that their one windshield wiper is not working. The destination airport TAF is reporting rain showers in the vicinity of the airport. Can this flight be dispatched?

No. The flight cannot be dispatched if precipitation is expected within 5 NM of the airport of takeoff or landing. "In vicinity" means that the phenomenon exists from 5 to 10 SM of the airport. Since 5 SM is less than 5 NM, precipitation might exist within the distance specifically prohibited by the MEL.

21. Can any anti-collision light be inoperative at any time?

Yes, the red beacons can be inoperative providing that the white wing/tail strobes still work normally.

22. Can any position lights be inoperative at any time?

Yes, but only during daylight operations.

23. What limitations apply to an aircraft with an inoperative altitude alerting system?

RVSM operations are generally prohibited. The autopilot altitude capture and hold functions must be working normally. Also, the aircraft cannot depart an airport at which repairs could be made and all repairs must be complete within 3 flight days.

24. Can an aircraft be operated with a malfunctioning thrust reverser?

Yes, as long as it is deactivated (thrust lever locked in forward position) and appropriate performance amendments are made.

10

Airports, Crew, and Company Procedures

A. Airport Diagrams, Charts, and Symbols

Although many air carriers utilize private enroute and terminal chart providers, the symbology in and the principles of the FAA's Terminal Procedures Publication charts are very similar to other providers' charts. Use these chart identification questions as a guide to what should be studied on the specific charts used by your company.

For questions 1–4, refer to the airport diagram of Tampa International Airport shown in Figure 10-1.

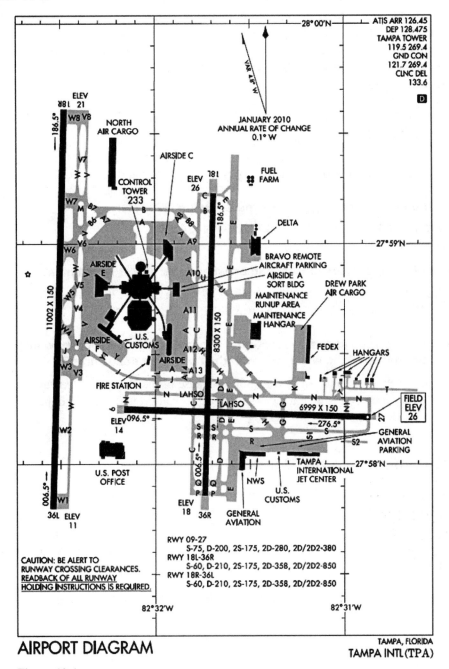

Figure 10-1.

1. **You retrieve Notices to Airmen (NOTAMs) for an upcoming flight from this airport. Taxiway W, W1, W2, W3, W4, and W5 are closed. The current METAR and TAF show that winds are currently and expected to remain out of the north. What impact can you expect on flights at this airport and what will you communicate about this closure to flight crews?**

Under these conditions, it can be expected that runways 36L and 36R would be in use. However, access to runway 36L is limited due to the taxiway closures. Several things should be considered. One possibility is that arrivals will be permitted to use runway 36L with the need to exit beyond W5. This could potentially reduce the arrival rate of the airport. Flight crews should be briefed on these closures with highlights or notes included in the dispatch release paperwork package, even though these closures will appear in NOTAMs. It may be wise to view airport arrival rates via the air traffic control command center products page and/or see how these closures may be affecting departures. Additional fuel may be considered for possible delays.

2. **You see a NOTAM indicating that the last 3,000 feet of runway 36L is closed. How much runway is available for takeoff and landing?**

Note the "11002 × 150" to the left of the runway. That is the normal length and width of the runway. If 3,000 feet are closed, the remaining runway is 8,002 feet.

3. **During your preflight planning you see the following NOTAMs:**

   TPA RWY 18L/36R CLSD WEF 1009271200-1011242200

   TPA TWY J CLSD

   What parts of the airport are closed, and on what dates and at what times?

Runway 18L/36R is closed from 2010, September (09), 27th day at 1200 Zulu to 2010, November (11), 24th day at 2200 Zulu. Taxiway Juliet is closed.

4. **If your aircraft is parked at airside A with the above closures in place, how might operations be affected if the winds are from the northwest at 20 knots?**

Departures are likely to occur from runway 36L. Because of the closure of taxiway J, aircraft will have a long taxi from airside A. Some additional ground fuel might be a prudent consideration.

B. Crew Qualifications and Limitations

1. **What are the minimum certification requirements for flight crew in terms of Ops Specs?** (FSIMS website)

Flight crews are required to have all certifications required by the FAA. These must be presented for inspection if required. Further, all flight crew must carry an approved form of photo identification such as a driver's license or passport.

2. **What are the minimum certification requirements to act as captain of a large transport aircraft?** (FSIMS website)

Captains are required to have an airline transport pilot (ATP) certificate with type rating, as well as a valid first-class medical certificate. They must also have an FCC radio telephone license if operating international flights and/or using HF communications.

3. **What are the minimum certification requirements to act as first officer of a large transport aircraft?** (FSIMS website)

   First officers are required to have a commercial pilot certificate with the appropriate category, class, and (in some cases) type ratings. They must also hold a valid first- or second-class medical certificate (some air carriers require a first-class). If they fly international flights and/or those using HF radio, they are required to hold an FCC radio telephone license.

4. **Are there any additional requirements for first officers who are a required third crewmember for international, long-haul flights (International Officers, or IOs)?** (FSIMS website)

   Yes, such first officers are required to have a type rating and normally must have a minimum number of hours as first officer.

5. **Are flight crews normally allowed to do commercial flying (for hire) outside of work?** (FSIMS website)

   Normally, no, as this affects their legality to fly at work (as it counts towards maximum flight times). Special authorization is required to do any such flying outside of work.

6. **Prior to working in any position, what type of training must flight crews (and dispatchers) go through?** (FSIMS website)

   Initial training.

7. **Each flight crewmember must (within/by the appropriate time duration/deadline) complete recurrent training that includes what subjects/activities?** (FSIMS website)

   - Ground training
   - Hazardous materials training
   - Differences training (if applicable)
   - Emergency training
   - Simulator proficiency check (for PICs this must occur every 6 months)

8. **What is "right seat dependency training"?** (FSIMS website)

   Captains must complete this if they are permitted to be scheduled to serve as first officers. This is essential to re-familiarize them with flying from the right seat.

9. **What is a "line check"?** (FSIMS website)

   A line check is an annual evaluation of the PIC during a regularly scheduled air carrier flight.

10. **What special requirement exists for PICs who have not previously been captain on a large, turbojet aircraft?** (FSIMS website)

    The FAA must observe this pilot in scheduled operations. Some air carriers require a special authorization to conduct their own observation flights.

11. **New captains and first officers are required to accumulate _____ flight hours within _____ days after completing training.** (FSIMS website)

    100 hours; 120 days.

12. What is meant by the term "high minimums captain"?

This is a PIC who has not yet accumulated 100 hours as captain on the aircraft. When evaluating approach minimums for destination airports, such captains must add 100 feet and ½ SM to all minimum altitudes and minimum visibilities.

13. Can requirements to alleviate high minimums restrictions be reduced?
(FSIMS website)

Yes, they can be reduced down to 50 hours with each landing counting as one flight hour.

14. Is there any restriction to allowing a new captain and new first officer to fly together? (FSIMS website)

Yes, unless one has 75 hours in the aircraft, they cannot be paired together.

15. Are there normally any restrictions to the types of operations or conditions in which first officers are allowed to fly if they have less than 100 hours?
(FSIMS website)

As is often the case, first officers with less than 100 hours are restricted from flying in/during the following:
- Designated special airports
- Contaminated runways (snow, water, ice)
- Braking action less than good
- Crosswinds in excess of 15 knots
- Wind shear
- Less than 4,000 RVR or ¾ SM visibility
- Any other condition determined by the PIC

16. Do high minimums restrictions apply to takeoff minimums? (FSIMS website)

No.

17. Do high minimums restrictions apply to the determination of alternate airports?
(FSIMS website)

No, the 100 and ½ are not added to alternate weather requirements.

18. Do high minimums restrictions apply to all Category I or II operations?
(FSIMS website)

Some Ops Specs allow for special exemption if flight crews are qualified at the next lower approach category. For example, if both the captain and first officer are qualified for Category II operations, the high minimums restrictions for Category I operations may be lifted. Some automation requirements may exist.

19. What recent experience requirements exist for flight crews? (FSIMS website; 14 CFR §121.439)

Three takeoffs and landings must be accomplished in the last 90 days. These can be conducted in a flight simulator as long as some additional training items are covered (such as approach to lowest authorized minimums, engine failure training).

20. Normally, how soon prior to departure must flight crews report for duty?
(FSIMS website)

Most air carriers require crews to report an hour prior to departure for domestic flights and slightly longer before international flights.

21. What if a pilot discovers that they have lost their pilot or medical certificate?
(FSIMS website)

Air carriers can request facsimile copies from the FAA 24 hours a day/7 days a week. These authorizations are good for 60 days.

22. What items, in addition to pilot and medical certificates, must a flight crewmember have with them when serving in such a capacity? (FSIMS website; 14 CFR §121.549)

A flight kit (bag) with the appropriate manuals, charts, forms needed for the flight, performance data, a company ID prominently displayed on an exterior piece of clothing, and a functional flashlight. Note that requirements vary from carrier to carrier.

23. Are crewmembers required to be available to company communication on layovers? (FSIMS website)

Although crewmembers are not obligated to communicate during their rest periods, most air carriers have a policy asking crews to check their messages during their layovers.

24. Can a dispatcher declare an emergency? (FSIMS website)

Yes, this is normally done if the PIC cannot be contacted and the status of the aircraft mandates the declaration of an emergency.

25. What kind of reporting requirements exist following emergencies? (FSIMS website)

Incidents and accidents require immediate reporting. Following an emergency, dispatchers and pilots should file a report as soon as possible, but no later than 10 days following the event (for pilots, the requirement is 10 days following return to their base).

C. Dispatch Area, Routes, and Main Terminals

1. What is Class I navigation? (FAA-H-8261-1)

This is navigation that takes place within the service volumes of applicable standard navigation aids, such as VORs or NDBs.

2. What is Class II navigation? (FAA-H-8261-1)

This is navigation that takes place outside the service volumes of applicable standard navigation aids (such as VORs or NDBs). Class II does not always require a long-range navigation system; however, flights outside Class I standards for more than an hour generally do require long-range navigation systems.

3. What is meant by the term "long-range navigation system"?

These are systems that authorize extended operations under Class II standards, such as oceanic and remote-area flights. Examples of this type of navigation system are GPS, LORAN, and inertial navigation.

4. On what routes/areas are aircraft permitted to be dispatched? (FSIMS website)

Aircraft are permitted to be dispatched only to those routes and areas specifically approved in Ops Specs. These normally show preference for remaining in controlled airspace, within radar contact, and within service volumes of the applicable navigation system(s). Exemptions to these preferences are normally provided in most Ops Specs, but under specific circumstances.

5. Are flights required to be dispatched on airways? What are the minimum certification requirements for flight crew in terms of Ops Specs? (FSIMS website)

Typically, no. If aircraft are dispatched outside the service volumes of ground-based navigation aids (if required to use them), the flight must be able to comply with Class II navigation requirements.

6. Can an aircraft be dispatched using Class I navigation standards if the position of the aircraft cannot be reliably fixed at least once an hour? (FSIMS website; FAA-H-8261-1)

No, this is normally not permitted. Instead, the aircraft should be dispatched under Class II standards, if authorized.

7. Are there any exceptions to the requirement to comply with Class II standards when outside of navigational service volumes? (FSIMS website)

Yes, one exception is if a flight is limited to no more than one hour outside the NAVAID service volumes; the other is when operating along an airway with a published MEA gap.

8. What type of navigation systems are authorized to be used on flights? (FSIMS website)

Each authorized system is specifically mentioned in Ops Specs. Only those in the Ops Specs are permitted to be used or relied upon.

9. How can a dispatcher determine if the failure of a navigational component will affect the flight? (FSIMS website)

The dispatcher should refer to the MEL and Ops Specs for possible negative consequences. Also, the route (including departure, enroute, arrival, and approach) should be referenced to see what navigation systems might be needed.

10. Are there time limits to the RNP capabilities of long-range navigation systems? (FSIMS website)

Some navigation systems (such as FMC with dual or triple IRS) are limited to eight hours (or other value) of use in areas that require the use of long-range systems.

11. What is meant by the term "RNP-10"? (FSIMS website)

RNP-10 means that navigation systems must accurately fix the aircraft position within 10 NM with a 95% confidence level.

12. What is "NAT/MNPS"? (FSIMS website)

This refers to the airspace above the North Atlantic in which minimum navigation performance standards apply. These standards require that aircraft remain within 6.3 NM of their track and have a minimal statistical chance of deviating beyond 30 NM (and an extremely low statistical chance of going beyond 50 NM). The aircraft must have a display in the cockpit to allow for monitoring of the aircraft navigational status and accuracy.

13. What is "RVSM"? (FSIMS website)

Reduced vertical separation minimums (RVSM) is when aircraft are vertically separated by 1,000 feet. Certain aircraft instrumentation is required and special training is needed for flight crews and dispatchers who are involved in operations in this airspace.

14. What is an example of an area of magnetic unreliability? What special requirements are needed to operate in such areas? (FSIMS website)

Such areas are where crews cannot rely upon their magnetic compasses for navigation. An example would be at extreme latitudes near the poles. In these areas, enroute navigation is conducted using true rather than magnetic headings. Normally, magnetic is still used in the approach environment.

15. What is a "redispatch" or a "rerelease"? (FSIMS website)

These terms refer to situations in which an aircraft is intending to go to a far away destination, but is originally released to a closer airport. As the aircraft approaches the closer destination, the fuel status (and other issues) are evaluated. If the aircraft is capable of continuing on to the further destination, it is redispatched/rereleased to go on. This must be planned ahead of departure and cannot be improvised.

16. What should dispatchers reference to ensure a redispatch/rerelease can be conducted? (FSIMS website)

Two hours prior to arrival at the redispatch/rerelease point, the dispatcher should evaluate weather, ground facilities, and the status of destination and alternate airports. This data should be conveyed to the PIC.

17. Where would the authorized areas for enroute operations be published? What are some examples of potential authorized areas? (FSIMS website)

This is published in Ops Specs (normally section B050). Examples include:
- Arctic
- Asia
- Atlantic (several different regions)
- Australia
- Canada
- Caribbean
- Europe
- Pacific
- Russia
- Sensitive international area overflights (e.g., Angola, Lebanon, Syria)
- South America
- U.S.A. (several regions)

18. When examining authorized areas for enroute operations, what else should dispatchers look for to ensure compliance with all requirements in Ops Specs? (FSIMS website)

There are typically limitations, provisions, and special requirements. These should be referenced to be sure that all mandates are met for legal operations in such areas.

19. Are revenue turbojet flights authorized to be conducted under VFR? (FSIMS website)

No, this is generally prohibited.

20. Does the certification of long-range navigation systems for use under Class II standards automatically qualify their use in NAT/MNPS or Pacific Airspaces? (FSIMS website)

No, these systems must be specifically authorized for such use in Ops Specs.

21. In order to conduct operations in Polar regions, what authorizations and provisions must exist? (FSIMS website)

Authorization to conduct operations in Polar regions must be specifically mentioned in Ops Specs, a recovery plan must exist and be reevaluated regularly, and a diversionary airport (or airports) must be provided.

22. An aircraft you are dispatching calls to say they have an emergency and need to dump fuel. Where can they expect to do this in a busy terminal area? (FSIMS website)

Most busy terminals have designated dumping locations away from populated areas. They should contact air traffic control for assistance.

23. When planning flights to and from busy terminal environments, what should dispatchers be aware of in terms of flight planning and terminal instrument procedures? (FSIMS website)

Dispatchers should check for IFR-preferred routes between busy terminal areas. Dispatchers should also plan to use Standard Instrument Departures (SIDs) and Standard Terminal Arrival Routes (STARs) for departing, arriving to or from large airports. In general, dispatchers should pick the procedure that is aimed in the general direction to or from which the flight is operated. They should verify that the aircraft can comply with the procedure's navigation requirements (e.g., some SIDs/STARs are RNAV only) and that the procedure is meant for the appropriate aircraft type (e.g., some SIDs/STARs are for turbojet aircraft only).

D. Authorization of Flight Departures and Company Departure Procedures

1. Can a flight depart without concurrence of the dispatcher and/or the captain?

No, both must agree that the flight is safe to conduct and complete.

2. What are standard takeoff minimums? (14 CFR §121.651)

- For aircraft with one or two engines: 1 SM or 5,000 RVR.
- For aircraft with more than two engines: ½ SM or 2,400 RVR.

3. Are there any provisions to allow for takeoffs below standard minimums? (FSIMS website)

Yes, if the air carrier is authorized to do so in their Ops Specs.

4. Can an air carrier reduce takeoff minimums if the existing published minimums are above standard? (FSIMS website)

No.

5. What is required to reduce takeoff minimums to 1,600 RVR or ¼ SM? (FSIMS website)

This normally necessitates the following:

- Touchdown zone RVR is controlling (if available).
- High intensity runway lights (HIRL) must be operational.
- Centerline lights (CL) must be operational.
- Adequate visual reference or a combination of lighting and markings that allow pilots to have enough visual data to keep the aircraft on the runway.

6. What is required to reduce takeoff minimums to 1,000 RVR? (FSIMS website)

This normally necessitates the following:

- A minimum of two RVR reports: touchdown zone and rollout RVR must both be 1,000 (mid-point RVR can be substituted for touchdown zone if it is inoperative).
- Centerline lights (CL) must be operational.

7. What is required to reduce takeoff minimums to 600 RVR? (FSIMS website)

This normally necessitates the following to be operational:

- Centerline lights (CL).
- Runway centerline markings (RCLM).
- Touchdown and rollout RVR sensors, or three RVR sensors, one of which may be inoperative (all of which should indicate a minimum of 600 RVR).

8. If operating at a foreign airport that reports RVR in meters, what is the approximate value used to equate to 600 RVR? (FSIMS website)

175 meters.

9. When is a takeoff alternate required? (14 CFR §121.617)

A takeoff alternate is required whenever the weather at the departure airport is less than the minimums for landing at that field.

10. A flight that you are dispatching is departing a remote airport for which there are no practical takeoff alternate airports. The lowest authorized approach minimums are a minimum descent height (MDH) of 500 ft AGL and 1 SM visibility. The reported ceiling is 300 ft AGL overcast and the visibility is 2 SM. Are you legal to depart? (FSIMS website)

Yes, because approach minimums technically only refer to visibility. Under these circumstances, considering no close-by alternatives exist, it might be wise to wait for better weather.

11. **A flight that you are dispatching is departing a remote airport for which there are no practical takeoff alternate airports. The weather is currently below authorized landing minimums. Can the flight depart?** (FSIMS website)

No.

12. **What is the maximum distance that a takeoff alternate can be from the departure airport for a Boeing 737?** (14 CFR §121.617)

For aircraft with two engines, the alternate cannot be further than one hour cruise in still air with one engine inoperative.

13. **What is the maximum distance that a takeoff alternate can be from the departure airport for a Boeing 747?** (14 CFR §121.617)

For an aircraft with three or more engines, the alternate cannot be further than two hours cruise in still air with one engine inoperative.

14. **You are dispatching a flight with a high minimums captain. Does this affect the minimum weather to determine if the flight requires a takeoff alternate?** (FSIMS website)

Yes. For example, the airport has an ILS approach with minimums of 200 feet and ½ SM. The weather would need to be 300 feet and 1 SM in order for this flight not to have to file a takeoff alternate.

15. **Do transport aircraft have to comply with VOR receiver check requirements in 14 CFR §91.171?** (FSIMS website)

Yes; however, this is usually handled by maintenance so flight crews do not need to make logbook entries, unless specifically mandated in Ops Specs.

16. **Are flights authorized to leave the gate prior to departure time?** (FSIMS website)

There is commonly a provision to allow flights to leave early if all passengers and bags are onboard prior to departure. Company publications will outline this procedure and the amount of time a flight is permitted to leave prior to the published departure time.

17. **What is the general procedure for handling an inoperative item while the aircraft is still sitting at the gate?** (FSIMS website)

The flight crew will reference the MEL to determine if the item can be deferred. If authorized in Ops Specs and the MEL, crews may be allowed to placard the item themselves. Depending on the issue, they may or may not have to notify maintenance and/or dispatch. Serious problems will require corrective actions by maintenance personnel.

18. **Are flight crews required to contact dispatch if they receive a reroute from air traffic control?** (FSIMS website)

Yes, as this can affect the safety of flight in terms of weather, fuel, or other factors.

19. **Are flight crews required to contact dispatch if they are expecting extended delays in the air or on the ground?** (FSIMS website)

Yes. This can affect fuel consumption and may demand alternative action planning.

20. How often must maximum thrust takeoffs be performed in most transport aircraft? (FSIMS website)

A majority of transport aircraft must perform a maximum thrust takeoff once every seven days. Dispatchers should note this requirement on the release, if applicable.

21. When departing an airport with obstacles in the vicinity, what should dispatchers do in order to ensure a safe departure? (FSIMS website)

All climb gradient requirements should be checked to ensure that the aircraft can comply with them. Referencing performance data/charts, dispatchers should confirm the necessary climb rates to meet climb gradient mandates. If special procedures (such as maximum thrust takeoff or maximum performance climbs) must be used to meet these requirements, these extraordinary needs should be conveyed to the flight crew on the release or briefed by the dispatcher.

E. Airport/Facility Directory

1. What publication should dispatchers use to find out details about airports such as runway lengths, hours of operation, special procedures or requirements, and telephone numbers?

The *Airport/Facility Directory* (A/FD).

For questions 2–12, refer to the Airport/Facility Directory *excerpt shown in Figure 10-2.*

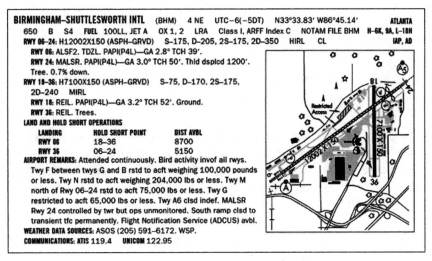

Figure 10-2.

2. What is the airport identifier code for Birmingham-Shuttlesworth International airport? (*Airport/Facility Directory,* or A/FD legend)

BHM. Also, remember that ICAO airport identifiers for the 48 contiguous U.S. start with the prefix "K" so the ICAO identifier is KBHM.

3. If a dispatcher wanted to find the low-altitude enroute chart on which this airport is displayed, where would they need to look? (A/FD legend)

KBHM is located on the L-18H low-altitude enroute chart available from AeroNav (FAA). Other private chart publishers organize their charts differently, so their contents listing would need to be researched to find the chart you're looking for.

4. Does this airport have instrument approaches? (A/FD legend)

Yes. See the note "IAP" for instrument approach procedure in the upper right above the airport diagram.

5. How long is runway 06? (A/FD legend)

Runway 06 is 12,002 feet long and 150 feet wide, is hard surfaced (H), is asphalt (ASPH) and is grooved (GRVD).

6. Is jet fuel available at this airport? (A/FD legend)

Yes, see the note "Jet-A."

7. Does runway 06 have centerline lights? (A/FD legend)

Yes, see the note "CL" and the dots on the runway in the airport diagram box.

8. You are dispatching a Boeing 757 to this airport. What is the maximum it can weigh when it lands on runway 06? (A/FD legend)

350,000 lbs is the limit for a two-dual-wheels-in-tandem type landing gear aircraft.

9. What type of approach lights does runway 06 have? (A/FD legend)

ALSF-2, which are one of the more helpful types of systems as they extend well away from the threshold and have special features that can assist flight crews to land in low visibility.

10. What are "TDZL"? (A/FD legend)

Touchdown zone lights (TDZL) are a series of in-pavement lights along the sides of the centerline that extend from close to the threshold to a point 3,000 feet down the runway. These assist flight crews in landing in poor weather. The combination of TDZL and CL sometimes allows for the reduction in required landing visibility for a category I ILS from 2,400 RVR to 1,800 RVR (but only if published).

11. How much runway is available for landing if arriving on runway 24? (A/FD legend)

10,802 feet, as there is a displaced threshold 1,200 feet long.

12. When determining where a flight should be diverted because of an emergency, what important data in the airport/facility directory should a dispatcher reference? (A/FD legend)

The proposed diversionary airport should be evaluated for the availability of airport rescue and fire fighting (ARFF) services. Refer to the second line of the KBHM entry. Class I refers to airports that handle large, scheduled operations. The index letter denotes how much equipment is available and the type of services offered. The further down the alphabet, the better the equipment and services. In the case of KBHM, it is an Index C airport, meaning it has a minimum of two to three vehicles and has 450–500 lbs of firefighting agent and 3,000 gallons of firefighting water supply.

For questions 13–15, refer to the A/FD directory excerpt shown in Figure 10-3.

```
COMMUNICATIONS: ATIS 119.4    UNICOM 122.95
     RCO 122.2 123.65 (ANNISTON RADIO)
Ⓡ APP/DEP CON 127.675 (231°–049°) 123.8 (050°–230°)
     TOWER 119.9 118.25    GND CON 121.7    CLNC DEL 125.675
       PRE–TAXI CLNC 125.675
AIRSPACE: CLASS C svc continuous ctc APP CON
RADIO AIDS TO NAVIGATION: NOTAM FILE ANB.
     VULCAN (H) VORTAC 114.4    VUZ    Chan 91    N33°40.21' W86°53.99'    129° 9.8 NM to fld. 750/02E.    HIWAS.
     MC DEN NDB (HW/LOM) 224    BH    N33°30.68' W86°50.74'    059° 5.6 NM to fld.    NOTAM FILE BHM.
     ROEBY NDB (LOM) 394    RO    N33°36.46' W86°40.73'    235° 4.6 NM to fld.    NOTAM FILE BHM.
     ILS 110.3    I–BHM    Rwy 06. CLASS IIE.    LOM MC DEN NDB.
     ILS/DME 109.5    I–ROE    Chan 32    Rwy 24. CLASS IE.    LOM ROEBY NDB.
     ILS/DME 111.3    I–BXO    Chan 50    Rwy 18.    (LOC only).
```

Figure 10-3.

13. What is the meaning of the "R" in a circle adjacent to APP/DEP? (A/FD legend)

This indicates that radar service is available from arrival/departure controllers.

14. In order to remain within the service volume of VUZ VORTAC, an aircraft flying at FL300 would need to stay within _____ NM of the facility. (A/FD legend)

130 NM. VUZ is a high-altitude facility (H).

15. What is the meaning of the term "CLASS IIE" in reference to the I-BHM ILS?

This localizer meets ILS category II approach standards. "E" means it meets these standards to within 2,000 feet of the far end (landing) of the runway.

11

Routing, Rerouting, and Flight Plan Filing

A. Air Traffic Control Routing

1. Describe how a dispatcher should decide on what route to use when planning a flight. (AIM)

Most air carriers have developed their own catalog of routes to use for each destination to which they fly. Otherwise, the route selection process should include a variety of considerations. First, dispatchers should check the Airport/Facility Directory or ATC Command Center website for the availability of IFR-preferred routes. These predetermined routes are used between large terminal environments to ensure the smooth, expeditious flow of traffic in between these points. If dispatchers fail to reference preferred routes, crews will likely be assigned them anyway, requiring the last-minute recalculation of fuel consumption and other critical factors. If no preferred route is available, the dispatcher should try to choose the route with the shortest distance, taking into consideration the navigation aids usable by the aircraft and flight crew. Of course, weather should be considered, which often necessitates routings around severe weather. Other considerations include the availability of arrival/departure procedures, air traffic control delays and re-routes, terrain, minimum IFR altitudes, driftdown performance, as well as enroute diversionary airports (if applicable). North American route program (NRP) routing may also be considered, providing for more direct and efficient flight routes. NRP are exempt from obligations for preferred IFR routes. Lastly, survival equipment requirements may exist for certain routes, such as those that involve overwater operations.

2. How can a dispatcher choose the appropriate standard instrument departure (SID) to use at a particular airport?

Most SIDs identify specific runways of departure that are applicable to their use. Dispatchers can try to identify the runway of departure by checking current weather conditions and confirming aircraft performance abilities for individual runways. Most SIDs guide aircraft in a general direction (e.g., northeast, southwest), which should coincide with the desired path towards the destination airport. SIDs are often designated for specific aircraft, such as "turbojet only." Lastly, SIDs sometimes include climb gradient requirements, which the dispatcher should ensure the aircraft can comply with. Once the SID is selected, the transition that best directs the aircraft towards the destination should be used. The first waypoint in the enroute part of the flight plan should be the point at which the SID and transition (if used) ends.

3. What if none of the published SIDs coincide with the direction of departure of a particular flight?

There are many airports that have only a limited number of SIDs, some of which are not applicable for departures heading in certain directions. Dispatchers should not feel compelled to use SIDs that do not make sense for the direction of flight. Simply choose a nearby NAVAID as the first waypoint in the flight plan.

4. How can a dispatcher distinguish between a vector and pilot navigation SID?

Vector departures normally only depict the NAVAIDs surrounding the departure airport and do not include pictorial/textual route descriptions. There are no transitions, per se, for vector departures.

5. How can a dispatcher include a vector SID in the route section of the flight plan?

Vector departures cannot be filed for and should therefore be excluded from the route description in the flight plan. Pilots will simply receive the vector SID as part of the IFR clearance. Dispatchers should use one of the NAVAIDs listed on the SID as the first waypoint in the flight plan.

6. What is the minimum enroute altitude for a jet route/airway?

In the United States, J routes have a minimum enroute altitude of 18,000 feet unless otherwise specified.

7. What considerations should a dispatcher make when considering an enroute cruise altitude?

The selection of a cruise altitude should include the following considerations:
- Minimum IFR altitudes
- Route limiting altitudes (some airways are unidirectional or require the use of specific altitudes)
- Weather, such as precipitation tops, turbulence, or icing
- Correct altitude for direction of flight
- Performance, such as optimum fuel consumption altitudes and driftdown considerations
- Length of flight
- Airspace, e.g., Military Operations Areas (MOAs)
- Any other factor relating to the efficiency or safety of flight

8. When using VOR navigation, what is the maximum distance between NAVAIDs that a dispatcher should use when planning a direct (non-airway) route? (AIM)

From 18,000 to 45,000 feet, the maximum distance should be 260 NM. Above 45,000 feet the limit is 200 NM. Below 18,000 feet the limit is 80 NM, unless the NAVAID is designated a high-altitude type and the flight is conducted from 14,500 to 17,999 feet, in which case the limit is 200 NM.

9. What are the requirements to create a direct (random) RNAV route? (AIM)

Dispatchers planning to create direct (random) RNAV routes should still use SIDs and STARs. The first point for the enroute portion of the flight plan should be the last point of the SID transition, while the last point should be a fix/NAVAID at the start of a STAR transition. The route should be described by fixes, which should be defined as named fixes or with degree-distance references to NAVAIDs. A minimum of one fix should be listed for each ATC center airspace through which the aircraft will fly. Each of these fixes should be within 200 NM of the previous center airspace boundary. An additional fix should be included for each point at which the route requires a turn. Special use airspace should be avoided by a minimum of 3 NM. Radar coverage is required for random/direct RNAV routes.

10. **What are the requirements for random RNAV routes for aircraft using latitude/longitude coordinate-capable navigation systems?** (AIM)

   SIDs and STARs should be used where available. The enroute portion of the flight plan should begin at the terminating point of the SID and should end at the starting point of a STAR. Enroute waypoints should be defined as latitude/longitude coordinates or by navigation reference system (NRS) waypoints. The minimum altitude for this type of flight planning is FL390.

11. **How does a dispatcher code 35 degrees 05 minutes North and 110 degrees 22 minutes West as a waypoint in the route section of the flight plan?** (AIM)

   This would be coded 3505/11022 and should be inserted in the route section of the flight plan just like any other waypoint/NAVAID.

12. **What does "NRR" stand for?** (AC 90-99)

   NRR stands for "non-restrictive routings," which are RNAV routings that allow for more direct, efficient conduct of IFR flights.

13. **What is "NRS"?** (AC 90-99)

   NRS (navigation reference system) is a network of named RNAV waypoints for use in designing NRR or more direct routes in high-altitude airspace.

14. **How can a dispatcher convey that an aircraft for which they are responsible is NRR capable?** (AC 90-99)

   Dispatchers should insert "HAR" into the remarks section of the flight plan if the aircraft is equipped with a navigation system that contains all NRS waypoints. Alternatively, dispatchers can use "PTP" to indicate that the aircraft has all "traditional" waypoints, but may not have all NRS waypoints installed.

15. **What is a "pitch waypoint"?** (AC 90-99)

   A pitch waypoint is the point at which a flight begins the NRR or NRP portion of its route.

16. **What is a "catch waypoint"?** (AC 90-99)

   A catch waypoint is the point at which a flight ends the NRR or NRP portion of their route.

17. **What responsibilities do dispatchers have concerning special use airspace when using NRR?** (AC 90-99)

   Dispatchers should avoid special use airspace that may impact the flight.

18. **What is the minimum altitude to use NRR?** (AC 90-99)

   It currently is FL390.

19. **How can dispatchers check the status of special use airspace?** (AC 90-99)

   Dispatchers can get real-time special use airspace status information from the website sua.faa.gov or by phoning a flight service station.

20. What special requirements may be applicable to flights operating over water? (FSIMS website)

The applicable requirements depend on how far away from shore a flight operates. For flights that travel more than 50 NM from shore, specific safety equipment requirements apply, including life preservers for each occupant, life rafts, survival equipment, and pyrotechnic signaling devices. Some air carriers are authorized by their Ops Specs to fly more than 50 NM from shore without the aforementioned equipment as long as they are above a specified altitude. Ops Specs will also address any additional demands made upon the carrier to operate flights in such areas.

21. You are planning a flight from Miami to San Juan, Puerto Rico. The aircraft scheduled to make the flight is not equipped for overwater flight. Can you operate this flight? (FSIMS website)

If you review the geography along that route, you should see available routes that keep the aircraft within 50 NM of shore, albeit some of the "shores" are small islands, but this fact alleviates the need for having the overwater equipment. An alternative option is to do a tail-swap to an aircraft that is equipped for overwater flight in order to have more routing flexibility.

22. What concerns should you have about dispatching a non-overwater equipped aircraft on the flight described in the previous question if there are areas of convective activity along the route? (FSIMS website)

If the flight is required to deviate, it must remain within 50 NM of shore. If the convective activity is widespread, especially along the centerline of the route, it may be advisable to switch to an overwater-equipped aircraft for routing flexibility, or even to delay the flight.

23. When looking at route options, you note an airway that is brown. What does this mean? (AIM)

Brown airways rely upon LF/MF NAVAIDs (e.g., NDBs) for guidance.

24. Can RNAV-capable aircraft use brown airways?

Yes, in almost all cases the required fixes to fly such airways will be available in RNAV databases.

25. When looking at route options, you note an airway that is blue. What does this mean? (AIM)

These are RNAV airways. Q routes are for high-altitude (18,000 MSL to FL450) use, while T routes are for low-altitude (below 18,000 MSL) use.

26. Should dispatchers plan direct/off-airway routes in remote or oceanic areas?

No, these areas typically require flights to remain on airways, mostly because of poor radar coverage. The use of published routes allows controllers to more easily track flight locations for separation purposes.

27. While planning a flight, you notice that an airway you want to use is labeled "V2-154." How should you enter this in the route section of a flight plan form?

You must choose one airway designation, in this case either V2 or V154. It is advisable to choose the option that allows you to fly the furthest in the desired direction. It is sometimes possible to traverse a large geographic area on one airway. However, do not feel compelled to use a single airway if it makes the route longer or takes you out of the way from where you want the flight to travel.

28. While flight planning, you notice a line of severe storms that cross the intended route. What should you do?

If possible, try to route the aircraft around the most severe parts of the weather system. "Soft spots" or holes may exist that the route could be planned near or through to allow pilots to evaluate the conditions before attempting to cross the line of weather. Ground-based weather radar tends to overstate the severity of weather, so pilots may find once they are airborne that they can traverse areas of weather. It is helpful if the dispatcher finds out if/how aircraft are making it through the area of concern by talking to other company aircraft, communicating with air traffic control, or monitoring systems such as aircraft situational display. Dispatchers should always fuel plan for the worst-case scenario, such as the longest possible route around the weather, or at the very least allow for extra fuel so that pilots can deviate freely as necessary.

29. How can a dispatcher be assured that flight planning data is legal to use in the dispatch of an air carrier flight?

All approved flight planning software, systems, and/or procedures should be specified in Ops Specs. Dispatchers should only use those items and procedures authorized by Ops Specs. In the case of a web-based system, the site from which the weather is accessed must have an "https" URL that indicates it is secure. This security can also be verified by a small padlock symbol in the lower corner of the browser window.

30. Should dispatchers plan to route aircraft around areas of turbulence?

Turbulence is not typically significant enough to warrant a circuitous route. The exception may be when an area of severe or extreme turbulence is expected or in the case of PIREPs indicating the same levels of turbulence. Dispatchers should also consider different cruise altitudes to avoid the turbulence, but should not choose extremely low altitudes (e.g., 28,000') due to the decrease in fuel efficiency in doing so.

31. When planning a flight to a destination that is receiving or expecting to receive snow, what special considerations should a dispatcher make?

Any weather event has the potential to slow down traffic and cause delays. It is wise to add additional fuel in these cases. Snow adds another element—the need for its removal from landing surfaces. It is possible that the runway(s) at the destination may be temporarily closed for snow removal. Contingency fuel should be added for possible delays. Dispatchers should consider alternate airports even if not legally required.

B. Rerouting

1. Are flights permitted to deviate from their filed flight plan route? (FSIMS website)

Ops Specs denotes what types of routes (airway and non-airway/direct) are permitted to be used during flight. Flights may deviate from these routes to avoid weather or per ATC requests. Flight crews should contact dispatch as soon as practical when these reroutes may result in fuel consumption significantly different than planned due to changes in ground speed and/or distance.

2. Should flight crews contact dispatch if they are assigned a different cruise altitude than originally planned? (FSIMS website)

Yes, if it is significantly different than what was planned. A large difference between the planned and actual cruise altitude could influence the total fuel burn, especially for longer flights. Also, the new altitude could have different winds than were accounted for in the original flight planning process, again potentially causing differences in fuel consumption.

3. Where can dispatchers find all active ATC reroutes in effect? (ATCCC website)

These can be found at the ATC Command Center website under "Current Reroutes."

4. How are current reroutes conveyed on the ATC Command Center website? (ATCCC website)

These advisories include the area impacted, the reason, the traffic included, the time frame in which the reroutes can be expected, and a list of the actual reroutes.

5. Decode the following reroute advisory: (ATCCC website)

ZDV ZLC ZMP   EWR   J584 SLT FQM1

Traffic arriving from Denver, Salt Lake, and Minneapolis Centers destined for Newark (KEWR) should file Jet route 584 to SLT then the FQM1 arrival.

6. How should reroutes be handled by flight crews and dispatch? (FSIMS website)

If the aircraft is still on the ground and at the gate, the dispatcher and flight crew should coordinate regarding the reroute and a new release should be printed. If the flight has left the gate or is in the air, crew-dispatcher coordination should take place to amend the release by penning in the changes, noting the time, and including the initials of the dispatcher. The dispatcher should confirm that the fuel value onboard the aircraft still allows for a legal flight to the destination.

7. Where can dispatchers find any restrictions to flight operations requested by various ATC facilities? (ATCCC website)

This information can be found at the ATC Command Center website under "Current Restrictions."

8. What types of restrictions are listed on the ATC Command Center website? (ATCCC website)

Examples of restrictions include the requested miles-in-trail spacing (which typically slows traffic flow), the runway(s) in use for route/arrival planning, desired arrival gate waypoint(s), and any other route specifications.

9. When a dispatcher sees restrictions listed for an area to which they are dispatching a flight, what should they do?

They should evaluate the potential impact of the restrictions on the flight, most notably fuel requirements. For example, in-trail spacing restrictions tend to lead to speed reductions and/or holding; therefore, the dispatcher may want to consider increasing contingency fuel just in case such restrictions do influence the flight.

10. What should a dispatcher do if they notice a flight is being rerouted (for example, on aircraft situational display or a similar system)?

The dispatcher should attempt to contact the flight via radio, SELCAL, or ACARS. They should get an update of the new routing and then use that to recalculate fuel.

11. What if a flight is rerouted but the new route compromises the legal fuel requirements for the flight?

If it is possible to choose a different route that does not cause this problem, then that should be done as soon as possible. Otherwise, a diversion will be necessary so the aircraft can refuel.

12. What is the ATC national playbook? (ATCCC website)

This is a preset array of alternate routes in congested areas in case of bad weather. This listing of alternative routes allows controllers, pilots, and dispatchers to plan accordingly when large pieces of airspace or entire airways are constrained or closed due to weather.

13. How can dispatchers find real-time delay information, including ground stops, ground delays, and the possibility for deicing? (ATCCC website)

This can be found in the Operational Information System (OIS) section of the ATC Command Center website.

C. Flight Plans

1. Dispatchers planning a flight with a magnetic course of 080 should select what kind of flight level for cruise: even or odd? (AIM)

Odd, so FL290, FL310, FL330, FL350, and FL410 are options in RVSM airspace.

2. Dispatchers planning a flight with a magnetic course of 180 should select what kind of flight level for cruise: even or odd? (AIM)

Even, so FL300, FL320, FL340, FL360, FL380, and FL400 are options in RVSM airspace.

3. Why is it so important that a dispatcher use the correct aircraft equipment code (suffix) on a flight plan? (AIM)

This allows air traffic control to be aware of the navigation capabilities of the aircraft. For example, if controllers know the aircraft has RNAV, they may clear the aircraft for direct routes. Also, the correct code should be used to reflect the ability of the aircraft to fly in RVSM airspace. Without such a code, delays or inefficient routings/altitudes may be issued to the aircraft.

4. What is the significance of a "/R" equipment code? (AIM)

A /R aircraft is RVSM capable and has the capability to perform advanced RNAV with RNP. This aircraft is also Mode C equipped. See AIM Table 5-1-2 for all available codes.

5. What are the meanings of the prefix aircraft codes "H/" and "T/"? (AIM)

H/ is used to denote a heavy aircraft and T/ is used to denote that the aircraft is TCAS equipped.

6. Can dispatchers plan direct routes that fall outside the service volumes of ground-based NAVAIDs? (AIM)

Yes, if the aircraft has a self-contained navigation system and the aircraft receives radar flight following.

7. Which flight plan form is applicable to non-RNAV operations that will be exclusively conducted in U.S. domestic airspace? (AIM)

FAA Form 7233-1.

8. Why should FAA Form 7233-1 not be used for filing a flight plan? (AIM)

Filing with this form may prevent that aircraft from being given RNAV SIDs and STARs.

9. How soon prior to departure is it recommended that an IFR flight plan be filed? (AIM)

A minimum of 30 minutes prior to departure, although it is recommended that nonscheduled operations file at least four hours in advance for operations above FL230.

10. What are the flight planning requirements for filing a RNAV direct flight plan? (AIM)

The route should include a SID and a STAR, if appropriate, with direct routing in between defined by either named waypoints or degree/distance fixes based on NAVAID (within service volumes). A waypoint must be included within each ARTCC airspace. These designated waypoints must be within 200 NM of the boundary of the previous center airspace. The route must avoid conflictive airspace (restricted, prohibited) by 3 NM. Any turns in the route must include a waypoint to mark the location of the turn. In certain cases, latitude/longitude or national reference waypoints can be used to define the route.

11. How should N36° 07' W106° 15' be conveyed on a flight plan form route description? (AIM)

3607/10615.

12. What is the significance of "KD34U" as a waypoint in a flight plan route? (AIM)

This is a lat/long fix in Denver ARTCC airspace. These types of "named" fixes are becoming more popular as direct RNAV routings become more mainstream. These are now being printed on IFR enroute charts.

13. If an aircraft is predicted to be able to climb to FL410 later in flight but can only initially hold FL370, what altitude should a dispatcher place in the requested altitude block on a flight plan form?

Only the initial altitude should be used (FL370). Pilots will request the higher altitude when appropriate. Note on the release a point along the flight at which the flight crew should climb to a higher cruise altitude.

14. Do air traffic controllers know what airport has been selected as the destination alternate? (AIM)

No, block 13 (alternate airport) is not transmitted to air traffic facilities.

15. When should FAA Form 7233-4 (International Flight Plan) be used? (AIM)

This form is recommended for use among all IFR flights, but must be used for IFR flights leaving U.S. airspace and for those planning on using RNAV procedures (SIDs and STARs).

16. Should an air carrier use the aircraft "N" number for item 7 (aircraft identification) on FAA Form 7233-4? (AIM)

No, they should use their company designator (e.g., AAL for American Airlines).

17. What letter(s) should be used for item 8 (flight rules and type of flight) on FAA Form 7233-4? (AIM)

The letter "I" should be used for IFR flights and "S" for scheduled air service. This designation is optional for flights conducted entirely within U.S. airspace.

18. Item 9 on FAA Form 7233-4 requires the input of a wake turbulence category. Your aircraft has a maximum certified takeoff weight of 325,000 lbs but only weighs 290,000 lbs today. What category should be used?

The actual weight of the aircraft is not the determinant of the category; therefore, the category would be based upon the MTOW of 325,000 lbs. This would place the aircraft in the "H" (heavy) category.

19. What is considered "standard" equipment for aircraft in U.S. domestic airspace in reference to item 10 (equipment) on FAA Form 7233-4? (AIM)

VHF radio, ADF, VOR, and ILS navigation are considered standard equipment. All other equipment should be listed.

20. How should an airspeed of 400 knots be conveyed for item 15 (cruise speed, level, route) on FAA Form 7233-4? (AIM)

N0400, where "N" is for knots.

21. How should an airspeed of Mach 0.80 be conveyed for item 15 (cruise speed, level, route) on FAA Form 7233-4? (AIM)

M080, where "M" is for Mach.

22. How should an altitude of 35,000 feet be conveyed for item 15 (cruise speed, level, route) on FAA Form 7233-4? (AIM)

F350, where "F" is for flight level.

23. How should an altitude of 12,000 feet be conveyed for item 15 (cruise speed, level, route) on FAA Form 7233-4? (AIM)

A120, where "A" is for altitude in feet.

24. How should a direct route between points be conveyed for item 15 (cruise speed, level, route) on FAA Form 7233-4? (AIM)

"DCT" for direct. For example "BIL DCT LVM" would mean from Billings direct to Livingston.

25. Is it possible to use a route such as "V325 V49" in which the transition from one airway to another will simply be done where the two cross (i.e., there is no named fix at this intersection) on FAA Form 7233-4? (AIM)

Yes; however, this may cause the rejection of the flight plan in some cases.

26. Are alternate airports listed on FAA Form 7233-4 transmitted to air traffic control facilities? (AIM)

No.

27. Does FAA Form 7233-4 have a place for SELCAL codes? (AIM)

Yes, SELCAL codes can be placed in item 18 (other information), written as "SEL/" followed by the selective calling (SELCAL) code.

28. Is the information listed in item 19 (supplementary information) on FAA Form 7233-4, such as endurance, persons on board, and survival equipment, sent to air traffic control facilities? (AIM)

No, this information is retained for search and rescue purposes but has no air traffic control function.

29. If polar survival equipment is not carried on the aircraft, how should this be noted on FAA Form 7233-4? (AIM)

The box adjacent to this item should be crossed out.

30. Does the filing and subsequent acceptance of an international flight plan constitute permission to enter a particular country's airspace? (AIM)

No, certain countries may require additional authorizations. Dispatchers should check on these clearance requirements prior to flight.

31. What special considerations must be made for flights arriving from outside the U.S.?

Such flights will need to clear customs upon entry. This normally means the aircraft cannot be serviced (internally) without prior clearance from customs or their designated representatives. Crews must also clear customs. If customs or their designated representatives do not meet the aircraft, crews should not take it upon themselves to open doors or disembark. This could lead to serious fines and/or other types of persecution.

32. Unless otherwise notified, air traffic control will likely delete an IFR flight plan after what time period following the lapse of estimated time of departure? (AIM)

One hour. This can be precluded if dispatchers or pilots notify ATC of a revised ETD.

33. What are the different ways that IFR flight plans can be cancelled? (AIM)

At airports with an operating control tower, this is handled by controllers upon landing. Otherwise, pilots must close their flight plan with an air traffic control facility or flight service station once they are on the ground. Pilots can elect to "cancel IFR" while airborne with the local air traffic control facility. As always, Ops Specs should dictate the procedure used.

34. If GPS is the sole means of providing RNAV/RNP for a given IFR flight, what must be conducted prior to this operation? (AIM)

A RAIM prediction must be made prior to this flight. This can be conducted using www.raimpredicition.net, by contacting a flight service station, by using a third-party provider, or by using the RAIM prediction capabilities of the unit itself. WAAS-enabled GPS users are exempt from this requirement as long as WAAS is available over the entire route.

35. What are pre-taxi clearance procedures? (AIM)

These exist at certain busier airports (locations can be found in the AFD) and give pilots the option to receive their IFR clearance prior to starting their taxi for departure. The provisions of these procedures include:

- Optional participation.
- Calls should be made no more than 10 minutes prior to taxi.
- Pilots then call ground for taxi, but do not normally need to tell ground they have their IFR clearance (unless they have not yet received such a clearance).

36. What is "PDC"? (AIM)

Pre-departure clearance (PDC) is an automated clearance delivery system. Aircraft equipped with ACARS will receive their clearance electronically. Aircraft not ACARS equipped can receive their clearance via a designated printer location. PDC eliminates frequency congestion and controller/pilot workloads. In order to participate, users must have subscribed to the appropriate service provider, only the first filed flight plan will be issued within a 24-hour period, and clearances amended prior to delivery will be dropped from PDC.

37. What special caution should dispatchers be aware of if they file multiple flight plans for the same flight? (AIM)

Dispatchers in this situation should make a note on the revised release (or while talking to crews during the release revision process) in order to ensure that pilots receive a full-route clearance. This would preclude them from erroneously assuming to fly a route from an "old" flight plan when they receive a "cleared as filed" clearance from air traffic control.

38. What is a "clearance void time"? (AIM)

Aircraft departing airports without a control tower will be issued an IFR clearance with an expiration time known as a "void time." This is to ensure that the airspace around that airport is protected from other IFR traffic, but only for a reasonable amount of time. Void time windows are usually 30 minutes. If the aircraft does not depart by the void time, they must call and get a revised clearance. If air traffic control does not hear back from the aircraft, they will assume that search and rescue may be required.

39. What is a "hold for release"? (AIM)

Aircraft departing airports without a control tower may be told to "hold for release" when air traffic control has other IFR traffic departing or arriving from the airport. This is an instruction for the aircraft not to depart following the receipt of their IFR clearance.

40. What is a "release time"? (AIM)

This is the earliest time that an IFR departure can leave an airport for separation purposes. This is used at airports without a control tower.

41. What is an "EDCT"? (ATCCC website)

An expect departure clearance time (EDCT) is the time that an IFR is released to fly its intended flight plan. EDCTs are in place when there are flow restrictions into airports or through certain airspace.

42. How can a dispatcher check to see if an EDCT has been issued for a flight? (ATCCC website)

The dispatcher can check by using the "EDCT lookup" feature on the ATC Command Center website. Clearance delivery will tell the pilots of this restriction when they call for their IFR clearance.

D. Amended Release Procedures

1. What is the most desirable way to convey an amendment to the release to flight crews? (FSIMS website)

The most desirable way is to send an entire new release to the station at which the aircraft is to depart. This new document replaces the old release.

2. If an aircraft has already left the gate or there is some other reason a new release cannot be given to the flight crew, how can an amendment be made to the release? (FSIMS website)

Any changes can be penned in on the flight release by crews, with a notation about the nature of the change, the time, and the initials of the dispatcher.

3. Does a flight release need to be amended when the flight crew and dispatcher decide to go to the alternate listed on the release? (FSIMS website)

No.

4. Does a flight release need to be amended when the flight crew and dispatcher decide to go to an alternate other than the one listed on the release? (FSIMS website)

Yes.

5. Does a flight release need to be amended when it is necessary to bypass a non-refueling intermediate stop? (FSIMS website)

Yes.

6. Do MEL items need to be on the release? (FSIMS website)

Yes.

7. If a new MEL item is discovered, how must this be handled in terms of the release?

The MEL item must be added, verbatim, to the release. This can be done through coordination between the crew and dispatch, and penning it in on the release, noting the time and initials of the dispatcher.

E. Diversion and Alternate Procedures

1. What airports, per Ops Specs, are authorized for use as alternates? (FSIMS website)

Any airport designated as regular, provisional, refueling, or alternate in Ops Specs can be used as an alternate airport.

2. Can an airport be planned as an alternate if the flight will arrive above the maximum structural or conditional (e.g., runway length/conditions) landing weight? (FSIMS website)

No. This makes sense, as this essentially makes such an airport unusable.

3. What is the definition of a "diversion"? (FSIMS website)

A diversion is an occurrence when an aircraft lands at an airport other than the originally intended destination.

4. If a flight bypasses an intermediate stop, is this considered to be a diversion? (FSIMS website)

Yes, as the aircraft is not landing at the airport it originally intended as its current destination.

5. What coordination between flight crews and dispatch is required prior to diverting? (FSIMS website)

Crews are advised to consult with dispatch prior to diverting because the selection of a diversionary airport may be based on factors currently unknown to crews. Also, the most favorable diversionary airport may be one other than a listed alternate. Factors that might influence the selection of the diversionary airport are weather, passenger handling, and whether the selected airport is the next scheduled stop on a multi-leg flight.

6. What considerations should be taken into account when selecting an alternate or diversionary airport?

The following are primary considerations when picking an alternate or diversionary airport:
• Proximity
• Weather
• NOTAMs
• Delays/traffic saturation
• Fuel availability
• Passenger handling capabilities
• Gate space and availability
• In-house/company services and employees
• Maintenance or equipment required by MEL or other issues (for example, a ground start cart in the case of an inoperative APU)

F. Intermediate Stops and Airport Types

1. What is a "technical stop"? (FSIMS website)

A technical stop is when an aircraft (typically in a scheduled service operation) makes a stop at an airport, as planned during the flight planning process, to refuel. An example of when this may occur is if the flight is operated out of an airport with a short runway or other performance limitation. The flight can then go to an airport without such limitations and fuel to the required level to complete the remainder of the flight.

2. How long is a release valid if the flight stops at an intermediate point? (14 CFR §121.593, 121.595)

One hour for domestic flights; six hours for flag flights.

3. What is a "regular airport"? (FSIMS website)

This is the airport authorized for use as the normally utilized facility that serves a community. Regular airports authorized for use by an air carrier are listed in Ops Specs.

4. What is an "alternate airport"? (FSIMS website)

This is an airport authorized for use if landing at the original destination is not possible. Alternate airports authorized for use by an air carrier are listed in Ops Specs.

5. What is a "refueling airport"? (FSIMS website)

This is an airport authorized for use as a refueling stop only (no on/off loading of payload or passengers is permitted). Refueling airports authorized for use by an air carrier are listed in Ops Specs.

6. What is a "provisional airport"? (FSIMS website)

This is an airport other than the regular airport that serves a particular community and which is authorized for use when/if the regular airport is not available for use. Provisional airports authorized for use by an air carrier are listed in Ops Specs.

G. Airport Weather Requirements

1. Can a flight be dispatched to an airport for which no weather information is available? (FSIMS website)

No. In order to legally dispatch a flight, the weather reports or forecasts (or combination thereof) must indicate the weather conditions will be equal to or better than the authorized approach minimums for that airport at the estimated time of arrival.

2. What airport(s) must have weather reporting for legal dispatch of a flight? (FSIMS website)

Weather reports must be available for the departure, intermediate stops, destination, and (if required) alternate airport(s).

3. From what kind(s) of weather source(s) are dispatchers permitted to retrieve reports and forecasts to use in the planning and dispatch of flights?

Only those approved in the Ops Specs and retrieved through a secure network (https or "padlocked" website).

12

Air Traffic Control and Navigation Procedures

A. Air Traffic Control

1. What is the purpose of Air Traffic Control? (AIM)

The primary purpose of air traffic control is to provide air traffic services to IFR traffic to ensure the "safe, orderly, and expeditious flow of traffic." Air Traffic Control (ATC) may provide additional services to both IFR and VFR aircraft when time permits.

2. What is an "ARTCC"? (AIM)

An air route traffic control center (ARTCC) is an air traffic management facility that provides air traffic services to aircraft that are primarily operating in the enroute environment.

3. How many ARTCCs are there? (AIM)

There are twenty centers in the contiguous 48 United States. Centers have a three-letter identifier that begins with a Z:

- Seattle (ZSE)
- Oakland (ZOA)
- Los Angeles (ZLA)
- Salt Lake City (ZLC)
- Denver (ZDV)
- Albuquerque (ZAB)
- Dallas (ZFW)
- Houston (ZHU)
- Kansas City (ZKC)
- Memphis (ZME)
- Atlanta (ZTL)
- Jacksonville (ZJX)
- Miami (ZMA)
- Minneapolis (ZMP)
- Chicago (ZAU)
- Indianapolis (ZID)
- Cleveland (ZCB)
- Washington, D.C. (ZDC)
- New York (ZNY)
- Boston (ZBW)

An additional center exists in the Caribbean near Puerto Rico—San Juan (ZSU).

4. What is an "ATCT"? (AIM)

An air traffic control tower (ATCT) is responsible for traffic in the vicinity of the airport. IFR separation is provided by control towers authorized to do so. Towers also handle local traffic flow (the movement of aircraft on the ground).

5. What is an "FSS"? (AIM)

A flight service station (FSS) is an air traffic facility that provides peripheral services such as weather briefings, flight plans, and lost/missing aircraft assistance as well as search and rescue coordination. An FSS may also assist in IFR clearance delivery/cancellation as well as handle NOTAMs and PIREPs.

6. Are air traffic control communications recorded? (AIM)

Yes, all ATC communications are recorded, including telephone conversations.

7. What different methods can pilots use to receive their IFR clearance at non-towered airports? (AIM)

Pilots can get their clearance via telephone, via a remote VHF communications outlet, or with a local air traffic control facility (once airborne).

8. What frequency should pilots use to announce their position at non-towered airports? (AIM)

The correct frequency is designated as the common traffic advisory frequency (CTAF).

9. What is "ATIS"? (AIM)

Automatic Terminal Information Service (ATIS) is a recording of the current weather and operational information for an airport. This eliminates the need for controllers to repeat the same information over and over for arriving and departing pilots. Busy terminal areas may have two ATIS broadcasts, one for arrivals and one for departures.

10. What is "D ATIS"? (AIM)

Digital ATIS is a computerized form of ATIS that allows pilots to access it using ACARS.

11. What is "radar traffic information service"? (AIM)

This is a service provided by air traffic control to notify pilots of other traffic proximate to their position.

12. What is a "safety alert" and what types of alerts are available? (AIM)

A safety alert is issued to pilots who are in (or imminently approaching) a safety compromised situation. Safety alerts are issued as terrain or obstruction alerts or aircraft conflict alerts.

13. What is "TEC"? (AIM)

Tower enroute control (TEC) allows pilots to fly between metropolitan areas with linked approach control areas to avoid having to enter the traditional enroute air traffic structure.

14. What is the purpose of a transponder? (AIM)

A transponder is a device that replies to interrogations by air traffic control radar. The unit can be set so that the message it sends back is coded for identification purposes. For example, the controller would ask Flight 123 to "squawk" 5512. The pilots would set their transponder to 5512. The position of the aircraft would then be known and immediately identified as Flight 123 on air traffic control radar. The controller could then "tag" the flight (known as a radar target) with pertinent information such as flight number, destination, route, etc. Altitude information is displayed for aircraft that are properly equipped to provide this data and ground speed is automatically calculated by the radar system.

15. What is "Mode C"? (AIM)

Mode C is a transponder that reports altitude information. The aircraft senses its altitude in relation to the standard datum (29.92 inches Hg) and transmits this data with the reply message. The air traffic control radar then makes a local altimeter setting correction and displays the aircraft altitude in MSL on the radar screen.

16. Where is Mode C required? (AIM)

Mode C is required at or above 10,000 MSL, within 30 NM of Class B airports, within and above Class C airports, within certain Class D airports, and for aircraft traversing an Air Defense Identification Zone (ADIZ).

17. What kinds of flight operations are subject to slot control? (AIM)

Slot control is the requirement for non-scheduled flights to make reservations to fly to a certain airport.

18. What is an "STMP"? (AIM)

A special traffic management program (STMP) is issued when an airport is constrained due to a special event or reduced capacity. These will be made known on the Air Traffic Control Command Center website and through NOTAMs. An example of a STMP would be the special procedures issued for airports near the Super Bowl.

19. When facing potential weather delays, what options will ATC utilize to optimize traffic flow (in order of preference)? (FAA)

- In-trail spacing changes
- SWAP advisories
- Reroutes
- Ground delay programs
- Airspace flow programs
- Ground stops

20. What does it mean when air traffic control states that SWAP advisories are in effect? (FAA)

Severe weather avoidance plan (SWAP) advisories are issued by the ATC Command Center in order to reduce the impact of severe weather events on the flow of air traffic. These advisories can include reroutes, suggested avoidance routes, and traffic management initiatives.

21. What is meant by the term "in-trail spacing"? (FAA)

This refers to the number of miles aircraft must be separated from one another as they flow along a route. As weather deteriorates enroute or in a specific terminal environment, air traffic control will often expand in-trail spacing to allow for a reduction in flow rate.

22. What is a "ground delay program" (GDP)? (FAA)

This is a means air traffic control uses to meter the number of aircraft departing to specific destinations by sequencing departures appropriately. This generally occurs when poor weather conditions prevail at the destination and the arrival acceptance rate at that airport is reduced for an extended period. Aircraft affected by a GDP will be issued an expected departure clearance time (EDCT). This is a Zulu time at which the aircraft will be expected to takeoff. Aircraft must depart within +/- five minutes of the EDCT in order to avoid further delays.

23. What is an "airspace flow program" (AFP)? (FAA)

When air traffic control airspace capacity is strained, an AFP will be issued. Aircraft affected by an AFP will be issued an expected departure clearance time (EDCT). This is a Zulu time at which the aircraft will be expected to takeoff. Aircraft must depart within +/- five minutes of the EDCT in order to avoid further delays.

24. Are there any options for a flight affected by an AFP to avoid the delay? (FAA)

The flight could be filed for an amended route around the constrained airspace.

25. How can a dispatcher check to see if an EDCT applies to a flight they are dispatching? (FAA)

The ATC Command Center has an EDCT look-up page. Dispatchers can also communicate with the appropriate ATC facility. Pilots can also check with clearance delivery/ground control at the departure airport.

26. How might a dispatcher plan ahead for the potential for delays at particular destinations? (FAA)

Other than good flight planning and monitoring weather and traffic conditions, dispatchers can view airport arrival demand charts at the ATC Command Center website under "Products—Airport Arrival Demand Chart (AADC)." This shows the acceptable arrival rate of an airport versus predicted demand. In the alert mode, if the airport is expected to be constrained, color coding (red, yellow, and green) are used to bring this to the attention of the user.

27. Where can dispatchers find any reroutes currently in use by ATC? (FAA)

Reroutes can be found by the associated advisory (the area being affected) at the ATC Command Center website under "Products—current reroutes."

28. What is the phonetic alphabet? (AIM)

The phonetic alphabet is the system used to communicate letters and numbers in communications per FAA and ICAO standards. For example, the letter "A" is phonetically pronounced "Alpha."

29. There are several numbers that have unique phonetic pronunciations. Name them. (AIM)

Three (3) is pronounced "tree"; five (5) is pronounced "fife"; and nine (9) is pronounced "niner." These special pronunciations are outlined to prevent confusion in communications across the globe. For example, "nine" is not used because it sounds like "nein," which means "no" in German.

30. What is the correct way of saying an altitude of 4,500 in radio communications? (AIM)

Four thousand five hundred.

31. What is the correct way of saying an altitude of 11,000 in radio communications? (AIM)

One one thousand.

32. What is the correct way of saying an airway, such as "V14" or "J544"? (AIM)

Victor fourteen (or one four); Jay five forty-four (or five four four).

33. What is the correct way to convey a communications frequency such as 134.5? (AIM)

One three four point five (ICAO: One three four decimal five).

34. In the U.S., altitudes above 18,000 feet should be referred to as _____? (AIM)

Flight levels (FL). Note: not all countries use 18,000 feet as the division line between altitudes and flight levels.

35. What is the correct way to express airspeed, such as "250 knots"? (AIM)

Two five zero knots.

36. What is the correct way to express airspeed in terms of Mach number, such as "M0.80"? (AIM)

Mach point eight zero (ICAO: Mach decimal eight zero).

37. When should airspeed typically be expressed in terms of Mach versus airspeed?

This cutoff is usually from 25,000 to 28,000 feet; in general this change takes place at high altitude.

38. Where can dispatchers find the conversion from local time to Zulu time (UTC)?

In the AIM or in the A/FD.

39. How should the time "0912 UTC" be expressed in voice communications? (AIM)

Zero niner one two Zulu.

40. What are the six legs of a standard traffic pattern at an airport? (AIM)

- *Upwind:* Parallel to landing runway and in direction of landing, but not the departure leg (i.e., aircraft departing the runway are not considered to be on upwind).
- *Crosswind:* Perpendicular to the landing runway departure end.
- *Downwind:* Parallel to the landing runway but in the opposite direction (reciprocal heading).
- *Base:* Perpendicular to the landing runway and the downwind leg.
- *Final:* The path aligned with the landing runway on the landing end.
- *Departure:* The leg extending from the departure end of the runway along the centerline.

41. What is meant by the term "left traffic"? (AIM)

This means that all turns in the traffic pattern will be made to the left.

42. What is meant by the term "left downwind"? (AIM)

This means that the aircraft will always have the runway on the left (and also that the aircraft will be to the left of the runway from the perspective of the landing runway heading). Lastly, all turns made within the pattern are made to the left.

43. What is a "calm wind runway"? (AIM)

This is a runway that is preferred for use by traffic when the winds are less than 5 knots. Dispatchers should consider this in their performance calculations when practical; however, pilots and dispatchers should not feel pressured to use this runway if its safety is questionable.

44. What is "LLWAS"? (AIM)

The low level wind shear alert system (LLWAS) is a network of wind sensors scattered around an airport that is capable of detecting wind shear and microburst activity. Activation of LLWAS alerts, particularly microburst alerts, should preclude aircraft operations.

45. What is "TDWR"? (AIM)

Terminal Doppler weather radar (TDWR) allows for the detection of severe weather and shear conditions in the local terminal environment.

46. What is "WSP"? (AIM)

A weather system processor (WSP) is an enhancement to airport surveillance radar (ASR)-9 facilities that allows for the display of severe weather on air traffic radar displays.

47. What is meant by the phrase "braking action advisories are in effect"?

This is used by air traffic controllers to note that braking action reports (of poor or zero) have been issued for some runways, or that braking conditions on them are changing rapidly and deteriorating.

48. What is meant by a report that there is a MU (μ) of 40?

Braking friction capacity on a given runway can be measured with special devices. The resultant measure of this friction capacity is represented by MU (pronounced myew). MU values below 40 mean aircraft braking performance will likely be compromised. The scale of MU is 0 (no braking) to 100 (perfect braking).

49. What should dispatchers consider if braking action NOTAMs are being issued at an airport used for flights they are dispatching?

Dispatchers should consider how this might affect takeoff and landing performance and should consult contaminated runway charts or data. If the conditions are questionable, phone calls should be made to local airport operations and/or ATC facilities.

50. What is "LAHSO"? (AIM)

Land and hold short operations (LAHSO) are when aircraft are instructed to land on one runway, but hold short of another runway that intersects the landing runway. LAHSO distances are available from the AFD. Operators should not be compelled to use LAHSO (some air carriers prohibit this type of operation).

51. What is "SMGCS"? (AIM)

The surface movement guidance control system (SMGCS) is a taxi procedure, including special lighting and markings, for low-visibility situations (less than 1,200 RVR). These generally include special routes from the terminal area to and from the most common runways used in low-visibility conditions.

52. Victor airways usually extend from _____ to _____ feet. (AIM)

1,200 AGL; 17,999 MSL.

53. Victor airways are Class _____ airspace. (AIM)

They are Class E airspace.

54. Jet airways usually extend from _____ to _____ feet. (AIM)

18,000 MSL to FL450.

55. Jet airways are Class _____ airspace. (AIM)

They are Class A airspace.

56. What are the normal items that are conveyed in an air traffic control clearance? (AIM)

- Clearance limit—this is the point to which an aircraft is cleared; this is usually the destination.
- Departure procedure
- Route
- Altitude—initial altitude and an altitude to be maintained within a given time or distance are usually issued in case of a radio communication failure.

57. What is a "CDR"? (AIM)

A coded departure route (CDR) allows for rapid route filing. Instead of having to use or convey an entire route in a clearance, an eight-digit CDR can be used—for example,"INDORDS2" for a route between Indianapolis and Chicago O'Hare. The use of CDRs must normally be agreed upon between an air carrier and local air traffic control facilities.

58. What are the standard IFR aircraft separation requirements for aircraft being operated at the same altitude? (AIM)

The requirement is 3 NM separation within 40 miles of the radar antenna, and increases to 5 NM separation beyond 40 miles from the radar antenna.

59. What is "ASDE"? (AIM)

Airport surface detection equipment (ASDE) is an enhancement to local air traffic control that allows for the monitoring of aircraft and vehicles on the ground through the use of radar.

60. When dispatchers use special departure procedures for the augmentation of performance data (for example, assuming pilots will fly an obstacle departure procedure in order to gain a higher allowable takeoff weight), should they do anything to convey this to flight crews?

Yes, they should make a note on the release or applicable document that "performance data based upon" the specific procedure(s) utilized. This will ensure that the pilots are aware of the use of specialized performance data for normal (and in case of abnormal) flight operations. An example of this notation is: "performance data based upon the use of the special engine out procedure for runway 18L."

61. How is communication with ARTCCs assured over large geographic areas? (AIM)

A network of remote center air/ground (RCAG) receivers and transmitters is scattered in strategic locations to ensure the best communication coverage. These consist of both VHF and UHF (and in some cases HF) sites.

62. What is "CPDLC"? (AIM)

Controller pilot data link communications (CPDLC) is a means for controllers and pilots to "text message" one another. This textual depiction of clearances can serve as a backup to voice communications and helps alleviate frequency congestions as well as the possibility of read back or comprehension issues.

63. What should dispatchers and pilots do in the case of air traffic control communications failure? (AIM)

Dispatchers should attempt to relay air traffic control messages, if applicable, via any means possible. Pilots should comply with the applicable loss of communications regulations and procedures while attempting to coordinate air traffic control communications with FSS, CPDLC, or via company frequencies (dispatch).

64 What items should be included in a position report? (AIM)

- Aircraft identification
- Position
- Time
- Altitude
- Type of flight plan (if not IFR)
- Estimated time of arrival at the next reporting point
- The name of the next reporting point along the route
- Remarks (such as instructions to pass on a copy of the position report to dispatch; this is often used in oceanic and remote operations)

Position reporting is only required when aircraft are not in radar contact or are specifically instructed to make such reports.

65. What are "colored airways"? (AIM)

Colored airways are low/medium frequency (L/MF) airways depicted in brown and lettered G, R, A, and B (named by the colors green, red, amber, and blue, respectively). Green (G) and red (R) generally run east and west while amber (A) and blue (B) are aligned north and south.

66. What are Q and T routes? (AIM)

These are RNAV airways. Q routes are for high-altitude use (18,000 to FL450) and T routes are for low-altitude use (below 18,000). Unless otherwise specified, these are RNAV-2 (RNP of 2.0).

67. When may an aircraft be instructed to hold? (AIM)

Holding patterns—regimented circular flight paths—are used by air traffic control to delay aircraft for various reasons, such as traffic saturation, poor weather, or runway closures. Pilots can also request to hold in order to work through abnormal aircraft issues or to wait for local weather to improve.

68. If a dispatcher receives notice that one of the aircraft for which they are responsible has been instructed to enter a hold, what are the priorities of this dispatcher?

In this situation, the dispatcher should evaluate the current fuel status of the airplane and compare this to the estimated length of the delay. Dispatchers should also explore the possibility of having the aircraft divert to an alternate destination by checking nearby stations for weather, the availability of ground services (with preference to those operated by the company), passenger handling capabilities, fuel, and proximity. Fuel burn value(s) should be calculated for each possible alternate. Pilots should be informed of a critical fuel value—the fuel level at which they should divert and to which alternate airport(s). Also, the aircraft's estimated time of arrival should be updated so that it can be conveyed through the proper channels for operational purposes (for example, so departure times of flights using the ship number can be updated).

69. What is an "FMSP"? (AIM)

A flight management system procedure (FMSP) is the equivalent of an RNAV STAR, but is specifically designed for aircraft with FMS or GPS navigation suites.

70. What is a local flow traffic management program? (AIM)

These are augmented arrival/departure procedures that enhance safety, reduce noise, and/or reduce fuel consumption of aircraft. This is made possible by uninterrupted descents or other special directions.

71. What is an "MSA"? (AIM)

A minimum safe altitude (MSA) is a minimum altitude published on approach charts for emergency use. It is typically given in reference to a point on the approach, such as the final approach fix, and normally provides protection out to 25 NM from this fix.

72. What is a "TAA"? (AIM)

A terminal arrival area (TAA) allows aircraft to transition from the enroute structure to a GPS/RNAV approach with minimal maneuvering (such as the need for a procedure turn). TAAs are defined by courses to fixes on the approach and distances from such fixes. The TAA provides a safe altitude at which aircraft can operate within the confines of the area.

73. What is an "MVA"? (AIM)

A minimum vectoring altitude (MVA) is a minimum altitude available only to air traffic controllers (displayable on their radar screens) that provides adequate obstacle clearance (1,000 feet in non-mountainous areas; 2,000 feet in mountainous areas) for aircraft which they are controlling.

74. What is "GLS"? (AIM)

A GBAS ("ground-based augmentation system") landing system, or GLS, is a precision satellite-based navigation (GPS) instrument approach. These are currently not yet in use and require the installation of LAAS.

75. What determines the approach category in which an aircraft falls? (AIM)

Approach category is based upon 1.3 times the maximum certified weight V_{S0}.
- Category A: up to 91 knots
- Category B: 91 to 120 knots
- Category C: 121 to 140 knots
- Category D: 141 to 165 knots
- Category E: 166 knots or more

76. Describe the three types of radar approaches that may be available from an air traffic control facility. (AIM)

- *Airport surveillance radar (ASR) approaches* provide lateral guidance to the runway, provided by radar vectors. Recommended altitudes are given as the aircraft moves closer to the airport.

- *Precision approach radar (PAR) approaches* are precision approaches that utilize vertical and lateral radar for controllers to guide the aircraft down to near ILS minimums.

- *No gyro approaches* are for emergency use when an aircraft loses pitch/bank information. Controllers simply tell pilots when to start and stop turns to guide them to the runway. Recommended altitudes are given as the aircraft moves closer to the airport.

77. What is the difference between dependent and independent parallel ILS approaches? (AIM)

Dependent instrument landing system (ILS) approaches require staggered separation (thus reduced flow rates) of aircraft arriving on parallel runways separated by 2,600 feet or more. Independent ILS approaches do not require such staggered separation (these are separated by 4,300 feet or more, or less than that value if the airport has ILS/PRM simultaneous close parallel approaches).

78. How far apart can parallel ILS approaches be conducted with a PRM system? (AIM)

These runways can be separated by less than 4,300 feet, but at least 3,400 feet for parallel final approach courses — a minimum which can be reduced to 3,000 feet if the approach courses are offset by 2.5 to 3.0 degrees.

79. What is a "simultaneous converging instrument approach"? (AIM)

When airports have converging runway/approach courses (such as the north/south runways and the northwest/southeast runways at Dallas-Fort Worth International), instrument approaches can converge as long as the approach minimums are raised and the missed approaches do not cross paths. The missed approach points on converging approaches must also be a minimum of 3 NM apart. If the runways actually intersect, the lowest minimums are 700 feet and 2 SM visibility.

80. What special equipment is required to reduce ILS visibility requirements from ½ SM (2,400 feet RVR) down to 1,800 feet RVR?

If specifically published, 1,800 RVR can be used as the approach minimum visibility if touchdown zone lights (TDZL) and centerline lights (CL) are operational.

81. What is SAAAR? (AIM)

Special aircraft and aircrew authorization required (SAAAR) approaches/procedures necessitate specialized avionics and crew training to conduct. Examples include RNAV RNP approaches, Category II ILS approaches, and Category III ILS approaches.

82. What is a "side-step"? (AIM)

This is a maneuver where a pilot will conduct an approach to one runway and then "side-step" to an adjacent (parallel) runway.

83. What is a "circling approach"? (AIM)

This allows an aircraft to conduct an approach to one runway but "circle" to another. Protection from obstacles is assured to a distance from the approach end of each runway at the airport, depending upon the approach category. Protection distances are 1.3, 1.5, 1.7, 2.3, and 4.5 miles for categories A, B, C, D, and E, respectively.

84. When are circling-only minimums published? (AIM)

When the final approach course is not aligned within 30 degrees of the runway heading and/or a high rate of descent would be required to get from the MDA to the runway, circling-only minimums will be published. The approach will not have a runway designation; it will instead be denoted with a letter (for example, instead of "VOR RWY 9" the approach title would be "VOR-A").

85. When can visual approaches be conducted? (AIM)

A minimum visibility of 3 SM and ceiling of 1,000 feet must exist; however, weather higher than these values is typically needed to conduct visual approaches. Whenever visual approaches are in use, the arrival rate of the airport will be much higher. Conversely, when an airport suspends visual approaches, arrival rates go down and may lead to delays. Dispatchers can project if visual approaches are possible by comparing the final approach minimum altitudes of the common approaches to a particular airport with the existing weather conditions The weather will normally need to be at least as high as these values to reliably utilize visual approaches.

B. Departure Procedures

1. What is a "DP"? (FAA-H-8261-1)

A departure procedure (DP) is any instrument procedure that has a function of guiding departing aircraft from a particular airport. DPs include ODPs and SIDs.

2. What is an "ODP"? (FAA-H-8261-1)

An obstacle departure procedure (ODP) is a method for aircraft to safely depart an airport and get to the enroute structure. An ODP is specifically designed to keep aircraft at a safe distance from terrain.

3. What is a "SID"? (FAA-H-8261-1)

A standard instrument departure (SID) is an instrument procedure that provides routings out of terminal areas to connect to the enroute environment. Although SIDs provide obstacle clearance, they are primarily designed to simplify or expedite traffic flow in busy terminal areas.

4. What two types of navigation might be expected on a SID? (FAA-H-8261-1)

SIDs rely on either pilot navigation or radar vectors to get the aircraft safely out of the airport area. Vector SIDs (normally indicated with just NAVAIDs rather than routings/altitudes) cannot be filed for during the flight planning process (the air traffic control computer system will not accept them).

5. When would non-standard takeoff minimums or departure procedures be published? (FAA-H-8261-1)

Non-standard minimums normally apply when obstacles exist in close proximity to the airport and/or a climb gradient of more than 200 feet per NM is required (an obstacle penetrates the 152 feet per NM obstacle clearance plane, which slopes upward from an altitude of 35 feet at the departure end of the runway).

For questions 6–10, refer to the takeoff minimums and departure procedures information for Columbus Metropolitan Airport shown in Figure 12-1.

COLUMBUS, GA
COLUMBUS METROPOLITAN
TAKE-OFF MINIMUMS: **Rwy 24,** 1100-2 or std. with a min. climb of 220' per NM to 1800. **Rwy 31,** 300-2, or std. with a min. climb of 300' per NM to 700.
DEPARTURE PROCEDURE: **Rwy 6,** climb via heading 056° to 1400 before turning southbound. **Rwy 13,** climb via heading 070° to 1900 before turning southbound. **Rwy 24,** climb via heading 280° to 1900 before turning southeastbound. **Rwy 31,** climb via heading 307° to 1400 before turning southbound.

Figure 12-1.

6. What are the takeoff minimums when departing runway 6?

They would be standard (1 SM for one- or two-engine aircraft; ½ SM for more than two engines) as non-standard minimums are not listed.

7. What are the takeoff minimums when departing runway 24?

The weather would need to be equal to or better than a 1,100-foot ceiling and 2 SM visibility. The other option would be standard (1 SM or ½ SM as applicable) as long as the aircraft could climb at 220 feet per NM to 1,800 MSL. Normally, when non-standard takeoff minimums are published, users are not authorized to reduce them per Ops Specs.

8. Aircraft departing runway 31 should do what prior to proceeding towards the south?

The aircraft should climb via a 307 heading to 1,400 feet before turning southbound.

9. Aircraft departing runway 31 should do what prior to proceeding towards the north?

No special procedure is required.

10. How should dispatchers ensure that pilots are aware of the special procedures that exist at an airport?

It might be helpful for dispatchers to note somewhere on the release or during their briefing that non-standard takeoff minimums and/or departure procedures exist.

For questions 11–18, refer to the ENDED THREE departure procedure out of Tampa International Airport shown in Figure 12-2.

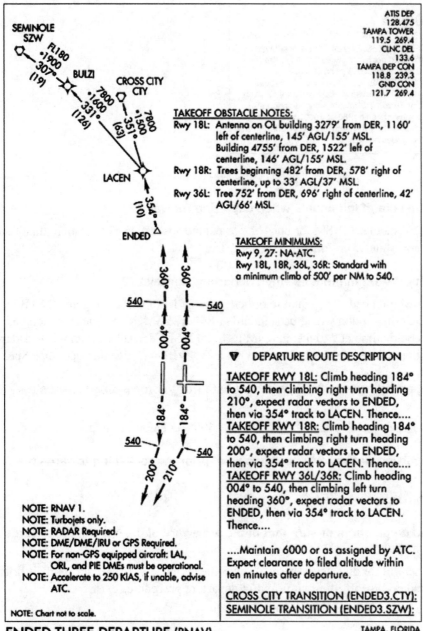

ENDED THREE DEPARTURE (RNAV)
(ENDED3.ENDED) 10154

TAMPA, FLORIDA
TAMPA INTL (TPA)

Figure 12-2.

11. You are planning a flight from Tampa to Atlanta. The preferred route calls for an arrival over Seminole (SZW) VORTAC. Is the ENDED THREE an appropriate departure for this planned route if aircraft are departing to the south out of Tampa?

Yes, although this SID directs traffic to the north, it has a provision for aircraft departing runways 18L/18R.

12. The aircraft that you are dispatching has an initial climb airspeed of 180 knots. What climb rate is required to comply with the climb gradient requirements for this SID if the departure is from runway 18R?

This SID requires a climb gradient of 500 feet per NM to 540 feet MSL (middle right of the chart). To convert from climb gradient to climb rate, first determine how many miles per minute the aircraft is traveling. At 180 knots, this value is 3 NM per minute (180 ÷ 60 = 3). Then multiply this by the climb gradient (3 × 500). The result is a required climb rate of 1,500 feet per minute. Check this value against climb charts for the aircraft. Crews should be notified of this requirement on the release documentation, particularly if they will be required to hold a particular climb rate to a higher altitude. An example citation would be "performance data predicated on a minimum climb rate of 1,500 feet per minute to 540 MSL."

13. What is the distance between ENDED and LACEN?

Ten NM (this is indicated by the "10" in parentheses).

14. What is the difference between ENDED symbolized with a triangle and LACEN symbolized by a star-like image?

ENDED is a "regular" intersection and LACEN is an RNAV waypoint.

15. What is the minimum enroute altitude (MEA) between LACEN and Cross City (CTY)?

7,800 MSL.

16. SIDs are named for a primary fix from which _____ radiate from this point in several directions.

Transitions. This case includes two: the SZW and the CTY transitions.

17. The notes include the term "RNAV 1." What does this mean?

Aircraft flying this procedure must have at least a RNP of 1.0.

18. How would this SID be denoted in a flight plan form route section if the aircraft is to use the SZW transition?

ENDED3.SZW

19. What are some concerns if an aircraft must return to the departure airport following an emergency?

Of course, the weather is a major concern, because if it is not good enough for a safe and legal arrival, the aircraft will need to divert or proceed to its takeoff alternate (if planned). Also, if the emergency requires crash and fire rescue, this will need to be requested. The same applies if medical assistance is needed. The landing weight of the aircraft might be over limits and may necessitate fuel dumping. The ground station will also need to be notified to ensure that personnel are available to work the gate and guide the aircraft in for parking. Customer service personnel should also be notified to plan for rerouting passengers, booking hotels, or other applicable solutions. Dispatchers should be prepared to file unusual occurrence paperwork and should notify their supervisors of the emergency. If it is possible for the flight to depart again in the near future, the dispatcher should start work on re-dispatching the flight as the current release will no longer be valid.

20. What concerns should dispatchers have about airports with obstacles in the vicinity and/or special departure procedures?

Dispatchers should see if an aircraft can meet climb gradient requirements following an engine failure. Most airports where this is an issue have special engine-out departure procedures. If dispatchers predicate performance on these procedures, flight crews should be made aware of this fact on the release.

C. Terminal Area Charts

1. What is the purpose of an IFR area chart?

Area charts provide greater detail for congested terminal environments. This allows the user to more clearly see airways, intersections, and airports. These charts use the same basic symbology found on low-altitude IFR enroute charts.

For questions 2–6, refer to the area chart excerpt shown in Figure 12-3.

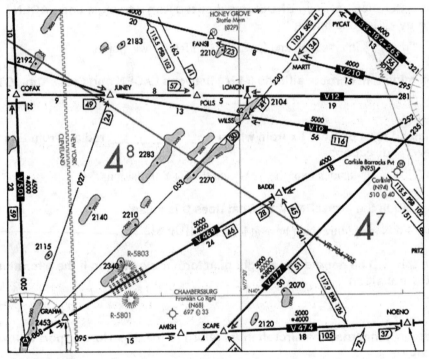

Figure 12-3.

2. How could an aircraft identify BADDI intersection?

It could be identified by 28 DME from the VORTAC on the bottom left, or 18 DME from the facility to the northeast. It could also be identified by the intersection of the 252 radial from the facility to the northeast and the 341 radial from EMI.

3. What are the areas of shading outlined with a solid line such as those found under WILSS and to the southwest of the intersection?

This is terrain. Note the "2000" following the line encircling the shading. That indicates the terrain in that area is at least 2,000 MSL. The highest point of the terrain is often indicated with a dot and the height, in MSL, of this point. For example, the highest point of the terrain area shown below WILSS is 2,104 MSL (in the upper right).

4. What is the minimum safe altitude an IFR flight could fly direct from BADDI to JUNEY?

The minimum off route obstruction clearance altitude (OROCA) near BADDI is 4,700 (indicated by the 4^7) and 4,800 near JUNEY (indicated by the 4^8). Thus, the minimum IFR altitude would be 4,800 feet; however, flights should plan for 6,000 feet correct altitude for this direction of flight (even-numbered altitudes are used for westbound flights).

5. Why might a dispatcher want to avoid using V469 for IFR flights?

Note the dashed lines that highlight the airway just northwest of the VORTAC in the bottom left of the excerpt. This indicates that the airway is compromised by nearby special use airspace—in this case, Restricted area R-5803. If this area was in use, flights may be diverted around this area, so dispatchers should avoid flight planning this route unless it is known that flights will be permitted to use the airway.

6. Why are the three altitudes listed for V377?

The top altitude is a minimum enroute altitude (MEA), the second is a GPS MEA (which can only be used by aircraft using GPS RNAV), and the third (with the *) is the minimum obstruction clearance altitude (MOCA).

D. Arrival Procedures

1. When flight planning to larger terminal airports, what kind of procedure(s) should dispatchers expect might be available?

These airports typically have standard terminal arrival routes (STARs). These are standardized arrival routes that help direct the flow of traffic into the terminal area in a manner that is expeditious and that avoids departing traffic. Dispatchers should plan on filing for a STAR if they exist.

2. How should dispatchers select the most appropriate STAR?

Dispatchers should review the available STARs and choose the one that best aligns with the route inbound to the terminal area. STARs are normally set up to come from general directions (north, northeast, south, west, etc.). Simply pick the one that is the most logical, preferably using one that has a transition from a VOR/waypoint close to or on the desired route. The dispatcher should also verify that the STAR is appropriate for the aircraft type, as many STARs are only for turbojets.

3. What is a "STAR transition"?

Most STARs have several different routes that feed from the enroute structure to the procedure itself. These are called transitions.

For questions 4–10, refer to the GOSHEN FIVE STAR shown in Figure 12-4.

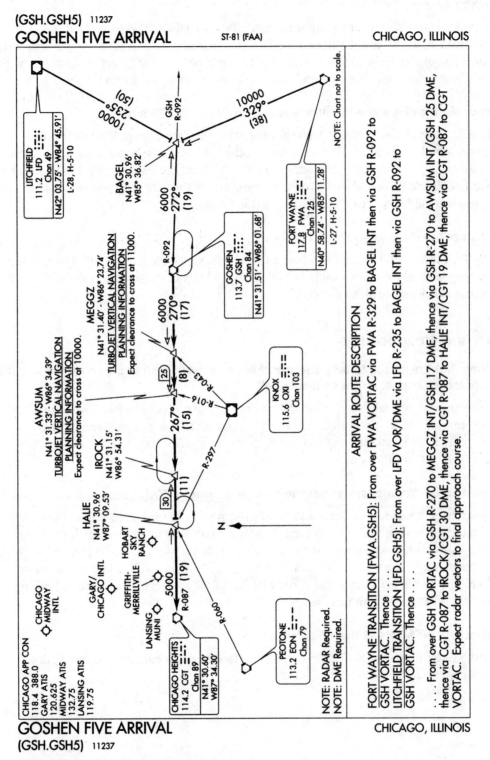

Figure 12-4.

4. How should a dispatcher indicate on the flight plan that their flight will fly the procedure from Fort Wayne VORTAC inbound?

In this case, the dispatcher should file for the FWA transition for the GOSHEN FIVE ARRIVAL. This should be done by using the computer code "FWA.GSH5" adjacent to the transition route description.

5. Does the dispatcher need to include all the waypoints along the FWA transition in the route filed on the flight plan?

No. The filing of the transition and STAR includes all of the appropriate intermediate waypoints.

6. What is the minimum altitude that should be expected from FWA to BAGEL?

10,000 feet is the MEA for this part of the transition.

7. How can a dispatcher be sure that the Chicago-area airport to which the aircraft is flying uses this arrival procedure?

NACO charts show all the airports that are included in the arrival on the chart. For example, if the flight was being dispatched to Chicago Midway, this would be an appropriate arrival. However, this arrival does not apply to Chicago O'Hare. Other chart providers print individual arrival plates for each airport to which the procedure applies.

8. Where should aircraft expect to start receiving radar vectors to the final approach course?

After crossing the CGT VORTAC (see STAR text).

9. If airborne flight delays begin into Chicago Midway airport, where might aircraft inbound on the GOSHEN FIVE be asked to hold?

Controllers will normally issue holding instructions to published holding patterns such as those at HALIE, IROCK, and GOSHEN. Dispatchers should look to see if there are diversionary airports close to or in the same general direction as these points. They should also start to calculate a critical fuel level to convey to flight crews so the crews know when they must divert.

10. What is the total distance from FWA to CGT on this STAR?

127 NM. This can be determined by adding up each leg distance, which are the numbers in parentheses below each segment.

For questions 11–14, refer to the GRNPA ONE ARRIVAL shown in Figure 12-5.

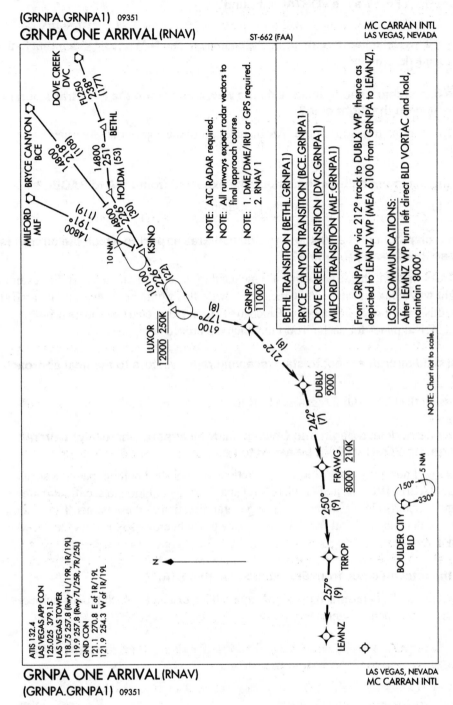

Figure 12-5.

11. The aircraft being dispatched only has VOR/DME navigation. Is this STAR appropriate for this aircraft? Why or why not?

The GRNPA ONE ARRIVAL is an RNAV procedure. Aircraft without RNAV capability cannot fly the procedure, thus dispatchers should not file such aircraft on this STAR. This procedure specifically requires DME/DME/IRU or GPS RNAV.

12. What is the RNP for this STAR?

This is an RNAV 1 procedure, meaning the RNP is 1.0 NM.

13. What are the numbers enclosed in lines adjacent to the FRAWG intersection?

The 8000 is a mandatory crossing altitude (lines above and below the number) and the 210K is a mandatory airspeed of 210 knots.

14. How many transitions are available for this STAR?

Four: Bethl, Bryce Canyon, Dove Creek, and Milford.

E. Instrument Approach Procedures

1. What is the difference between a precision and non-precision approach?

Precision approaches provide vertical guidance while non-precision approaches do not. Both approach types provide lateral guidance.

2. How does a dispatcher know what approaches can be used by flights?

Air carriers receive authorization to fly specific types of approaches within Ops Specs.

3. Why should dispatchers favor airports with precision approaches when selecting an alternate or diversionary airport?

Precision approaches normally allow for lower weather minimums. Because of this and the precision allowed by these approaches, flights are more likely to get into the airport in poor weather.

4. Can aircraft still use an ILS approach if the glide slope is out of service?

The localizer is still available, so the aircraft could still use this portion of the approach. Of course, this lateral-only guidance would mean the approach is therefore a non-precision type.

5. An aircraft that is being dispatched has GPS RNAV. It is being dispatched to an airport that has only an NDB approach available due to NOTAMs applicable to other approaches. Can this flight be dispatched?

No. But if the title of the approach was "NDB or GPS", this flight could be dispatched as long as the carrier's Ops Specs authorize the use of GPS approaches.

6. What types of NOTAMs are regulatory in nature and may affect approach procedures, minimums, and requirements?

Flight Data Center (FDC) NOTAMs cover these important changes and should be referenced by dispatchers prior to planning a flight.

7. What is a "visual approach"? (FAA-H-8261-1)

This is a means to allow pilots to visually proceed to an airport for landing instead of having to conduct an instrument approach. Flow rates into airports are substantially higher when pilots are able to conduct visual approaches, and thus the likelihood of delays is much lower. Air traffic control can provide vectors for a visual approach as long as the ceiling is a minimum of 500 feet above the minimum vectoring/IFR altitude and the visibility is at least 3 SM. The minimum weather, overall, is a 1,000-foot ceiling and 3 SM visibility.

8. What is a "charted visual flight procedure" (CVFP)? (FAA-H-8261-1)

These are published visual approach procedures generally for turbojet aircraft to avoid excessive amounts of noise.

9. What is a Category I ILS? (FAA-H-8261-1)

A Category I instrument landing system (ILS) is a precision approach that allows pilots to descend to 200 feet above the touchdown zone of the runway in visibilities as low as 1,800 RVR. However, a Category I ILS normally has a minimum visibility of ½ SM or 2,400 RVR.

10. What must be available to allow for a Category I ILS to have a minimum visibility of 1,800 RVR? (FAA-H-8261-1)

In order to reduce the required visibility from 2,400 RVR to 1,800 RVR, the runway must have operational touchdown zone lights and centerline lights. The 1,800 RVR minimums must be published in order to use them on a runway equipped in this way.

11. What is a Category II ILS? (FAA-H-8261-1)

A Category II ILS allows pilots to descend to a decision height of 100 feet above the touchdown zone in visibilities as low as 1,200 RVR. Special aircrew and aircraft authorization, training, and equipment are required to fly these approaches.

12. What is a Category IIIa ILS? (FAA-H-8261-1)

A Category IIIa ILS allows pilots to descend to a decision height as low as 100 feet above the touchdown zone in visibilities no lower than 700 RVR. Special aircrew and aircraft authorization, training, and equipment are required to fly these approaches.

13. What is a Category IIIb ILS? (FAA-H-8261-1)

A Category IIIb ILS allows pilots to descend to a decision height no lower than 50 feet above the touchdown zone in visibilities less than 700 feet but not lower than 150 feet RVR. Special aircrew and aircraft authorization, training, and equipment are required to fly these approaches.

14. What is a Category IIIc ILS? (FAA-H-8261-1)

A Category IIIc ILS allows pilots to land without decision height and/or visibility limitations. Special aircrew and aircraft authorization, training, and equipment are required to fly these approaches.

15. What is an ILS/PRM approach? (FAA-H-8261-1)

These are ILS approaches, supported with precision runway monitoring (PRM), to parallel runways that are separated by at least 3,400 feet but not more than 4,300 feet. They can also exist at airports with runways separated by 3,000 feet if the localizer to one runway is offset by 2.5–3.0 degrees. PRM approaches exist at airports with special radar systems providing a faster update rate than normal approach radar systems to allow for precision monitoring of these specialized approaches. Part 121 and 135 operators must have completed specialized training to conduct these approaches.

16. What is a "converging ILS approach"? (FAA-H-8261-1)

These are approaches to runways where the final approach courses converge. Converging ILS approaches cannot have overlapping missed approach procedures and the missed approach points must be at least 3 NM apart. The minimums of these approaches cannot be lower than 700 feet and 2 SM.

17. Do any instrument approach procedures utilize radar vectors instead of ground-based NAVAIDs? (FAA-H-8261-1)

Yes. The airport surveillance radar (ASR) approach uses radar to provide lateral guidance to the runway. The precision approach radar (PAR) system uses lateral and vertical radar to guide an aircraft both laterally and vertically to the runway (and thus is considered a precision approach). Not all operators are permitted to conduct these approaches; consult individual Ops Specs for details.

18. When might air traffic control give an aircraft priority handling?

Aircraft in distress are always given priority handling. Aircrews and dispatchers should not hesitate to declare an emergency if special assistance or expediency is needed. Also, if an aircraft is low on fuel, they should declare "minimum fuel" so as to preclude any unnecessary delays inbound to the arrival airport.

For questions 19–22, refer to the plan view of the approach plate shown in Figure 12-6.

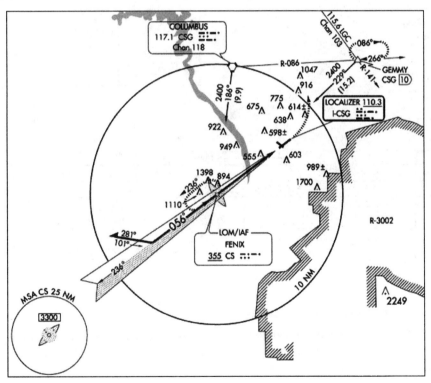

Figure 12-6.

19. What kind of approach is shown?

This is an approach that has a localizer. To determine if it is an ILS, LOC, or LDA, reference the approach title.

20. An aircraft is arriving at this airport late at night when approach control is closed. How could the aircraft get from the enroute structure to the approach without radar vectors?

The aircraft can transition via the CSG VORTAC by flying the 186 radial for 9.9 NM at a minimum altitude of 2,400 feet or it could fly a 229 heading from GEMMY for 15.2 NM at a minimum altitude of 2,400 feet. These transitions end at FENIX (which is the initial approach fix [IAF]) where the aircraft would fly outbound on a 236 heading along the localizer. It would then perform a procedure turn to the right to reverse course back inbound in the localizer.

21. Where would an aircraft hold following a missed approach?

At GEMMY or FENIX. Note the holding patterns depicted by a dashed line. Read the textual description of the missed approach to determine which was the primary hold and which was for an alternate missed approach.

22. What is the minimum safe altitude (MSA) for this approach? Upon what NAVAID is it based?

The MSA is 3,300 and is based upon a 25 NM radius of CS LOM (FENIX); see the lower left of the plate.

For questions 23–27, refer to the profile view of the approach plate shown in Figure 12-7.

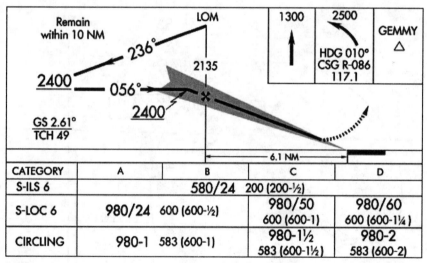

CATEGORY	A	B	C	D
S-ILS 6	580/24 200 (200-½)			
S-LOC 6	980/24 600 (600-½)		980/50 600 (600-1)	980/60 600 (600-1¼)
CIRCLING	980-1 583 (600-1)		980-1½ 583 (600-1½)	980-2 583 (600-2)

Figure 12-7.

23. What are the minimums for this approach?

Technically, all that is required to conduct approaches is visibility, which in this case is 2,400 feet RVR (½ SM). The decision altitude (DA) is 580 feet MSL and the decision height (DH) is 200 feet above touchdown zone.

24. Where would an aircraft intercept the glide slope on this approach?

Just outside the LOM at the point indicated by the arrow with the lightning bolt appearance if the aircraft was at 2,400 feet.

25. To what point/location would a flight crew decide to go missed approach on the ILS approach; that is, where is the missed approach point (MAP)?

Pilots fly the glide slope down to decision altitude (DA) and then decide to land or go missed approach. Therefore, the MAP is on glide slope at DA, which will occur approximately ½ SM from the end of the runway.

26. What are the minimums for this approach if the glide slope was inoperative?

Aircraft would be limited to conducting the localizer-only approach, which has a minimum visibility of 5,000 RVR (1 SM) for Category C aircraft.

27. What are the arrows and numbers in the upper right corner of the excerpt?

These are the missed approach instructions in pictorial format. They read: climb to 1,300, then climbing left turn to 2,500, fly a 010 heading until intercepting the 084 radial from CSG, then fly to GEMMY. The textual description would provide the remaining instructions.

For questions 28–30, refer to the profile view of the approach plate shown in Figure 12-8.

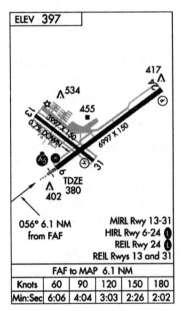

Figure 12-8.

28. Where is the missed approach point (MAP) for the localizer-only approach?

The MAP is located 6.1 NM from the FAF, which would be identified by time. An aircraft flying at 150 knots would take 2:26 from the FAF (which in this case would be the LOM, marked by the Maltese cross symbol on the profile view) to the end of the runway (which is the MAP).

29. What kind of lighting is available for runway 6?

This runway has approach lights, PAPI on the left side (indicated by the P in the circle), and high-intensity runway lights (HIRL). All of these lights are pilot controlled when the control tower is closed. (This is indicated by the dark backgrounds of the light symbols and the "L" next to the HIRL details.)

30. What are the dimensions of runway 6?

The runway is 6,997 feet long and 150 feet wide.

For questions 31–34, refer to the profile view of the approach plate shown in Figure 12-9.

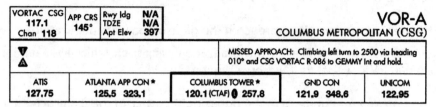

VORTAC CSG 117.1 Chan 118	APP CRS 145°	Rwy ldg N/A TDZE N/A Apt Elev 397		VOR-A COLUMBUS METROPOLITAN (CSG)
▼ ⚠			MISSED APPROACH: Climbing left turn to 2500 via heading 010° and CSG VORTAC R-086 to GEMMY Int and hold.	
ATIS 127.75	ATLANTA APP CON ★ 125.5 323.1	COLUMBUS TOWER ★ 120.1 (CTAF) 257.8	GND CON 121.9 348.6	UNICOM 122.95

Figure 12-9.

31. What is indicated by the "T" symbol in the middle left of the excerpt?

This means that either non-standard takeoff minimums or a departure procedure, or both, exist for this airport. Dispatchers should look in the "T" symbol pages in the front of the approach plate book for more information. Other chart publishers print this information on the airport diagram page.

32. What is indicated by the "A" symbol in the middle left of the excerpt?

This means there are non-standard alternate minimums for individuals wanting to rely on this specific approach to file this airport as an alternate. Dispatchers should look in the "A" symbol pages in the front of the approach plate book for more information. Other chart publishers print this information on the airport diagram page.

33. Why does this chart say "VOR-A" instead of indicating an approach to a designated runway?

Final approach courses not aligned within 30 degrees of the runway or approaches that require steep descents from the MDA to the runway are circling only and are designated with a letter rather than a runway number. Thus this is a circling-only approach.

34. Why do some of the frequency station names have a star next to them?

This indicates that the facility (e.g., Columbus Tower) is not open 24 hours a day. Refer to the A/FD for operating hours.

For questions 35–39, refer to the profile view of the approach plate shown in Figure 12-10.

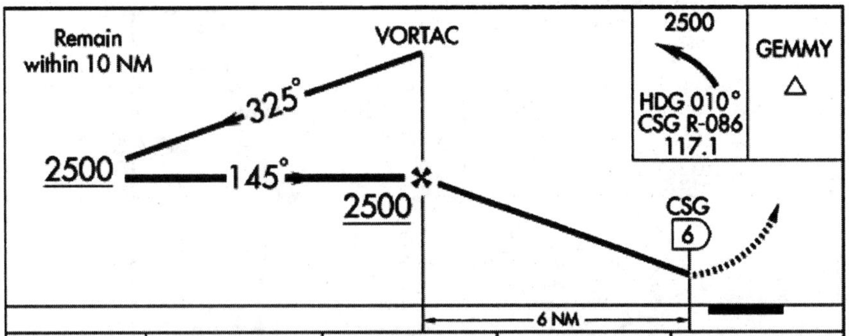

CATEGORY	A	B	C	D
CIRCLING	980-1	583 (600-1)	980-1½ 583 (600-1½)	980-2 583 (600-2)

Figure 12-10.

35. Is this a precision or non-precision approach?

This is a non-precision approach. This is evident from the lack of glidepath symbols, such as the lightning bolt arrow and shaded glidepath shown in Figure 12-11.

Figure 12-11.

36. Where is the final approach fix (FAF) for this approach?

The FAF is located at the VORTAC. It is indicated by the Maltese cross symbol.

37. Where is the missed approach point (MAP) for this approach?

The MAP is 6.0 DME from the VORTAC, just short of the runway.

38. What are the minimums for this approach?

Caution is necessary when evaluating circling approach minimums. Many air carrier Ops Specs have circling minimums no lower than 1,000 feet AGL and 3 SM visibility. In any case, although an aircraft may technically be Category C, the actual speed at which the aircraft will circle should be used in determining the approach category minimums to be used. Therefore, a Category C aircraft might need to instead use Category D minimums. In this case that would require a minimum visibility of 2 SM and an MDA of 980 feet.

39. What is meant by "Remain within 10 NM" in the upper left of the excerpt?

This instructs flight crews to remain within 10 NM of the VORTAC while conducting a course reversal (procedure turn).

For questions 40–42, refer to the profile view of the approach plate shown in Figure 12-12.

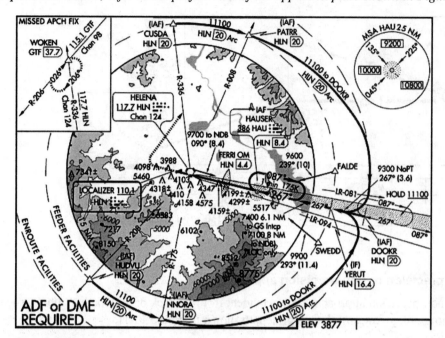

Figure 12-12.

40. Assuming no radar service is available into this airport due to the mountainous terrain, how should a dispatcher route plan an arrival to this airport from the south if the winds are favoring this approach?

Dispatchers could file a route so that the last waypoint is NNORA and the aircraft could then fly the DME arc to conduct the approach. However, if the weather changes to favor a different runway later, it makes more sense to file to HLN, from which the aircraft could transition to the approach and conduct a course reversal.

41. What is the highest obstacle on this approach plate?

It is the terrain at 8,775 feet in the southeast corner. The highest obstacle is noted with slightly larger lettering (other plate publishers use an arrow symbol to denote the highest obstacle).

42. An aircraft being dispatched to this destination has GPS RNAV but does not have an ADF or DME. Can it be dispatched to this airport if this was the only approach available and the weather was low enough to require its use?

Yes, GPS can be substituted for DME as long as it was authorized in Ops Specs.

13

Communication Procedures and Requirements

A. Communication Procedures

1. List some means by which aircraft and dispatchers can communicate with one another?

- Two-way radio—very high frequency (VHF)
- Two-way radio—high frequency (HF)
- Two-way radio—satellite
- Datalink—ACARS (HF, VHF, or satellite)
- SELCAL
- ARINC
- JetComm
- Various private vendor radio networks such as Tokyo Radio or Atlanta Radio

2. When would it be preferable to try to contact an aircraft via HF versus VHF?

VHF is limited to around 200 NM or so, while HF can bounce (propagate) off of the ionosphere and travel over long distances. Therefore, at times when an aircraft is operating in a remote area, it might only be reachable by HF.

3. What is the general "rule of thumb" concerning the selection of an HF radio frequency—that is, selecting a lower frequency versus a higher one?

As the saying "the higher the sun, the higher the frequency" indicates, higher frequencies should be used during the day and lower frequencies at night. This is for a variety of reasons, but mostly relating to the charge-state of the ionosphere during the day (when it is more energized) versus at night (when it does not receive solar radiation).

4. How can a dispatcher determine which is the most expeditious means of contacting a flight?

Most air carriers publish communication coverage maps, making the selection of a communication system relatively simple. In most instances, direct VHF voice communication is preferred, if possible. Dispatchers can get the attention of the crew by using SELCAL, which should prompt them to call dispatch.

5. How should a dispatcher initiate communications using a relay radio network such as Atlanta Radio?

Some air carriers monitor relay service radio frequencies when they are outside the range of their normal communication system. The dispatcher would contact the radio network and provide the location of the aircraft. The radio network would then attempt to call the aircraft on a nearby frequency repeater. After successful contact with the aircraft, the dispatcher would be phone-patched to the radio frequency.

6. What is "ARINC"? (ARINC.com)

ARINC is a private company that provides aviation communication services via HF, VHF, satellite, and datalink. They also relay communications among facilities. Dispatchers can utilize ARINC to communicate with their flights, usually in remote areas. Coverage maps are provided to subscribers based upon the level and types of services utilized.

7. What is "JetComm"?

JetComm is a means of communication that uses designated ground facilities (such as NAVAIDs) to which crews "dial in," resulting in a phone-patch to dispatch. Subscribers to such systems have access to coverage maps.

8. How should time be conveyed in all communications and messages?
(FSIMS website)

All times should be in Zulu (UTC).

9. You have control over a flight and notice that the latest weather report at the flight destination indicates conditions much different than what was forecast. What should you do and how?

This weather should be brought to the attention of the flight crew. This can be done via ACARS. If further discussion or consultation is necessary, this can be noted on the ACARS message. Alternatively, the dispatcher can SELCAL the aircraft or use an alternative direct contact method.

10. What are some methods a dispatcher can use to monitor flight status and receive departure and arrival times? (FSIMS website)

- Two-way radio (VHF, JetComm, ARINC, etc.)
- SITA messages
- ACARS
- Telephone
- Fax
- Aircraft situation display (ASD)

B. Communication Requirements

1. What are the general communication requirements for all aircraft conducting domestic or flag operations under 14 CFR Part 121? (14 CFR §121.99)

All such aircraft must be in two-way radio communication, or another means of communication must exist between the aircraft and dispatch/flight control throughout the duration of the flight.

2. How long are communications records required to be kept? (14 CFR §121.711)

30 days.

3. What reports are aircraft required to communicate to dispatch? (FSIMS website)

Departure reports, enroute reports (if applicable), in-range reports, and arrival reports. In addition, any other special messages should be communicated as needed.

4. To what do "out, off, on, and in times" refer?

An "out time" is the Zulu time at which an aircraft leaves the gate. An "off time" is the Zulu time at which an aircraft takes off. An "on time" is the Zulu time at which an aircraft lands. An "in time" is the Zulu time at which an aircraft arrives at the gate following landing. These times are reported to dispatch for flight following purposes.

5. What minimum items should the departure message contain? (FSIMS website)

Although each air carrier has its own individual requirements, a departure message should at minimum contain:

- Out and off times
- Fuel uplift (added by the fueler) and the total fuel onboard
- Estimated time of arrival at the destination
- Total passengers on board
- Zero fuel weight and/or other aircraft weight(s)
- Takeoff power setting used
- Other information, as required or as necessary

6. What minimum items should be in an enroute report message? (FSIMS website)

- Errors in the estimated time of arrival at the destination exceeding 10 minutes
- Diversions (such as overflying an intermediate stop or going to an airport other than the originally planned destination)
- Weather conditions that could be helpful to other flights or dispatch
- Mechanical issues
- Others, as required or as necessary

7. What minimum items should be in an in-range report message? (FSIMS website)

Although each air carrier has its own in-range procedures, flights should notify the arrival station approximately 15–20 minutes prior to departure. At minimum, this communication should include:

- Revised estimated time of arrival
- Special needs (for aircraft, crew, or passengers)
- Gate assignment/parking location
- Aircraft maintenance status

8. What minimum items should be in an arrival report message? (FSIMS website)

The arrival report should include:

- On time
- In time
- Fuel onboard upon arrival
- Any other items that may be helpful to other flights or dispatch (e.g., airport conditions)

9. When is an aircraft considered to be overdue?

If an aircraft has not arrived within 30 minutes of the estimated time of arrival and its condition is unknown, it is considered missing. Dispatchers should then do everything possible to make contact with the aircraft.

10. Describe what a dispatcher should do upon realizing that an aircraft is overdue.

After exhausting means of communication with the aircraft, the local air traffic control facility should be notified so they can begin coordinating search and rescue operations. The dispatcher should also contact his or her supervisor(s) as well as the destination station. Each air carrier has an emergency response checklist for use in such situations; this document should be the primary source of guidance for whom to contact and in what order of priority.

11. How soon after an aircraft is found to be overdue must a report to the National Transportation Safety Board (NTSB) be filed if no wreckage is found? (49 CFR §830.15)

Seven days.

12. How soon after an aircraft accident must a report be filed to the NTSB? (49 CFR §830.15)

Ten days.

14   Abnormal and Emergency Procedures

A. Security Procedures

1. What is the "TSA"? (tsa.gov)

The Transportation Security Agency is the U.S. government agency charged with providing safe and secure transportation.

2. What types of searches of aircraft are normally conducted by air carriers for security purposes? (49 CFR Part 1544)

Daily aircraft security searches are conducted for domestic operations. International operations typically have more frequent or regimented search procedures. Customs and border patrol generally have an agreement with air carriers that such searches comply with narcotics search necessities.

3. What is the recommendation concerning discussions about air carrier security procedures? (49 CFR Part 1544)

It is recommended that air carrier personnel do not discuss security procedures or policies with persons who do not need to know the information and do not conduct such discussions in public places.

4. What is an "FFDO"? (tsa.gov)

A federal flight deck officer (FFDO) is a pilot who is trained and authorized to carry a firearm onboard an aircraft.

5. Are persons carrying firearms authorized onboard air carrier aircraft? (49 CFR Part 1544)

Yes, but only under certain conditions. Air carriers have procedures for accepting such passengers in their Ops Specs. Examples of persons authorized to carry firearms are:
- FFDOs
- Federal air marshals (FAMs)
- Law enforcement officers (LEOs)
- Military Ravens (similar to a FAM)

6. What is an "AOSC"? (49 CFR Part 1544)

An Aircraft Operator Security Coordinator (AOSC) is the primary point of contact within an air carrier who acts as the liaison to TSA.

7. What is a "GSC"? (49 CFR Part 1544)

A Ground Security Coordinator (GSC) is the individual responsible for the security of an aircraft while it is parked at the gate prior to block out and following block in.

8. What are some of the responsibilities of a GSC while the aircraft is parked at the gate? (49 CFR Part 1544)

GSCs are responsible for:
- Screening of passengers and carry-ons
- Controlling access to the aircraft
- Ensuring ground servicing is completed in a secure manner
- Handling emergency or disruptive passenger situations
- Briefing the Inflight Security Coordinator (ISC) of any known security issues prior to departure

9. Who normally is the GSC? (49 CFR Part 1544)

The GSC normally is a gate agent or station manager.

10. Who normally is the Inflight Security Coordinator (ISC)? (49 CFR Part 1544)

The captain is the ISC.

11. What if the ISC suspects an inflight security issue?

The ISC (captain) should coordinate with dispatch (operational control) to discuss the options, such as diversion to a nearby airport. Operations personnel should also contact the FAA Operations Control Center and /or federal law enforcement (FBI) per their air carrier's security procedures manual.

12. What if the dispatcher is made aware of a possible security issue?

Possible security issues should be made known to the GSC if the aircraft is on the ground. If it is in the air, operational control should coordinate with the ISC (captain) to discuss the options, such as diversion to a nearby airport. Operations personnel should also contact the FAA Operations Control Center and/or federal law enforcement (FBI) per their air carrier's security procedures manual.

13. What if a suspected explosive device is onboard the aircraft?

Air carriers have specific procedures to handle such situations for individual aircraft within their fleets. In addition, pilots and flight attendants receive special training on such procedures. Operational control should coordinate with the ISC (captain) to discuss the options, such as diversion to a nearby airport. Operations personnel should also contact the FAA Operations Control Center and/or federal law enforcement (FBI) per their air carrier's security procedures manual. Clearly, this type of scenario will affect the schedule of the aircraft in question and once security issues are handled, focus can be switched to dealing with the impact of the situation on dispatch and scheduling.

14. Are prisoners allowed to be carried on air carrier aircraft? (49 CFR Part 1544)

Yes. Specific procedures exist depending upon the type of prisoner in terms of their known "risk" to the safety of others.

15. What is required to carry a "high-risk" prisoner? (49 CFR Part 1544)

Only one high-risk prisoner can be carried on each flight unless authorized by TSA. A high-risk prisoner requires two armed escorts.

16. What is required to carry a "low-risk" prisoner? (49 CFR Part 1544)

For flights less than four hours, one armed escort can be responsible for up to two low-risk prisoners. For flights four hours or longer, two armed escorts are required and can be responsible for up to two low-risk prisoners.

17. What boarding procedures should be used for prisoners? (49 CFR Part 1544)

Prisoners should be boarded prior to all other passengers. They should remain seated until all passengers have exited the aircraft.

18. What seating requirements exist for prisoners? (49 CFR Part 1544)

Prisoners should be seated in the last row. Their escort must sit between them and the aisle.

19. Can prisoners be served alcoholic beverages? (49 CFR Part 1544)

No.

20. Do prisoners need to be escorted to the lavatory? (49 CFR Part 1544)

Yes.

21. Are prisoners required to be restrained? (49 CFR Part 1544)

Yes, and effort should be made to hide such restraints, if possible.

22. Can firearms be carried in checked baggage? (49 CFR Part 1544)

Yes, as long as the firearms are unloaded and in an approved container. They must be declared by passengers, who will then be required to fill out a special form.

B. Emergency Procedures

1. Is a dispatcher authorized to declare an emergency?

Yes. Dispatchers can declare an emergency anytime a flight is in imminent danger or is overdue.

2. Name examples of some situations in which the declaration of an emergency is appropriate.

- Mechanical emergency (engine failure or fire).
- Aircraft is unable to determine its position (navigation system failure).
- Aircraft is overdue by more than 30 minutes and location or status of aircraft is unknown.
- Aircraft reports a distress condition.
- Insufficient fuel remains to reach the destination or other suitable alternate.
- Aircraft is deviating from its planned route and/or altitude without explanation.
- Known or suspected hijack.
- Any other threat to flight operations applicable to the aircraft.

3. When should a dispatcher declare an emergency? (14 CFR §121.557, 121.559)

Ideally, there should be communication between a flight crew and a dispatcher about the emergency and they should coordinate their actions (with the pilot/flight crew normally declaring the emergency). But if a dispatcher is unable to communicate with the flight crew, he or she should declare an emergency and take all actions necessary to deal with the emergency.

4. Who should be notified upon the declaration of an emergency?

The supervisor on duty should be notified. From that point, the communications procedures outlined in the air carrier's emergency procedure manual should be followed.

5. What type of record(s) should be kept during and following an emergency?

A chronological record should be kept about the occurrences relating to the emergency. All communications, paperwork, and other details should be retained for the filing of reports following the end of the emergency.

6. Must a dispatcher file a report following an emergency?

Yes, they must file the appropriate report within 10 days.

7. To whom does a dispatcher file reports concerning emergencies?

Each air carrier has a chain of command that should be followed (as outlined in operations manuals or other documents). The report normally will be filed with the vice president of flight operations or their equivalent.

8. When should a "minimum fuel" declaration be made?

Minimum fuel should be declared anytime that an aircraft, if it were to be delayed, might end up in a low fuel emergency situation. Most air carriers have a specific value at which this should be declared.

9. When should a low fuel emergency be declared?

A low fuel emergency should be declared anytime an aircraft falls below minimum fuel values and is in imminent danger of running out of fuel. Most air carriers have a specific value at which this should be declared.

10. Can military airports be used in an emergency?

Yes, and they should be considered viable alternates in such cases.

11. What is meant by "ditching" an aircraft?

This is when an aircraft must land in the water in an emergency situation. An example of when ditching might be required is following fuel exhaustion or power failure in a remote, overwater location.

12. What should a dispatcher do if suspecting that an aircraft is going to need to ditch?

The dispatcher should contact the local air traffic control facility and applicable Coast Guard or military agency responsible for that area. The last known position of the aircraft should be relayed to these facilities. Appropriate company personnel should be notified as soon as practical.

13. What information should a dispatcher collect for the reporting of an overdue aircraft?

Dispatchers should report:
- Aircraft route
- Last known position
- Last known communication
- Number of persons onboard
- Fuel onboard
- Any other pertinent information to assist in finding the aircraft or search and rescue operations

14. What document should a dispatcher utilize during an emergency or overdue aircraft situation?

Dispatchers should consult their emergency response manual and other applicable documents or manuals (such as the General Operations Manual [GOM]).

15. What are the responsibilities and services provided by the FAA in emergency or urgency situations?

The FAA will provide assistance to aircraft in emergency/urgency situations to the best of its ability. This may include priority handling and emergency response coordination. The FAA will also help in the coordination of search and rescue efforts. In the case of potential acts of terrorism, the FAA has personnel to help handle such situations—for example, in dealing with explosive devices.

C. NTSB Reporting Requirements

1. What is the definition of an "aircraft accident"? (49 CFR §830.2)

The National Transportation Safety Board (NTSB) defines an aircraft accident as "an occurrence associated with the operation of an aircraft which takes place between the time any person boards the aircraft with the intention of flight and all such persons have disembarked, and in which any person suffers death or serious injury, or in which the aircraft receives substantial damage."

2. What is the definition of an "aircraft incident"? (49 CFR §830.2)

The NTSB defines an aircraft incident as "an occurrence other than an accident, associated with the operation of an aircraft, which affects or could affect the safety of operations."

3. What are the three levels of injury, as defined by 49 CFR §830? Define each.

- *Fatal:* an injury that results in death within 30 days of the event.

- *Serious:* an injury requiring 48 hours or more of hospitalization that occurs within seven days of the event; bone fractures (excluding simple bones such as fingers, toes, and the nose); hemorrhages; tendon/nerve/muscle damage; internal organ damage; and/or second- or third-degree burns to more than 5% of the body.

- *Minor:* any other type of injury not described above.

4. What is the definition of "substantial damage"? (49 CFR §830.2)

Substantial damage is defined as "damage or failure which adversely affects the structural strength, performance, or flight characteristics of the aircraft, and which would normally require major repair or replacement of the affected component." Damage not considered to be "substantial damage" (for the purpose of Part 830), includes: "engine failure or damage limited to an engine if only one engine fails or is damaged, bent fairings or cowling, dented skin, small punctured holes in the skin or fabric, ground damage to rotor or propeller blades, and damage to landing gear, wheels, tires, flaps, engine accessories, brakes, or wingtips."

5. What is the definition of "minor damage"? (49 CFR §830.2)

Minor damage is that which is easily repairable and does not qualify as substantial.

6. Upon the occurrence of an aircraft accident, who must be notified, in addition to company personnel? (49 CFR §830.5)

The NTSB.

7. What types of occurrences require immediate notification of the NTSB?
(49 CFR §830.5)

The following require immediate notification of the NTSB:

- An aircraft accident.
- Flight control system malfunction or failure.
- Inability of any required flight crewmember to perform normal flight duties as a result of injury or illness.
- Failure of any internal turbine engine component that results in the escape of debris other than out the exhaust path.
- In-flight fire.
- Aircraft collision in flight.
- Damage to property, other than the aircraft, estimated to exceed $25,000 for repair (including materials and labor) or fair market value in the event of total loss, whichever is less.
- For large multiengine aircraft (more than 12,500 pounds maximum certificated takeoff weight):
  - In-flight failure of electrical systems which requires the sustained use of an emergency bus powered by a back-up source such as a battery, auxiliary power unit, or air-driven generator to retain flight control or essential instruments.
  - In-flight failure of hydraulic systems that results in sustained reliance on the sole remaining hydraulic or mechanical system for movement of flight control surfaces.
  - Sustained loss of the power or thrust produced by two or more engines.
  - An evacuation of an aircraft in which an emergency egress system is utilized.
- Release of all or a portion of a propeller blade from an aircraft, excluding release caused solely by ground contact.
- A complete loss of information, excluding flickering, from more than 50 percent of an aircraft's cockpit displays known as:
  - Electronic Flight Instrument System (EFIS) displays
  - Engine Indication and Crew Alerting System (EICAS) displays
  - Electronic Centralized Aircraft Monitor (ECAM) displays
  - Other displays of this type, which generally include a primary flight display (PFD), primary navigation display (PND), and other integrated displays.
- Airborne Collision and Avoidance System (ACAS) resolution advisories issued either:
  - When an aircraft is being operated on an instrument flight rules (IFR) flight plan and compliance with the advisory is necessary to avert a substantial risk of collision between two or more aircraft; or
  - To an aircraft operating in class A airspace.
- Damage to helicopter tail or main rotor blades, including ground damage, that requires major repair or replacement of the blade(s).
- Any event in which an operator, when operating an airplane as an air carrier at a public-use airport on land:
  - Lands or departs on a taxiway, incorrect runway, or other area not designed as a runway; or
  - Experiences a runway incursion that requires the operator or the crew of another aircraft or vehicle to take immediate corrective action to avoid a collision.
- An aircraft is overdue and is believed to have been involved in an accident.

8. How soon after an accident is a report required to be filed with the NTSB? (49 CFR §830.15)

A report must be filed within 10 days of an aircraft accident or within 7 days if the aircraft is still missing but no wreckage has been found.

9. What items should be included in the aforementioned report to the NTSB? (49 CFR §830.6)

- Type, nationality, and registration marks of the aircraft.
- Name of owner, and operator of the aircraft.
- Name of the pilot-in-command.
- Date and time of the accident.
- Last point of departure and point of intended landing of the aircraft.
- Position of the aircraft with reference to some easily defined geographical point.
- Number of persons aboard, number killed, and number seriously injured.
- Nature of the accident, the weather, and the extent of damage to the aircraft, so far as is known.
- A description of any explosives, radioactive materials, or other dangerous articles carried.

10. Is damage to an engine cowling following an engine failure considered substantial damage? (49 CFR §830.2)

No, unless damage has occurred to structural components unrelated to the engine.

11. An aircraft taxiing into the gate strikes its wingtip on a baggage cart. Is this considered substantial damage?

This type of incident is not considered to cause substantial damage, although the aircraft must be properly inspected by maintenance personnel to ensure no hidden structural damage occurred.